*Social Learning
and Personality Development*

Social Learning
and Personality Development

ALBERT BANDURA
Stanford University

RICHARD H. WALTERS
University of Waterloo

HOLT, RINEHART AND WINSTON, INC.

NEW YORK · CHICAGO · SAN FRANCISCO

TORONTO · LONDON

December, 1965
Copyright © 1963 by Holt, Rinehart and Winston, Inc.
Library of Congress Catalog Card Number: 63–17966
20798–0113
Printed in the United States of America

to Ginny and Glenys,
Mary, Carol, and Dave

Preface

In this book we have outlined a set of social-learning principles that emphasize the role of social variables to a greater extent than existing learning theories and consequently appear more capable of accounting for the development and modification of human behavior. Our socio-behavioristic approach represents an integration of our own research efforts and an attempt to relate these to findings obtained from controlled investigations in a number of areas, including child development and social psychology, as well as traditional experimental psychology. In order to illustrate the applicability of our social-learning principles to a wide range of important social phenomena, we have also drawn on data from other social sciences, notably anthropology and sociology, and from a number of clinical and psychiatric sources.

We have concentrated on child behavior, because studies conducted with children have in many cases yielded the most relevant data. Moreover, we are impressed with the continuity of social learning from childhood to maturity, and with the importance of the learning experiences of childhood and adolescence, both in the home and in extrafamilial social settings, for the eliciting, shaping, and maintaining of behavior patterns that are still evident, though of course in modified forms, in later years of life.

Much lip service has been given to the point of view that the same learning principles can account for the development of prosocial and deviant patterns of response. However, few people have accepted the full implications of this point of view, as a brief glance at any representative sample of books on psychopathology will indicate. The reader of such books will find little continuity between the principles and concepts of clinical theory and practice, on the one hand, and those of general and developmental psychology, on the other. Not only do we take the position that deviant and prosocial behavior can be accounted for by a single set of adequate social-learning principles, but we also question the theoretical significance of this dichotomy. Consequently, while we have focused primarily on the development of response patterns that occur in the repertories of the majority of children and adults, we have also attempted to demonstrate how our social-learning principles can account for the acquisition and maintenance of responses that deviate from social norms.

It is repeatedly stated that psychotherapy is a learning process. We concur with this view and therefore have tried in our final chapter to demonstrate how our social-learning principles may be applied both in clinical practice and for the socialization of children. We hope that the reader will find little or no discontinuity between our account of social development and the training or treatment we propose.

While this book was being written the authors made invited contributions to the *Nebraska Symposium on Motivation* (Bandura, 1962) and the *Yearbook of the National Society for the Study of Education* (Bandura and Walters, 1963). These contributions include preliminary presentations of some of the material included in Chapters 2 and 3 of the book. While some overlap was inevitable, we have refined our thinking on a number of issues on the basis of our own subsequent research and the considerable body of relevant research findings that have only recently become available.

A number of students, whose contributions are reflected in the joint authorship of many papers that are referred to in this book, have participated in our research, and we wish to express our gratitude for their assistance.

Many facilities in the California and Ontario areas were utilized in conducting our laboratory and field studies, on the findings from which we have relied heavily throughout the book, and financial assistance was obtained from a number of sources.

We are grateful for the cooperation of the Superintendents of Schools of Palo Alto, Menlo Park, Los Altos, and the City of Los Angeles; of the Directors of Education of the City of Toronto and Forest Hill Village; of the Superintendents of Public Schools of the Scarborough, Lakeshore District, and York Township Boards of Education; and of the Principals and Staffs of the schools in which our research was conducted. We wish also to thank Edith Dowley, Director, and Marilyn Haley and Patricia Rowe, Head Teachers, of the Stanford Nursery School; and William E. Blatz, formerly Director, and Dorothy Millichamp, Assistant Director, of the Institute of Child Study of the University of Toronto, for aid in arranging research facilities. Some of the more recent studies have been greatly facilitated by the support and cooperation of members of the staff of the Ontario Hospital, New Toronto, especially H. C. Moorhouse, Superintendent, Donald R. Gunn, Director of Clinical Research, and Edward Llewellyn Thomas, Medical Research Associate.

Our research was supported in part by Research Grants M-1734, M-4398, and M-5162 from the National Institute of Mental Health, Public Health Service, and the Lewis S. Haas Child Development Research Fund, Stanford University; and also by grants from the Canadian National Research Council (APA-47) and the Public Health Research Grant 605-5-293 of the (Canadian) National Health Grants Program. A grant for Research in the Humanities and Social Sciences from the University of Toronto in part defrayed the traveling expenses involved in this joint production.

We are especially grateful to Mrs. Mary E. Merrill for undertaking numerous responsibilities involved in the preparation of our manuscript.

Stanford, California   A. B.
Waterloo, Ontario R. H. W.
July 1963

Contents

*Social Learning
and Personality Development*

CHAPTER ONE

The Socio-behavioristic Approach

During the past half century, learning-theory approaches to personality development, deviant behavior, and psychotherapy have been favored by the majority of research-oriented psychologists. Generally speaking, however, these conceptualizations have not been highly effective in accounting for the processes whereby social behavior is acquired and modified. Indeed, most prior applications of learning theory to issues concerning prosocial and deviant behavior (Bijou and Baer, 1961; Dollard and Miller, 1950; Lundin, 1961; Rotter, 1954; Skinner, 1953) have suffered from the fact that they have relied heavily on a limited range of principles established on the basis of, and mainly supported by, studies of animal learning or human learning in one-person situations. In order to account adequately for social phenomena, it is necessary to extend and modify these principles, and to introduce new principles that have been established and confirmed through studies of the acquisition and modification of human behavior in dyadic and group situations (Sears, 1951).

Principles of Social Learning

THE ACQUISITION OF NOVEL RESPONSES THROUGH OBSERVATIONAL LEARNING

The weaknesses of learning approaches that discount the influence of social variables are nowhere more clearly revealed than in their treatment of the acquisition of novel

1

responses, a crucial issue for any adequate theory of learning. According to Rotter's social-learning theory (1954), for example, the probability of the occurrence of a given behavior in a particular situation is determined by two variables—the subjectively held probability (expectancy) that the behavior in question will be reinforced and the value of the reinforcer to the subject. Rotter's account of the learning process presupposes the existence of a hierarchy of responses that tend to occur in different situations with varying degrees of probability; it is therefore quite inadequate for explaining the occurrence of a response that has not as yet been learned and consequently has a zero probability value. A child who is unfamiliar with the Polish language would never emit the Polish phrase for "expectancy" even though the probability of reinforcement was 100 percent and the contingent reinforcer was exceedingly attractive. Obviously, in this particular example, the introduction of an important social variable—a verbalizing model—is an indispensible aspect of the learning process.

Although Rotter's social-learning theory is probably adequate for predicting the occurrence and modification of previously learned response patterns, it has had relatively little impact on theories of social behavior, perhaps because the dependent variables of the experiments generated by this approach have not generally dealt with social responses. For the most part, the experimentation has been limited to expectancy statements and conditions that lead to their modification, generalization, and extinction, but little attempt has been made to relate the expectancy variable to the types of social behavior that a social-learning theory should elucidate.

Other accounts of the acquisition of novel responses have frequently been limited to descriptions of behavioral change based on principles of operant or instrumental conditioning (Bijou and Baer, 1961; Lundin, 1961; Skinner, 1953). Skinner (1953) has provided a detailed account of the procedure of operant conditioning through *successive approximations*, whereby new patterns of behavior may be acquired. This procedure involves the positive reinforcement of those elements of available responses that resemble the final form of the behavior it is desired to produce, while component responses having little or no similarity to this behavior are left unrewarded. By gradually raising the requirement for reinforcement in the direction of the final form the behavior is to take, available responses can be shaped into patterns that did not previously exist in the repertory of the organism. From this point of view, novel responses never suddenly emerge but are always the outcome of a relatively prolonged process of operant conditioning.

> Operant conditioning shapes behavior as a sculptor shapes a lump of clay. Although at some point the sculptor seems to have produced an entirely novel object, we can always follow the process back to the original undifferentiated lump, and we can make the successive stages by which we return to this condition as small as we wish. At no point does anything emerge which is very different from what preceded it. The final product seems to have a special unity or integrity of design, but we cannot find a point at which this suddenly appears. In the same sense, an operant is not something which appears full grown in the behavior of the organism. It is the result of a continuous shaping process (p. 91).

Operant-conditioning procedures can be highly effective, particularly if stimuli that elicit responses in some respects resembling the desired behavior are already available in the learner's repertory. It is doubtful, however, if many of the responses that almost all members of our society exhibit would ever be acquired if social training proceeded solely by the method of successive approximations. This is particularly true of behavior for which there is no reliable eliciting stimulus apart from the cues provided by others as they exhibit the behavior. If a child had no opportunity to hear speech, for example, or in the case of a deaf-blind person (Keller, 1927), no opportunity to match the mouth and laryngeal muscular responses of a verbalizing model, it would probably be impossible to teach him the kind of verbal responses that constitute a language. In such cases, *imitation* is an indispensable aspect of learning. Even in cases where some other stimulus is known to be capable of arousing an approximation to the desired behavior, the process of acquisition can be considerably shortened by the provision of social models (Bandura and McDonald, 1963).

In *Social Learning and Imitation* (1941), Miller and Dollard emphasized the role of imitation in accounting for social-learning phenomena; however, in their later publication, *Personality and Psychotherapy* (Dollard and Miller, 1950), imitation receives only three passing references. This paradox can perhaps be explained by the fact that the authors conceptualized imitation as a special case of instrumental conditioning in which the social cues serve as the discriminative stimuli and the learner's responses are differentially rewarded or not rewarded according to whether they match or fail to match those made by the model. Since the experiments on which their theory was based included no instances of the acquisition of novel responses in the absence of rewards to the observers for imitative behavior, it is perhaps not surprising that Miller and Dollard summarily dismissed observational learning as a special case of instrumental conditioning.

The process of imitation is now receiving increasing attention from learning theorists, but is still usually treated as a form of instrumental conditioning, as conceptualized by Miller and Dollard. There is considerable evidence, however, that learning may occur through observation of the behavior of others even when the observer does not reproduce the model's responses during acquisition and therefore receives no reinforcement (Bandura, 1962a). It is thus evident that the learning principles set out by Hull (1943) and Skinner (1938, 1953) must be revised and extended in order to account adequately for observational learning. Moreover, these principles deal only with the role of direct reinforcement. Since the eliciting and maintaining of imitative behavior are highly dependent on the response consequences to the model, an adequate social-learning theory must also take account of the role of *vicarious reinforcement,* through which the behavior of an observer is modified on account of the reinforcement administered to a model.

PATTERNS OF REWARD

Imitative behavior is often rewarded by the model and, in addition, brings rewarding consequences, provided the model exhibits socially effective behavior; consequently, most children develop a generalized habit of matching the responses of successful models. Indeed, social behavior patterns are most rapidly acquired through the combined influence of models and differential reinforcement. While the principles of successive approximation and imitation are crucial for the understanding of the acquisition of social behavior patterns, maintenance of these patterns over a long period of time can best be explained in terms of principles derived from studies of the effects of the *scheduling of reinforcements* (Ferster and Skinner, 1957).

Under laboratory conditions it is possible to dispense reinforcers for every desired response or to dispense them intermittently according to some schedule or plan. Generally speaking, continuous reinforcement results in the more rapid acquisition of responses, but once learned, the behavior is more stable and more resistant to extinction if it has been acquired on an intermittent schedule.

Intermittent reinforcement may be provided on a variety of different schedules. The experimenter may reinforce responses according to a *fixed-ratio* schedule—he may reinforce only every other, every third, or every nth response. Or he may reinforce responses on a *fixed-interval* schedule; in this case, a selected interval of time separates the presentation of each successive pair of reinforcers. With a fixed-ratio schedule, very stable rates of response are set up, with the speed of response varying positively with the frequency of the reinforcements. On a fixed-interval schedule, the rate of response is low immediately after a reinforcement but increases markedly as the time for the next reinforcement approaches. Examples of fixed-ratio schedules of reinforcement in everyday life, particularly in child-training procedures, are difficult to find. On the other hand, in most modern social systems the socializing agents, who are dispensers of reinforcers, have to organize their lives on the basis of the time schedules of others. Consequently, in most families some responses of the children are reinforced on a relatively unchanging fixed-interval schedule. Feeding, the availability of the father or school-age siblings for social interaction, and, in general, events associated with household and family routines may serve as reinforcers, positive or negative, that are dispensed at relatively fixed intervals.

A study by Marquis (1941) demonstrates the influence of fixed-interval feeding schedules on the behavior of infants. Marquis compared the activity of infants fed on three-hour, four-hour, and "self-demand" schedules. Infants on fixed-interval schedules showed increased activity as the time for feeding approached; moreover, infants who had been shifted from a three-hour to a four-hour schedule showed rapidly increasing amounts of activity throughout the fourth hour. The effect of fixed-interval schedules on the behavior of older children in family situations has not as yet been the subject of systematic study. Informal observation, however, suggests that they control behavior in much the same way as they do in laboratory studies with animals. For example, in families in which the father is a positive reinforcer, the children (and the mother) can be observed to make "anticipatory responses" as the time for his arrival home from work approaches.

In everyday life, most reinforcers, apart from those associated with daily routines, are dispensed on variable schedules. In laboratory studies the effects of both *variable-ratio* and *variable-interval* schedules have been investigated. In the former case, instead of reinforcing every *n*th response, the experimenter varies the ratios around some mean value, so that a varying number of unreinforced responses occur between the presentation of successive reinforcers. In the case of variable-interval schedules, the experimenter varies the interval between the presentation of successive reinforcers. Variable schedules result in very stable rates of response and, generally speaking, in increased resistance to extinction. Characteristically, social reinforcers are dispensed on *combined schedules* by which the number of unreinforced responses and the time intervals between the presentation of reinforcers are both allowed to vary. Animal studies show that responses that are reinforced at variable intervals but only when the subject is responding at a high rate result in stable *high* rates of response; those that are reinforced at variable intervals but only when the subject is responding at a *low* rate result in stable *low* rates of response. The use of combined schedules thus permits the experimenter to sustain behavior at any desired rate.

In the training of children, the use of combined schedules certainly predominates. Let us take the example of attention-seeking behavior. Most young children attempt many times in the day to elicit a nurturant response from their mothers. Sometimes the mother will respond immediately, but more often she is busy. At varying intervals she will reward the child with interest and attention. Many mothers are inclined to ignore mild forms of attention-seeking behavior and to respond only when this behavior is frequent or intense. It can be predicted, on the basis of laboratory studies to which reference was made above, that these mothers should have children who show persistent attention-seeking behavior occurring at the rates and intensities that have previously brought reward. One may suspect that most "troublesome" behavior has been rewarded on a combined schedule by which undersirable responses of high magnitude and frequency are unwittingly reinforced. The behavior is thus persistent, difficult to extinguish, and baffling for the parents. Perhaps the genesis of much aggressive behavior is to be found in the use of schedules which reward *only* responses of high magnitude; these could be attention-seeking, food-seeking, and other so-called "dependency" responses, as well as responses of the kind more usually regarded as "aggressive."

In social situations, then, reinforcements are usually dispensed on a combined schedule, with both the number of unreinforced responses and the time-intervals between reinforcements continually changing. However, social reinforcement is not so chaotic a process as some writers have implied. The prevalence of mixed schedules of reinforcement in social situations is not due solely to the fact that human beings are less reliable than programmed machines or to their inability to be continuously present to witness the behavior they wish to control. It is due also to the complexity of social demands. Even if the socializing agents were consistent in their behavior and even if they were able to mediate all the child's responses, their scheduling of reinforcements would be dependent on the form, timing, intensity, and objects of the child's behavior.

GENERALIZATION AND DISCRIMINATION

Learned patterns of response tend to generalize to situations other than those in which they were learned, the extent of *generalization* being a function of the degree of similarity between the original learning situation and the novel sets of cues. Indeed, social behavior would be very inefficient if a new set of responses had to be acquired in every social situation. If that were the case, socialization would involve an interminable series of trial-and-error processes, since owing to the constant variability of the patterning of social cues, previously learned complex responses would rarely be elicited in novel situations.

Responses may overgeneralize or generalize on the basis of irrelevant cues, and in such cases maladaptive behavior may occur. Watson and Raynor (1920) have described an experimentally induced phobia in a year-old infant, Albert, whose "irrational" fears were largely the result of overgeneralization. Albert was first exposed to a white rat; then, just as he was about to touch the rat, a loud noise was produced behind his head. On again being presented with the rat, Albert behaved in a highly emotional manner. After several pairings of the rat and the loud sound, Albert displayed a violent fear response when the rat alone was presented. Further tests revealed that by this time Albert had developed a phobia; the fear had generalized to other fluffy objects including rabbits, dogs, a seal-fur coat, cotton, wool, and human hair. Thus, on the basis of stimulus generalization, the range of anxiety-evoking stimuli had grown much wider. Indeed, many "anxiety states" reflect overgeneralizations of this kind.

Inappropriate generalization may be illustrated by the following letter taken from the advice column of a leading metropolitan newspaper:

DEAR ABBY:

My girl friend fixed me up with a blind date and I should have known the minute he showed up in a bow tie that he couldn't be trusted. I fell for him like a rock. He got me to love him on purpose and then lied to me and cheated on me. Every time I go with a man who wears a bow tie, the same thing happens. I think girls should be warned about men who wear them.

AGAINST BOW TIES

DEAR AGAINST:
   Don't condemn all men who wear bow ties because of your experience. I know many a man behind a bow tie who can be trusted.

As the above document illustrates, a generalized response is inappropriate when it occurs to a stimulus element that is not regularly correlated with the other elements of the stimulus complex in which the response was originally learned. In the above example, the letter-writer had generalized a whole pattern of behavior to the bow tie, an object which one would not expect to be regularly associated with the response characteristics of the wearer. The "counselor" is, in effect, attempting to improve the writer's discrimination learning by pointing out that there are positive as well as negative characteristics associated with the wearing of bow ties.

Effective social learning requires both adequate generalization and sharp *discriminations*. Let us consider the handling of physical aggression in North American society. Mild physical aggression expressed toward peers is frequently rewarded as a "sign of masculinity" in boys, but more intense responses of this kind are usually punished. Physical aggression toward parents or siblings, even when mild, is considered undesirable and consequently goes unrewarded or, more often, is punished. On the other hand, physical aggression is permitted, encouraged, and rewarded in some social contexts, provided it is limited to specific forms. For example, in a boxing match a boy may punch with all the force he can muster, but biting or kicking even in this context will lead to prompt social disapproval. Thus, although on the surface it may appear that social reinforcements are dispensed in a haphazard manner, effective social training involves the establishment of fine discriminations. If reinforcements were haphazard, these fine discriminations, which are essential for effective social functioning, would never be acquired.

The social-learning history of an individual may modify his susceptibility to social influence that is exerted through reinforcement or modeling procedures. Children who have developed strong dependency habits are more influenced by social reinforcers than are children in whom dependency responses have been only weakly established (Baer, 1962; Cairns, 1961, 1962; Cairns and Lewis, 1962), and imitative behavior is more readily elicited in high-dependent than in low-dependent children (Jakubczak and Walters, 1959; Dorothea Ross, 1962). Thus, social behavior can be both more easily elicited and more strongly reinforced in children in whom strong dependency habits have been built up. Children who have had a history of failure, including negative reinforcement of independence behavior, are more likely to match the behavior of others and to be influenced by the social reinforcers they dispense (Gelfand, 1962; Lesser and Abelson, 1959). Experiences associated with institutionalization appear also to increase the responsiveness of children to social reinforcers (Stevenson and Cruse, 1961; Stevenson and Fahel, 1961; Zigler, Hodgden, and Stevenson, 1958).

Although there are individual differences in susceptibility to social influence, it is usually possible to predict what reinforcers will be effective for most members of a particular group, since group members share many common social experiences. Some sex differences in responsiveness to social reinforcers, dispensed by same-sex and different-sex experimenters, have already been identified (Epstein and Liverant, 1963; Gewirtz, 1954; Gewirtz and Baer, 1958a, 1958b; Hartup, 1961). Differences between sex of model and sex of child also influence the extent to which imitative behavior will be elicited (Bandura, Ross, and Ross, 1961, 1963a; Rosenblith, 1959, 1961), thus channeling social responses in the direction of sex-appropriate behavior. Moreover, reinforcement procedures are more effective when the agent of reward is a high-prestige person than when the reinforcers are dispensed by a person of low prestige (Prince, 1962), while models of high prestige are also more likely to serve as major sources of imitative behavior (Asch, 1948; Lefkowitz, Blake, and Mouton, 1955; Lippitt, Polansky, and Rosen, 1952). A reinforcer is, in addition, more effective if it represents a class of events that is highly valued (or greatly disvalued) in the recipients' reference group (Zigler and Kanzer, 1962).

The effectiveness of a reinforcer in changing the behavior of a given individual may vary from time to time. It may be enhanced if the individual has been deprived, for some time before its introduction, of reinforcers of this class; it may be reduced if reinforcers of the same class have been freely dispensed for some time preceding its presentation (Gewirtz and Baer, 1958a, 1958b). Deprivation may also result in increased imitative behavior (Rosenblith, 1961). Deprivation and satiation effects are readily observed in the case of reinforcers that are related to biological processes in the organism. In the case of social reinforcers, apparent deprivation and satiation effects are probably due to the occurrence of conditioned emotional responses, learned because of past association of physiological discomfort and pain with the absence of nurturant figures (Gerard and Rabbie, 1961; Schachter, 1959; Staples and Walters, 1961) or with prolonged social interaction resulting from fatigue. Evidence is accumulating that the effectiveness of social-influence procedures is greater if the observers or recipients of social reinforcers are emotionally aroused (Walters, 1962; Walters, Marshall, and Shooter, 1960; Walters and Ray, 1960), possibly because a moderate degree of arousal results in a restriction of attention to salient environmental events. One may suspect, however, that an extreme degree of emotional arousal may result in attention to too many irrelevent cues or in failure to attend to a sufficient number of relevant ones, and so disrupt the learning process (Bindra, 1959; Easterbrook, 1958).

Punishment, inhibition, and nonreward

In preceding sections, we have focused on the presentation of positive reinforcers (rewards) as a means of producing socially approved patterns of behavior. A good deal of social training necessarily involves also the suppression or *inhibition* of responses. In the first place, as we have already noted, response patterns learned in one situation tend to generalize to others in which they are regarded as socially undesirable. Moreover, social demands vary as a child grows older, so that a pattern of response that has been encouraged at one stage of development may later be considered inappropriate and consequently requiring modification. Finally, there are behavior patterns that are permitted to, and rewarding for, adults but that are not socially sanctioned for the child or adolescent. Smoking, drinking, sexual behavior, and many other adult-role activities are examples of adult-permitted, but child-prohibited, response patterns that children are likely to observe to be rewarding and to attempt to reproduce through imitation. In these cases, the goal of social training is the complete suppression of the behavior until the child has reached the age or social status that makes the activity acceptable or esteemed. Indeed, failure in adulthood to produce some of the responses that are prohibited for children can lead to strong social censure.

There are a number of procedures by which the child may be taught to comply with social demands. Undoubtedly, many of the desired changes are brought about by differential social reinforcement, which involves the reward of socially appropriate behavior and the *nonreward* of alternative responses. Selective reinforcement is a slow process and is more frequently used to shape manners and customs that have no serious social consequences than to eliminate activities that constitute a social threat. It is particularly inefficient when there is a strong dominant response and the alternative responses are only weakly developed or absent (Bandura and McDonald, 1963). In cases such as this, more active intervention is required. This may take the form either of the removal of a positive reinforcer (for example, through the deprivation of a privilege or possession) or of the presentation of an aversive stimulus such as physical punishment. While both procedures are techniques of "punishment," as this term is generally employed in the child-training literature, they may have very different effects on the behavior they are intended to control.

Theories and research relating to the effects of *punishment* have been primarily concerned with the direct administration of a noxious stimulus to an organism, the behavior of which it is intended to change. In the typical punishment study, an external cue is paired with a painful stimulus. As a result of this pairing, the formerly neutral cue acquires the capacity to elicit responses that were previously given only to the noxious stimulus. These conditioned avoidance responses are highly resistant to extinction (Solomon, Kamin, and Wynne, 1953). The presence of the conditioned stimulus can thus maintain the avoidant behavior for a long time. It can also lead to the learning of responses that were not made either to the noxious stimulus alone or to the pairing of the neutral and painful stimulus (Brown and Jacobs, 1949; Miller, 1948a). Thus the procedures used in avoidance training give rise to conditioned emotional responses that influence the course of future learning.

In social learning, punishment is used less often to produce avoidance responses to situational cues than to inhibit responses the child has already acquired. Mowrer (1960b) has recently distinguished "place-avoidance learning" from "response inhibition." In place-avoidance learning, an individual is taught to make a specified response in order to escape the noxious stimulus; in response inhibition, the "punished" individual eventually learns not to make a response and so to escape the punishment (Mowrer, 1960a). During the process of response inhibition, proprioceptive cues accompanying the response acquire the capacity to arouse the conditioned emotional reaction. Since some of these cues occur early in the response sequence that originally led to the commission of the disapproved act, the conditioned emotional reaction inhibits the completion of the sequence. Mowrer has made an important distinction but at the same time has indicated that there are similarities in the way in which place avoidance and response inhibition are learned. In social learning both external cues, particularly those associated with the presence of the socializing agents, and internal cues contribute to response inhibition. Conditioned emotional responses may, in fact, be elicited simply by the presence of an adult who has been the agent of punishment; in such cases, the external cue may result in response inhibition without the child's making any preparatory neuromuscular or postural adjustments associated with the commission of the act. Mowrer's analysis of the process of response inhibition has relevance primarily to the problem of "internalization" of prohibitions and the development of "self-control," processes whereby the individual learns not to commit a disapproved act in the presence of high instigation and in the absence of external punishing agents.

A distinction has sometimes been made between the removal of positive reinforcers and simple nonreward. In social training a continuum of procedures, ranging from the active confiscation of a valued privilege or possession to simple nonresponsiveness, is employed. An intermediate procedure consists in the withholding of reinforcers that have been regularly dispensed in the past. From the child's point of view, active confiscation is usually seen as a punishment, simple nonreward as mere disinterest. Intermediate procedures, which have wide use in the shaping of age-appropriate behavior and in many other circumstances, usually involve the withholding of social reinforcers and include some of the techniques that have been labelled as "threat of loss of love." The demonstration of "hurt" or "pain" reactions by the parents is sometimes also included in the latter category. This, however, differs from the withholding of reinforcers in procedure, and probably also in effects, and will be discussed in Chapter 4.

The methods described differ in the relative emphasis they place on the production of desired, and the elimination of unacceptable, responses; in their relative effectiveness in shaping behavior; and in the extent to which they result in undesirable "side effects." In simple nonreward, emphasis is placed on the removal of disapproved behavior. This procedure can be very effective if the desired substitute response already exists in the child's repertory or a model is provided, and if this response, once elicited, is immediately reinforced.

The presentation of aversive stimuli, as in physical and verbal punishment, is similar to nonreward in that it focuses attention on socially disapproved behavior. Its effects on this behavior are, however, very different. Whereas nonreward usually results in the extinction of responses, aversive conditioning suppresses rather than eliminates them (Azrin, 1959, 1960; Estes,

1944) and may sometimes result in generalized inhibition, involving responses other than the punished one (Estes and Skinner, 1941; Sidman, 1962). Moreover, emotional responses established through aversive conditioning may motivate socially undesirable behavior patterns that are highly resistant to extinction. These patterns may include avoidance of the punishing agents, a consequence that reduces the effectiveness of the agents for further social training. Aversive stimulation, like nonreward, can be very effective in changing behavior if desirable responses are elicited and rewarded while the undesirable response is suppressed. In these circumstances, it may be the quickest and most effective way of producing change (Whiting and Mowrer, 1943).

Active confiscation of privileges is almost invariably combined with verbal or physical punishment; it is therefore likely to result in the side effects associated with aversive training procedures. The withholding of positive reinforcers need have none of these disadvantages. Its immediate effect is probably to increase socially desirable responses that are aimed at reinstating the reinforcers. Since the socializing agent is the source of the reinforcers, this procedure, in contrast to aversive stimulation, tends to maintain approach responses that facilitate social training.

In the preceding discussion of the effects of various social-training procedures, attention has been primarily given to their influence on the person whose behavior it is intended to modify or control. However, the administration of punishment to one person may produce conditioned emotional reactions (Berger, 1962) and response inhibition (Bandura, 1962b; Bandura, Ross, and Ross, 1963b; Walters, Leat, and Mezei, 1963) in observers, effects that are very similar to those produced by direct negative reinforcement.

CONFLICT AND DISPLACEMENT

The pairing of noxious stimuli with social responses that an individual, because of past positive reinforcement, is strongly disposed to make gives rise to an *approach–avoidance conflict,* the outcome of which is dependent upon the relative strength of the approach and avoidance responses. Miller's

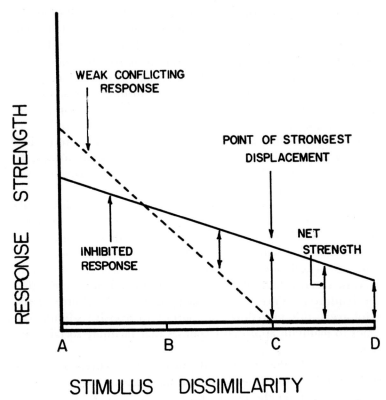

FIG. 1–1. *Miller's conflict paradigm. "Displacement produced by greater steepness in the gradient of generalization of the conflicting response (assuming linearity). It can be seen that displaced responses can occur and that the strongest displaced response will be expected at an intermediate point,* C *in the diagram on the*

(1948b, 1959) conflict model (Figure 1–1) is the best known attempt to predict, on the basis of learning-theory principles, what the outcome is likely to be. According to this model, inhibitory (fear or anxiety) responses and the responses with which they compete generalize to stimulus situations similar to those in which they were originally learned, the strength of the generalized responses being a function of the similarity between the original

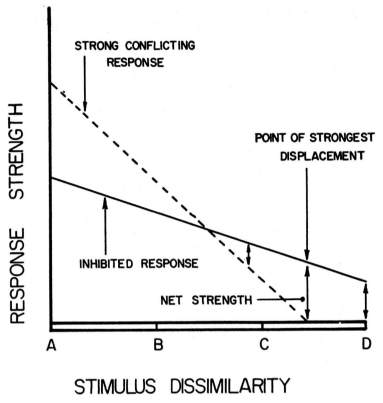

STIMULUS DISSIMILARITY

FIG. 1–1   (*Continued*)

left. Increasing the strength of the conflicting response weakens the strongest displaced response and causes it to be elicited by less similar stimuli, those between C *and* D *in the diagram to the right" (from Miller, 1948b).*

and the new situations. Miller assumes that the generalization gradient for an inhibitory response is steeper than that of the response which is inhibited and that, consequently, at some point on the stimulus dissimilarity continuum the approach tendency becomes the stronger and is therefore manifested in overt activity. A series of studies with animals (Brown, 1948; Kaufman and

Miller, 1949; Miller and Kraeling, 1952; Miller and Murray, 1952; Murray and Berkun, 1955) that supported Miller's basic assumptions have given wide acceptance to the conflict paradigm.

Social-learning applications of Miller's conflict model have largely been confined to attempts to account for the expression of aggressive frustration reactions toward persons other than the original frustrators. It has been assumed that a fear response learned in interactions with socialization agents may prevent punished behavior—in this case, aggression—from being displayed toward these agents, but that the aggressive response is likely to be diverted to other persons or objects. Moreover, the probability that a *displaced* aggressive response will be directed toward a particular target has been depicted as a function of the similarity of possible objects of aggression to the socialization agents and of the strength of the original aggressive and fear responses (Bandura and Walters, 1959; Sears, Whiting, Nowlis, and Sears, 1953; Whiting and Child, 1953; Wright, 1954). On account both of extremely arbitrary (and usually post-hoc) ordering and locating of targets of aggression on the similarity continuum and also of the introduction of additional assumptions designed to explain discrepancies between findings and predictions based on Miller's model, it is difficult to assess the theoretical implications of these applications.

Highly aggressive boys have been found to have parents who strongly disapprove, reprimand, and punish aggression *in* the home (Bandura, 1960; Bandura and Walters, 1959; Glueck and Glueck, 1950), a finding that has frequently been interpreted as an instance of displacement. However, since the parents of such boys encourage and reward aggression *outside* the home (Bandura, 1960; Bandura and Walters, 1959), the apparently displaced aggression may be primarily an outcome of discrimination training.

The hypothesis that when a frustrating agent is feared, aggression will be displaced to a less-feared scapegoat has been used to account for the occurrence of hostility and aggression toward minorities or members of "out-groups" that are identifiably different from the social groups to which the aggressor belongs. Evidence for the scapegoat theory of prejudice is, at best, equivocal (for example, Berkowitz, 1958, 1962; Cowen, Landes, and Schaet, 1959; Lewin, Lippitt, and White, 1939; Lindzey, 1950; Lippitt, 1939; Miller and Bugelski, 1948; Stagner and Congdon, 1955; Weatherley, 1961). Prejudices, like other "aggressive" responses, are acquired through imitation and direct training and make their appearance relatively early in a child's life (Radke-Yarrow, Trager, and Miller, 1952). Once a prejudice has been learned, hostile-aggressive responses are, by definition, high in the response hierarchies elicited by the target of prejudice. The "scapegoating" of out-group members can therefore be regarded as the outcome of discrimination learning in which a strong association has been developed between the sight or sound of individuals belonging to certain ethnic or religious groups (Allport, 1954), or known to hold certain beliefs (Rokeach, 1960), and hostile-aggressive responses. Since the aggressor is said to select for attack an individual or group who is *unlike* the frustrating agent, the kind of stimulus generalization assumed in the Miller displacement model seems to play little or no part in determining its occurrence (Buss, 1961).

The part that deliberate social training plays in fostering displacement of aggression is well illustrated by the behavior of parents and other members of white communities during the desegregation battles in the South. Children in these communities were provided with ample opportunities, through observation of their parents, to learn whom they should hate and for what reasons, and how they should express their aggression toward the hated objects.

One reason for the inadequacy of Miller's displacement model is that it adopts a basically nonsocial approach to a problem in social learning. According to this model, the objects and strength of displaced responses can be predicted from knowledge of three variables only—the strength of instigation, that is, of approach tendencies to the frustrating agent; the severity of punishment of these responses; and a stimulus-similarity dimension. The theory thus ignores the influence of the original agents of frustration and punishment in determining responses toward stimulus objects other than themselves. In fact, parents often through precept, example, and control of reinforcement contingencies determine rather precisely the kind of displaced responses that a child will or will not exhibit. Displaced aggression is further modified by the responses it elicits from other socializing agents and from the objects of the aggression themselves. Miller's generalization gradients thus become relatively meaningless for a human-learning situation in which the patterns of reward-punishment contingencies displayed by parents and other agents of socialization have no consistent relationship to the similarity of the parents to possible objects of aggression.

Moreover, the model makes no provision for the occurrence of self-generated inhibitory responses, which may be relatively independent of situational cues. When avoidance behavior is motivated by the anticipation of self-punishment, one would expect the slopes of the approach and avoidance gradients to differ less than when avoidance is motivated by fear of externally administered punishment.

One should probably reserve the term "displacement" for cases in which frustration is known to have occurred and the frustrated response is directed toward an object other than the frustrator. An adequate social-learning model for the prediction of displacement must take into account a number of variables that are ignored in Miller's paradigm. Knowledge of the extent of frustration and of the punitiveness of the primary socializing agents is, of course, needed. In addition, however, crucial for prediction are such variables as the hierarchy of frustration reactions the agent has acquired; the modeling (through overt behavior and attitudes) of responses to potential displacement objects by parents and other authority figures; and the reward-punishment contingencies adopted by these figures in respect to the relevant behavior, both when directed toward themselves and when directed toward other possible objects.

Social training consists largely in teaching a child to express aggressive, dependency, and other social responses only in certain ways. For example, he may be taught to "defend his principles" (or his parents') but not to attack an opponent physically. The substitution of more socially acceptable responses for less acceptable ones has been referred to as "response displacement" (Bandura and Walters, 1959). This, however, is also a case of discrimination learning, and no new principles are required to explain its occurrence.

PERSONALITY DEVELOPMENT
AND THE CONCEPT OF REGRESSION

As a consequence of the training procedures that have been outlined earlier, the child learns a variety of response patterns to the same social cues. These patterns vary in strength, forming a *habit hierarchy*. A particular habit of responding may dominate many hierarchies and consequently be elicited in many social situations; however, the nondominant habits may be different from one hierarchy to another and may vary in strength relative both to the dominant habit and among themselves. Dependency training provides a good example of how the relative strength of responses in a hierarchy may be changed through learning and how a single response pattern may become dominant in different social contexts. During a child's earliest years, parents encourage and actively reward the physical dependency expressed in the seeking of "contact comfort." However, in the course of independence training, they reward less and less frequently this type of response, when expressed toward themselves, and instead encourage and reward dependency behavior that takes the form of seeking attention, approval, and interest. Although eventually the latter predominates over the former in the response hierarchy, both response patterns are highly developed and may not differ widly in strength. It is not unusual, therefore, for older children, adolescents, and even adults, particularly under stress conditions, to exhibit occasional physical-comfort responses (clinging and holding) to parents and to other family members who may have reinforced such responses in earlier years. In contrast, physical dependency receives less reinforcement in interactions with same-sex peers, while attention-seeking responses are frequently and continuously rewarded. Since the physical-dependency responses toward peers are weakly developed, especially among males, they are very rarely elicited even when attention-seeking behavior brings inadequate reward.

Since some response patterns are dominant in many hierarchies, they are exhibited in a wide range of situations. In the traditional psychodynamic models, these response hierarchies are conceptualized as layers or levels of personality. In these models it is assumed that the dominant responses are superficial derivatives that obtain their engery from psychic forces operating in the lower levels of personality. In contrast, the social-learning model outlined above regards response tendencies low in the habit hierarchies as exerting little or no influence on overt behavior, which is a product of social learning. According to our view, preoccupation with ever-present underlying forces mitigates against the understanding of persistent patterns of behavior.

If the component habits in a response hierarchy differ widely in strength, the dominant response pattern may persist for a relatively long period of time in the face of non-reward and punishment. In contrast, when the habits activated in a particular social situation differ little in strength, any minor changes in consequences will result in response variability. Non-dominant responses are likely to be ones that the individual has learned at an earlier time; and if they are no longer age-appropriate, their emergence may be regarded as an instance of *regression*.

In most psychodynamic accounts, regression occurs when a person under stress, usually in the form of internally generated "ego-threat," reverts to a pattern of behavior characteristic of an earlier stage of development at which some degree of "fixation" has developed. According to Fenichel (1945), fixation may result either from excessive gratification or from excessive frustration at a given level of development. Of course, one would expect habits that had received a great deal of gratification through intermittent reinforcement to be maintained over a long period of time and to be relatively dominant in certain response hierarchies. On the other hand, although frustration may produce a temporary intensification of the nonrewarded response, in and of itself it provides no conditions conducive to the establishing or maintaining of a strong habit and, if prolonged, should eventually lead to extinction. Probably cases of fixation that have been described as originating from excessive frustration are ones in which the behavior in question has been intermittently reinforced. There is therefore no need to distinguish between "positive" and "negative" fixation (Whiting and Child, 1953) on the basis of different antecedent conditions. We suspect that, in the case of positive fixation resulting from excessive gratification, emphasis is placed on the reward trials, whereas in the case of negative fixation, the supposed antecedent of which is excessive frustration, emphasis is shifted to the nonreward trials; consequently, both kinds of fixation can be accounted for by principles relating to the scheduling of reinforcements.

According to our social-learning model, regression is most likely to occur if age-appropriate and age-inappropriate responses differ relatively little in strength, especially when the latter responses have received prolonged intermittent reinforcement and current reinforcement schedules are inadequate for maintaining the age-appropriate behavior. From this point of view, the occurrence of self-generated threat or threat of punishment by others is less important than current reinforcement schedules in determining whether regression will occur. For example, one would not expect regression when a pattern of behavior is both punished and rewarded; on the other hand, if the dominant age-appropriate behavior is a source of threat and alternative age-appropriate responses are inadequately rewarded, regression may readily occur (cf. Mowrer, 1940). Moreover, regressive behavior is often elicited in children through their observing a younger sibling rewarded for behavior which is appropriate for a younger, but not for an older, child. Imitation of the younger sibling may then occur because the older child mistakenly anticipates reward for matching the sibling's behavior. In such cases, the anticipation of reward rather than the occurrence of threat is the more important factor in eliciting the age-inappropriate responses.

CONTINUITIES IN SOCIAL DEVELOPMENT

Exponents of psychodynamic theories of personality, with the exception of Lewin (1935), have assumed that there are elaborate stage-specific modes of behavior which are typically displayed by individuals of specifiable chronological ages, and that regression involves a reversion to patterns of responding that are characteristic of a level of development through which an individual should have passed. From the point of view presented above, regressive reactions in most cases are likely to be relatively specific and to reflect changes in only a few response hierarchies.

Stage theories of personality development (Erikson, 1950; Freud, 1949 [1940];[1] Gesell and Ilg, 1943; Piaget, 1948 [1932], 1954 [1937]; Sullivan, 1953) have been widely accepted as providing explanations of prosocial as well as of regressive and other deviant forms of behavior. Although there is relatively little consensus among these theories concerning the number and characteristics of crucial stages, they all assume that social behavior can be categorized in terms of a relatively pre-fixed sequence of stages which are more or less discontinuous. Stage theories place emphasis on intraindividual variability over time and on similarities among individuals at specifiable age periods; consequently, they tend to minimize obvious and often marked interindividual variability in behavior due to biological, socioeconomic, ethnic, and cultural differences and to variations in the child-training practices of socialization agents. Since children from diverse backgrounds experience different reinforcement contingencies and are exposed to widely differing social models, there are marked group differences at any age level. Moreover, even children who come from similar social or cultural backgrounds and have similar biological characteristics may, as a result of differing social-training experiences, display marked interindividual variability in social behavior patterns. On the other hand, since familial, subcultural, and biological factors that partly determine an individual's social-training experiences are likely to remain relatively constant throughout much of his earlier lifetime, one would expect a good deal of intraindividual continuity in behavior at successive age periods. Thus, social-learning approaches, in contrast to stage theories, lay stress on interindividual differences and on intraindividual continuities.

---

[1] In the case of works first published in a language other than English, the date of the publication of the original book or paper has been placed in brackets after the date of the translation to which reference has been made. It is hoped that this device will help preserve the chronology of material and also facilitate its identification within the list of references provided at the end of the book.

Stage theories have at best specified only vaguely the conditions that lead to changes in behavior from one level to another. In some of these theories it is assumed that age-specific behavior emerges spontaneously as the result of some usually unspecified biological or maturational process. In others it seems to be assumed that the maturational level of the organism forces from socializing agents patterns of child-training behavior that are relatively universal, thereby predetermining the sequence of developmental changes. In contrast, social-learning theories would predict marked changes in the behavior of an individual of a given age only as a result of abrupt alterations in social-training and other relevant biological or environmental variables, which rarely occur in the social-learning histories of most individuals during pre-adult years.

The most widespread treatment of certain forms of social behavior as emergent stage-specific phenomena is to be found in the literature on adolescence. Adolescents are typically characterized as passing through a period of storm and stress and as struggling to emancipate themselves from their parents. They are depicted as striving for independence, resisting dependence on adults, and allying themselves with a peer group, to whom they are compulsively conforming, in a "conflict of generations" (Gallagher and Harris, 1958; Hurlock, 1955; Josselyn, 1948; Mohr and Despres, 1958; Parsons, 1950; Pearson, 1958). Consequently, on account of the conflicting values and standards to which they are supposedly exposed and also because they are assumed to be in a transition state in which they are neither child nor adult, adolescents are depicted as ambivalent, confused, and unpredictable in their behavior. There is very little research on representative samples of adolescents that would support this viewpoint; indeed, available studies of family interactions (Bandura and Walters, 1959; Elkin and Westley, 1955) and normative data concerning the behavior of high-school students (Hollingshead, 1949) suggest that the majority of adolescents have already achieved a considerable degree of independence and therefore have little need to resist dependence on adults. Moreover, they tend to choose friends on the basis of the values they have acquired from their parents; consequently, their peer group tends to reinforce the standards of behavior of which their parents approve, and there is thus no serious conflict of generations (Westley and Elkin, 1956).

Individual differences that are lawfully related to, and highly consistent with, preadolescent behavior can, of course, be as readily observed among adolescents as among younger children. Indeed, such differences are probably more marked during adolescence, by which time habits have become more stable and behavior more under internal-stimulus control.

In the literature on childhood psychopathology it is frequently implied that the vast majority of adolescents pass through a mildly delinquent phase and that delinquency is a stage-specific phenomenon. However, research into delinquent careers (Glueck and Glueck, 1930, 1950; McCord, McCord, and Zola, 1959; Powers and Witmer, 1951) clearly indicates that anti-social behavior does not suddenly emerge with adolescence and that histories of delinquency usually extend back at least into middle childhood years. Again, continuity of behavior is more evident than discontinuity.

THE INTERACTION OF SOCIAL-LEARNING AND BIOLOGICAL VARIABLES

In societies in which the possession of certain genetically determined attributes brings esteem and facilitates the acquisition of rewarding resources, constitutional factors inevitably influence the nature of the social-learning histories of individual persons. Moreover, biological and biochemical factors obviously interact with social-learning variables in subtle ways that have been frequently overlooked even by theorists who claim to present biosocial interpretations of human development.

Social manipulations can have relatively little influence on some biologically determined characteristics, such as the body type or facial features of an individual. Yet within a society that sets high value on the possession of certain physical attributes, the frequency with which social reinforcers are dispensed is partly dependent on the extent to which these cultural ideals are met. In North American society, where prestige and social rewards are bestowed for athletic ability and physique, boys who are small, lack muscular strength or dexterity, or who are obese and possess feminine-like physiques are relatively unsuccessful in obtaining positive reinforcement from peers. Similarly, a female who does not match the standards of beauty within her society evokes far fewer positive responses, especially from males, than one who possesses these socially esteemed characteristics. The slender, petite female has been highly admired in North American culture; she may, however, be the recipient of relatively few positive reinforcers and considerable aversive treatment in cultures lacking in labor-saving devices.

> Industriousness on the part of the girl is an even more important criterion of attractiveness than for a boy. The big, strapping woman, who could carry large loads of produce or firewood up the mountainside, and who could labor tirelessly were the females that caused Kwoma men to smack their lips and make lewd comments. Marok's sister, Uka, a powerfully built woman, was considered the most attractive girl in the hamlet (Whiting, 1941, p. 72).

Patterns of social reinforcement may be determined to some degree not only by the *type* of physical characteristics one possesses, but also by the *timing* of changes in physique in relation to one's age-mates. Because they temporarily depart from the physical ideals of their culture, early-maturing girls and late-maturing boys in North American schools gain relatively little prestige and popularity among their peer group (Jones, 1957; Mussen and Jones, 1957). It is thus apparent that within the framework provided by prevailing social models, physical characteristics may have a considerable *indirect* influence on the course of an individual's development.

When associations are discovered between constitutional factors and patterns of social behavior, many theorists are inclined to regard the genetically linked characteristic as a major causative influence when in fact the relationship may be far more indirect. For example, some investigators (Glueck and Glueck, 1950; Sheldon, Hartl, and McDermott, 1949) have noted an association between mesomorphic body build and the occurrence of antisocial aggressive behavior. They have failed to point out, however, that the possession of an athletic, muscular physique increases the probability that physically aggressive responses will be reinforced or, at least, not lead to harmful consequences. Indeed, it is reasonable to suppose that while mesomorphy may contribute to the maintenance of physically aggressive responses, it is of relatively little importance during the acquisition period.

Although intellectual development is highly modifiable through environmental manipulations (Hunt, 1961), there can be little doubt that genetic factors set some limits on the development of an individual's intellectual capacities and thus influence the relative proportion of experiences of success and failure which he receives, especially within societies that emphasize formal education. These experiences, however, will be highly dependent on the social models with which a child is presented and on the reinforcement patterns adopted by his parents and other adults in his immediate social subgroup. A child of below-average intelligence is likely to receive fewer negative reinforcements if he grows up in a lower-class home than if his parents have attained professional status. Similarly, responses to physically handicapped children vary considerably among social subgroups even within a single culture (Barker, Wright, and Gonick, 1946).

A number of investigators have observed stable individual differences among neonates in activity level, crying, autonomic reactivity, and patterns of tension and tension control (Aldrich, Sung, and Knop, 1945; Grossman and Greenberg, 1957; Kessen, Williams, and Williams, 1961; Wolff, 1959). If, as Kessen and Mandler (1961) have suggested, there are constitutionally determined predispositions to develop or inhibit anxiety, such factors will inevitably modify the effects of child-training practices and determine in part which methods of control parents and other socialization agents will learn to select for most effectively training individual children.

It is not our purpose to elucidate the little-understood role of constitutional factors in personality development and we shall refer to these only on rare occasions in the remainder of this book. Studies of identical twins who have been reared apart (Anastasi and Foley, 1949) lead to the conclusion that even when genetically determined attributes remain relatively constant, social-learning variables may produce marked differences in patterns of social behavior. It is probable that, until further advances in biochemistry and psychopharmacology have been made, there is more to be gained by studying the role of undoubtedly important social-learning variables in personality development than by seeking to establish relationships between constitutional factors and personality characteristics.

Social learning, deviant behavior, and psychotherapy

In spite of the fact that available research evidence (Sears, 1943) should long ago have raised serious questions concerning the wisdom of utilizing psychoanalytic constructs as a basis for scientific analyses of human behavior, some of the major attempts to present prosocial and deviant behavior within a single learning-theory framework (Dollard and Miller, 1950; Mowrer and Kluckhohn, 1944; Mowrer, 1950) have largely consisted of translations of Freudian principles and concepts, such as the pleasure principle, ego strength, repression, and transference, into terms more acceptable to experimental psychologists. Dollard and Miller, among others, claim that such translations permit psychoanalytic hypotheses to be more readily tested. However, theorists and practitioners who favor psychodynamic approaches are inclined to dismiss negative results, obtained from empirical tests of psychoanalytically derived hypotheses that are couched in learning-theory terms, on the grounds that the translations are inadequate; at the same time, they welcome results that confirm such hypotheses and claim these positive outcomes as reputable sources of support for their adherence to psychoanalytic theory and method. The net effect of these translations has thus been to entrench more firmly assumptions and concepts that have accumulated over the years through the uncontrolled trial-and-error experiences of practicing clinicians.

In some respects the widely accepted psychodynamically based theories of psychopathology are dominated by models provided by physical medicine. In accordance with these models, behavior deviations are frequently considered to be derivatives or symptoms of underlying disease processes which disrupt social functioning in a manner analogous to that in which toxic substances affect the functioning of the body. This symptom-underlying disease analogy is reflected in the use of terms such as "mental health," "mental disease," and "emotional disorder," and in the labeling of persons exhibiting atypical behavior as "sick" and as "patients" and even of cultural and subcultural patterns as "sick," "healthy," and "unhealthy." It is also reflected in discussions of theoretical issues in psychopathology, as in the question whether schizophrenia should be considered as a single "disease entity," and in the widespread and sometimes indiscriminate use of chemical and physical agents to modify or control deviant behavior patterns.

Some clinicians who have adopted this medical model hold the view that the basic pathology is somatic in nature; the majority, however, regard the underlying disturbance as a psychologic, rather than neurologic, dysfunction. The latter employ symptom-underlying disease models in which the "disease" is a function of conscious or (more often) unconscious inner agents akin to the supernatural forces that once provided the explanatory concepts of physics, biology, and (more recently) medicine. General medicine has progressed from the demonology that dominated it during the dark ages; as scientific knowledge has increased, magical explanations have been replaced by scientific ones. In contrast, theories of psychopathology, in which demons reappear in the guise of "psychodynamic forces," still reflect the mystical thinking that once predominated in science (Reider, 1955). These demonic agents are typically "ego-alien," buried under layers of personality, and held in check by counteragents or lines of defenses.

The psychodynamic "disease" model thus leads one to seek determinants of deviant behavior in terms of relatively autonomous internal agents and processes in the form of "unconscious psychic forces," "dammed-up energies," "cathexes," "counter-cathexes," "defenses," "complexes," and other hypothetical conditions or states having only a tenuous relationship to the social stimuli that precede them or even to the behavioral "symptoms" or "symbols" that they supposedly explain. In contrast, our social-learning theory, instead of regarding internal processes as primary links in causal sequences that generate deviant patterns of response, treats such processes as mediating events, the nature of, and modifications in, which must be inferred from the conjunction of certain manipulable stimulus conditions and observable response sequences. While these inferred events may play an important role within an explanatory system that generates predictions concerning behavioral change, they cannot be directly manipulated and consequently are of little importance in implementing programs for modifying behavior. Moreover, they have predictive value only to the extent that they are systematically related to both the manipulable stimulus conditions and the observable response variables, a condition that is rarely met in the cases of the constructs employed in psychodynamic theories.

To illustrate the differences in approaches, let us consider the concept of symptom substitution, which has played an important role in determining techniques of psychoanalytic therapy. The most detailed accounts of the functional value of symptoms and the manner in which these should be handled by the therapist are provided by Freud (1920 [1917]) and Fenichel (1945), who constantly introduce hydraulic-energy analogies. Neurotic symptoms are regarded as substitute or derivative discharges of warded-off and repressed impulses that constitute a threat to the ego and consequently cannot receive direct expression. These occur on account of insufficient ego-control, which may arise from excessive stimulation from libidinal forces or through the blocking of energy discharges (Fenichel, 1945). The energy is then channeled into, and bound up in, symptomatic behavior, which is consequently affect-laden and highly resistant to change. Since the symptom is an energy outlet and its removal in no way reduces the underlying motivating forces, symptom treatment results only in further blocking of energy, which must therefore find expression in some other form. Moreover, since the energy is bound in the symptom, which thus serves as a defense, there is a danger that symptom removal will result in the flooding or overwhelming of the ego with energy, forcing the ego to resort to pathological behavior that is often even more extreme than the disorder the patient originally displayed.

There is no reason to believe, on the basis of social-learning theory, that the direct modification of deviant behavior inevitably results in the appearance of new substitute deviant responses. According to our point of view, the symptom is a pattern of behavior that dominates the response hierarchies the patient has learned to a given set of stimulus conditions. If this symptom is eliminated through counterconditioning, extinction, or some other method of modifying behavior, the next most dominant set of responses in the hierarchies will tend to occur. These patterns of behavior may or may not be deviant. If they are not deviant, removal of the symptom effectively completes the treatment. However, if the patient has learned relatively few pro-social means of obtaining the rewards or relief which his deviant behavior was aimed at securing, it is always possible that, following elimination of one deviant pattern, another set of deviant responses will occur. This outcome can, of course, sometimes be forestalled by including in the treatment program procedures designed to elicit, shape, and strengthen desired alternative behavior.

Within this book we have made a number of comparisons between psychodynamic interpretations of social and developmental phenomena and those generated by our socio-behavioristic approach. These comparisons will reveal fundamental differences between the two points of view in respect to issues concerning both personality development and the genesis and treatment of deviant behavior. Indeed, we have attempted to demonstrate that a single set of social-learning principles can account for the development of both prosocial and deviant behavior and for modifications of behavior toward greater conformity or greater deviation. Consequently, we regard unique psychodynamic principles as superfluous and see little point in attempting to translate them into learning-theory terms.

Methodological Problems

DEFINITION OF THE DEPENDENT VARIABLE
IN CHILD PSYCHOPATHOLOGY

Much of the research into the determinants of deviant social behavior has been confounded by subjective value judgments of what constitutes "normal" or "abnormal" behavior. The dependent variables in these investigations are often defined in terms of an inferred global state of the organism—for example, mental or emotional disturbance, ego defect, emotional immaturity, superego defect—rather than being defined in terms of specific observable behavior. The investigator typically makes categorical judgments concerning children's states or conditions instead of attempting to order their behavior along measurable dimensions. The categorization of children as "disturbed" or "nondisturbed," "normal" or "abnormal," and mentally "ill" or "healthy" involves value judgments that are influenced not only by social and cultural factors (Hollingshead and Redlich, 1958) but also by personal biases related to the training, personal experience, and theoretical orientation of the individual who makes the judgment.

Judgments of this kind often result in referrals to clinics or other social agencies. Sometimes parents define the child as "mentally disturbed" and in need of diagnostic study or therapeutic attention. At other times the definition is initially provided by social agencies, public health agencies, schools, or legal authorities. The definition is then confirmed by physical and mental health practitioners, such as pediatricians, general practitioners, psychiatrists, psychologists, or psychiatric social workers. In contrast to adults, who frequently refer themselves for diagnosis or treatment, the children themselves are rarely the definers. A certain proportion of children who are defined by someone as exhibiting an "emotional disturbance" become residential or day "patients" in diagnostic, detention, or treatment centers. These children constitute the population from which subjects for research are typically drawn. In other words, the research workers rely on the institutional definition of psychopathology, that is to say, children who attend outpatient centers or hospitals for "emotionally disturbed" children or are in legal detention are regarded as psychologically deviant. In studies that are sophisticated enough to include comparison groups, these typically consist of noninstitutionalized children or children not in treatment, who by virtue of their nonmembership in deviant groups, as defined above, are considered to be "normal" and "psychologically healthy." Since a certain percentage of children who are defined by someone as displaying an "emotional disorder" are not to be found in clinics, hospitals, or detention homes, often because of parental reluctance to concur with the judgments of others or because facilities for diagnosis and treatment are not available, the institutional definition of "mental disturbance" may result in the inclusion of an unknown number of false negatives in the noninstitutionalized group. In addition, since the referral of a child to an agency may be the most convenient way for a parent or other adult to bring attention to his own problems or to obtain assistance in influencing the decisions of school and other authorities, this type of definition frequently results in the inclusion of an unknown number of false positives in the "emotionally disturbed" group.

Selection of subjects solely on the basis of their attendance at a treatment or custodial agency may yield somewhat misleading information concerning the antecedents of childhood disorders. For example, all kinds of deviant behavior—delinquency, autism, psychosomatic disorders, achievement and intellectual defects—have been attributed to the single nonspecific factor of parental rejection, which supposedly generates either anxiety or hostility. Since parents who are critical of, or displeased with, their children's behavior are more likely to seek remedial treatment than parents who accept their children's atypical patterns of response, it is not surprising to find a high incidence of rejection in parents of children drawn exclusively from clinic populations.

Once rejection is hypothesized as the crucial causative factor in childhood disorders, a child's deviant behavior tends to be regarded as a derivative or manifestation of the underlying anxiety or hostility resulting from the disturbed parent-child relationship. Moreover, the influence of specific social-training procedures, such as the direct reinforcement of certain classes of deviant responses or exposure to deviant models of particular kinds, is almost inevitably overlooked. Consequently, most studies of childhood deviation have yielded relatively little information concerning the differential etiology of varying forms of childhood deviation, other than elaborate accounts of intrafamily dynamics that are often inferred from the symptoms manifested by a particular child. There is consequently a paucity of general principles that can be applied to the understanding of childhood disorders. The position might be very different if comparisons were more frequently made between groups of non-institutionalized children who show atypical patterns of social behavior. For example, Bandura (1960) compared the child-training practices of parents of boys who were extremely inhibited in a wide variety of social situations with those of parents of highly aggressive boys. In this study, samples of deviant children were selected on the basis of careful behavioral observations. Although the children chosen for study displayed aggressive and withdrawn response patterns that were more extreme than those typically encountered in clinical populations, it was found that neither group of parents was particularly rejecting. On the other hand, there were considerable differences between the two groups of parents in their direct training procedures and their modeling behavior. Since the majority of the families regarded either aggression or social inhibition as a desirable attribute, they did not appear in clinics in spite of repeated pressure from school authorities for the families to seek therapeutic attention for their sons' behavioral problems.

The above discussion is not meant to imply that research workers should never make comparisons between institutionalized and noninstitutionalized children, or between children who are receiving treatment of certain kinds and children who are not. Such comparisons are justified, however, only if the variables under investigation are ones that, on the basis of theory or prior research, can reasonably be expected to vary systematically as a function of institutionalization or treatment procedures.

THE NORMAL–ABNORMAL DICHOTOMY

Failure to distinguish between value judgments and empirical issues has led to considerable confusion in clinical investigations of the antecedents of psychopathology. Categorization of behavior patterns as normal or abnormal involves a value judgment, and it should be recognized that issues revolving around such judgments cannot be resolved on the basis of empirical data. Consequently, since questions of value are independent of questions of causality, it is a mistaken belief to hold that research cannot profitably commence before "disorders" have been categorized. For example, much time has been spent in attempts to arrive at a consensus on what constitutes "alcoholism." There is a wide variety of behavioral indices that have been, or could be, used to support the judgment that a particular person is an alcoholic—the amount of alcohol consumed, the time of day during which drinking occurs, the occurrence of blackouts or withdrawal reactions, the proportion of an individual's income that is spent on alcohol, or a preference for solitary drinking. Because different judges select different criteria, which they also weight differentially, for determining the presence of alcoholism, consensus is difficult to achieve. To complicate the matter, the indices that are considered to indicate pathology vary greatly from one culture or subculture to another; in fact, in some cases there is virtually no overlap (Jellinek, 1960).

However, the research worker who is interested in identifying antecedents of one or more of the behavioral indices listed above gains nothing from establishing a prior definition of alcoholism, though he can of course employ the term as a convenient shorthand way of referring to the constellation of behavioral variables that he has selected for study. In this case, however, the dependent variables are measurable classes of behavior and not the abstract label of "alcoholism." Indeed, one may suspect that many of the contradictions and inconsistencies in findings relating to the "problem of alcoholism" spring in part from the fact that research workers frequently do not specify precisely their dependent variables but simply present the value label, which usually gets attached to their subjects merely on account of their having attended a clinic or hospital. A similar situation exists in respect to research on most syndromes, such as neuroticism, mental deficiency, delinquency, schizophrenia, and psychopathy, for which multiple criteria are employed. In all such cases, research workers have tended to rely on the subjective judgments of experts as the basis for selecting their subjects and have consequently failed to provide carefully specified dependent variables for which there could be specific antecedents.

It has frequently been claimed that normal behavior can be best understood by studying deviants, on the supposition that the latter exhibit extreme or more "pure" forms of the phenomena under investigation. This claim has no more foundation than the belief that the study of deviant behavior should be postponed until normal behavior is understood. Both positions, in fact, presuppose that social-value judgments must be made before research can be profitably undertaken. For a science of social behavior such judgments have no relevance; the task facing the scientist is to select behavioral variables which fall on some well-defined dimensions and to identify their antecedents and correlates. It is probable that many relationships between selected antecedent and consequent variables will not be linear ones; in such cases, extrapolation from one level of behavioral extremity to another would undoubtedly be erroneous if, in fact, only one level had been studied.

The belief that it is advantageous to base the study of "normal" behavior on observations of highly deviant individuals has generated a number of trait theories of personality (Cattell, 1946; Eysenck, 1947; Rosanoff, 1938), which attempt to evaluate the behavior of nondeviant individuals in terms of a set of dimensions or categories borrowed from descriptive psychiatry. In addition, it has inspired the construction of personality tests (for example, Hathaway and McKinley, 1943), which "quantify" human behavior on scales such as schizophrenia, hypochondriasis, and hysteria. Since the nosological categories of descriptive psychiatry are themselves based on a sampling of very diverse responses exhibited by different groups of patients, most of whom do not fall precisely into any available category, these categories can hardly be fruitful reference points for a scientific approach to personality. Indeed, the existence of such trait theories and related measuring devices has, in general, had the effect of encouraging imprecise, descriptive research and so of hampering progress in the discovery of the antecedent-consequent relationships that regulate social behavior.

"A more productive and less confusing approach to the understanding of behavior disorders is to examine carefully the process by which socialization of behavior is achieved and to select dimensions or variables of child behavior that appear to be of importance for the socialization process" (Bandura and Walters, 1959, p. 362). Similarly, one may select dimensions of behavior exhibited in varying degrees and intensity by parents and other agents of socialization, and seek for relationships between these socialization variables and the behavior exhibited by children. A dimensional approach of this kind "focuses on variables that are relevant to the normal study of the child and its findings can thus be more readily fitted into the context of general psychological theory" (Bandura and Walters, 1959, p. 363). Moreover, such an approach more readily permits an integration of findings from laboratory-experimental and field studies, since the variables under study can be manipulated, at least within certain limits, for the purpose of establishing the nature and direction of the causal relationships that influence personality development.

Because of the widespread acceptance of the abnormal–normal dichotomy, general principles of social learning and behavior that have been developed on the basis of laboratory-experimental studies have been largely ignored in textbooks on psychopathology and have consequently had little impact on the theorizing in this area. Over the past decade, a tremendous accumulation of empirical data relevant to theories and problems of psychopathology and behavioral modification has been secured through controlled experimental studies, particularly in the areas of social and developmental psychology. Data are now available concerning response acquisition, inhibition, and disinhibition in social situations; conflict, frustration, and stress reactions; avoidance and withdrawal learning; the acquisition and maintenance of aggressive and dependent behavior; the development of self-control and of reactions to transgression; personality correlates of conditionability and persuasibility; the processes of conformity, deviation, and group acceptance; and experimentally derived procedures of behavioral change and control. Generally speaking, these laboratory studies have yielded remarkably precise and consistent relationships which provide a basis for a reformulation of social-learning principles that may now be applied to the understanding and modification of deviant behavior patterns.

STRATEGY OF RESEARCH

In the development of principles of social learning, the researcher attempts to identify covariations between manipulable antecedent events and consequent response variables. In many cases, however, the antecedent variables cannot be readily manipulated in real-life or laboratory situations, a limitation that is particularly true of research into atypical forms or intensities of social responses. First, ethical considerations preclude real-life manipulations that might result in highly deviant behavior. Second, socially salient deviant response patterns—for example, generalized patterns of aggression and withdrawal—result from the interaction of a number of child-training variables that would be difficult to produce through experimental procedures. Interaction effects occur on account both of the complexity of social responses of any single socializing agent and of the number of these agents that play a part in the shaping of a child's behavior. Under these circumstances, it is sometimes advantageous to start with field studies that are essentially correlational in nature. Such studies often generate hypotheses concerning antecedent-consequent relationships, which must then be tested in more rigorously controlled laboratory situations in order to ascertain whether the covariations do in fact represent causal relationships.

Covariations in two classes of events, one of which has been regarded as the antecedent of the other, may be a function of changes in some as yet unidentified variables. For example, parental preference for nonaggressive psychological forms of discipline has often been regarded as an antecedent of guilt in children. However, a strongly moralistic nonaggressive orientation in a parent may both inhibit him from using physically and verbally aggressive methods of discipline (thus limiting the range of techniques at his disposal) and at the same time, through modeling, produce guilt in his children.

In other cases, the causal links may be even more remote. Aggressively demanding fathers frequently encourage their sons to adopt an orientation similar to their own as a means of getting ahead in life, and reward them for aggressive and demanding behavior, particularly in their social interactions outside the home. Such fathers are also likely to demand a great deal of their wives' time and attention, thus forcing them to reduce the time and attention they give to their children. In such cases, maternal frustration of dependency would be associated with aggressive orientations in children, but it would be erroneous to conclude that the former was an antecedent of the latter.

Although the field approach has the advantage of permitting observations of the simultaneous influence of a large number of interacting social-training variables, it is often difficult, if not impossible, to identify the crucial interaction effects. There is always the danger that the investigator who relies solely on field studies will wrongly conclude that one or other of the supposedly causative factors is a necessary or sufficient antecedent of the phenomenon under investigation. In addition, it is often difficult to determine the direction of relationships that are established in field studies. Degree of parental rejection is found to covary with seriousness of childhood antisocial behavior. However, one cannot conclude that the parent variable is the antecedent, since children who get into serious trouble with authorities are likely on this account to be rejected by their parents.

The laboratory-experimental approach has the advantage that, if experiments are well executed, it "generates relatively precise statements of cause and effect which are remarkably unambiguous" (Bijou and Baer, 1960, p. 141). While laboratory studies permit some variables to be held constant while others are manipulated and so provide some indication of the relative importance of variables that cannot be isolated in real-life situations, limitations placed on psychologists who are interested in social-learning sequences in children often prevent them from gaining many of the advantages that are usually associated with the use of experimental methods. In the first place, the experimental manipulations of the stimulus events can cover only a small range of those found in real-life situations, usually only those at the weak end of the stimulus continuum. For example, the experimental production of "anxiety" through the use of aversive stimuli is usually accomplished by methods that, it is assumed, will have no *adverse effects* on the child. A child psychologist who wishes to study the effects of punishment is debarred from attempting to reproduce the whole range of punishments that are administered to most children in real-life situations. In contrast, in some animal experiments the severity and range of punishments administered may extend beyond those that the animal is likely to encounter in its natural surroundings (Azrin, 1959, 1960). This corresponds more closely to procedures in the natural sciences, in which substances can be subjected to laboratory conditions considerably more severe than the natural conditions whose effects on the substances are being predicted.

The implications of results from experimental studies of social behavior are often discounted on the grounds that the artificiality of laboratory manipulations precludes generalization to real-life situations. This attitude reflects a misunderstanding of the manner in which knowledge is advanced. Indeed, experiments are not designed to reproduce the stimulus events that occur in real-life situations and they would be superfluous if they were. Let us consider the manner in which a scientist might study the effects on behavior of brain damage. In real life, brain lesions can occur as a result of a large variety of adverse circumstances, such as automobile accidents or falling objects, or as a by-product of disease. The brain lesions that nature provides may vary considerably in extent and location, thereby making it difficult for the investigator to make confident statements concerning their effects on behavior. Knowledge would be more quickly advanced if, instead of waiting for injuries to occur, an experimenter were to "artificially" produce lesions through surgical operations in which the locus and amount of damage were systematically varied. One would hardly expect him to attempt to reproduce the traumatic stimulus events that occur in nature, for example, by striking or dropping his subjects on their heads or infecting them with syphilis and waiting for paresis to develop. Of course, ethical considerations prevent the experimental induction of brain injury in human subjects; consequently, experimenters are forced to confine their laboratory studies to infrahuman organisms, on which they perform controlled operations. If, in fact, they were to attempt to duplicate traumatic events that occur to animals in nature, they would be unlikely to make any substantial contribution to knowledge.

Although the laboratory experiment is not designed to reproduce real-life stimulus events, extrapolation of results to everyday situations is justified only when the experimental manipulation involves the stimulus elements that appear to be essential for producing the real-life effect. For example, if the experimenter is interested in the socialization process and wishes to test a hypothesis concerning the effect of family interactions, his grounds for extrapolation will be firmer if he experimentally creates an analogue of the nuclear family, in which male and female adults serve as the mother and father figures, than if he simply observes the child's responses to mother and father dolls. In the former case, he can systematically vary the behavior of the experimental "parents" and observe the effects upon his child subjects.

Similarly, if one wishes to develop principles of social learning, the dependent variables should overlap with the social responses concerning which the experimenter wishes to make statements. For example, if one is attempting to establish the role of some presumed antecedent of overt aggression, it is better to record children's responses in a controlled social situation permitting interpersonal aggression than to obtain some fantasy measure. Unfortunately, the relevant social-stimulus elements have frequently been neglected in child experimentation, and the dependent variables have been responses that are only attenuated analogues of those that children make in everyday life.

As long as conditions that obtain in real-life situations cannot, for ethical or practical reasons, be reproduced in laboratory settings, experimental studies alone cannot provide the data for an adequate science of social learning. Theory-based naturalistic and longitudinal studies are thus indispensable adjuncts to laboratory methods. Consequently, it is important to seek out conditions in nature in which certain stimulus and response variables are present and others in which they are absent and to note how these covary. Ideally, a concerted attack on problems of social development should include both field and laboratory studies, and the latter should be designed in such a way

as to reproduce as closely as possible the social stimuli and responses that occur in real-life situations. In some respects, the
results obtaind from laboratory and field studies will not be
directly comparable. Positive results yielded by laboratory studies
will nevertheless serve to increase confidence in conclusions drawn
from field studies and will often bring to light important main
and interaction effects, the precise nature of which cannot be
assessed from field data. However, it should be noted that negative
results obtained in laboratory studies may sometimes simply reflect the weakness and the limited character of the experimental
manipulations or the inappropriateness of the response variables.

This book focuses on a series of laboratory-experimental and field studies that provide empirical support for a set
of social-learning principles accounting for the development and
modification of prosocial and deviant social behavior. Although
many of these studies were carried out by the authors and their
co-workers during the past few years, most of the evidence in
support of the principles that are developed in subsequent chapters has inevitably been supplied by the laboratory and field
research of other investigators, on whose findings we have sometimes drawn quite heavily. The techniques of research used in
these studies have been too diverse to summarize and consequently will be briefly described in the contexts in which the
findings are presented.

Summary

Previous attempts to conceptualize social phenomena, including deviant patterns of response, within the framework of modern learning theories have, generally speaking, relied
on a limited range of learning-theory principles that have largely
been developed and tested on the basis of studies of animal
subjects and of human subjects in one-person situations. Because
of their neglect of social variables, these attempts have been
particularly ineffective in accounting for the acquisition of novel
social responses. Moreover, the exponents of learning-theory
approaches to the problems of social and antisocial behavior have,

for the most part, tacitly accepted the basic tenets and concepts of psychodynamic models and have merely translated these into terms familiar and acceptable to the learning theorist. In this book we have attempted to extend and modify existing learning-theory principles and to suggest additional principles in order to account more adequately for the development and modification of human social responses. In addition, we have tried to avoid any uncritical acceptance of psychodynamic tenets and have, both within this chapter and elsewhere throughout this book, re-examined a number of the psychological "mechanisms" postulated in psychodynamic theories in the light of the tentative set of social-learning principles we have proposed as a starting-point for a more adequate theoretical approach to both social development and psychotherapy.

Our social-learning principles seek to explain deviant behavior in terms of classes of events that appear to be equally important for the establishing of nondeviant patterns of response. This approach carries the implication that the distinction between deviant and nondeviant behavior represents a value judgment and that categorical value judgments of this nature, though important for determining the decisions and actions of agents of social control, are of little theoretical significance. Consequently, in subsequent chapters we shall attempt to explain the development of all forms of social behavior in terms of antecedent social stimulus events such as the behavioral characteristics of the social models to which a child has been exposed, the reinforcement contingencies of his learning history, and the methods of training that have been used to develop and modify his social behavior. Although we do not deny the importance of constitutional variables in the development of personality, we have not attempted to examine their role in any detail; indeed, we are of the opinion that more is to be gained at the present time through the study of social-learning influences.

Much research into the determinants of personality patterns has been confounded by subjective value judgments of what constitutes "normal" or "abnormal" behavior and by conceptualizations of personality structure that are based on psychiatric diagnostic categories. The dependent variables in research studies are consequently often defined in terms of categorical judgments concerning hypothetical internal states or conditions such as "emotional disturbance," "abnormality," "mental illness," or other descriptive labels often encompassing relatively heterogenous behavioral phenomena. In order to identify the antecedents and correlates of socially deviant response patterns, the researcher must first select a set of objectively defined response variables. In seeking out the social-training antecedents of these response patterns, it is possible to choose one of two general research strategies. The first type of approach involves the study of covariations among stimulus and response variables as they occur in naturalistic situations. Carefully designed theory-based field studies have the advantage of permitting observations of the effects of a wide range of stimulus events that cannot be readily reproduced in laboratory situations because of practical or ethical considerations. Field studies also make it possible to assess the simultaneous influence of a large number of social-training variables that would be difficult to manipulate simultaneously through experimental procedures. It is often difficult to know, however, whether the covariation between two classes of events observed in field studies in fact represents a causal relationship, since both classes of events may be a function of changes in some other unidentified variable or set of variables. In addition, it may at times be difficult to determine the direction of the causal relationships that are established in field investigations. The laboratory-experimental approach, on the other hand, permits precise manipulation of stimulus variables and controlled observations of the changes that occur in the dependent behavioral events. Laboratory experimentation is thus capable of yielding relatively precise statements about causal relationships.

A concerted attack on the problem of identifying determinants of prosocial and deviant behavior should combine field and laboratory approaches, the results of which will not, however, be directly comparable in all respects. For example, results from laboratory experiments that fail to confirm hypotheses generated by field studies may primarily reflect the inappropriateness or limited range of the stimulus or response variables which are observed under the laboratory conditions. Moreover, extrapolation of results from laboratory to everyday social situations is justifiable only when the experimental manipulation involves social-stimulus elements that appear to be essential for producing the real-life effect. For such reasons, it is advantageous to design laboratory studies in such a way as to reproduce as closely as possible the social stimuli and responses that occur in the real-life situations concerning which the experimenter wishes to make causal statements. However, this does not imply that laboratory experiments should be designed to reproduce real-life situations *in toto;* if they were, the experimenter would necessarily relinquish the crucial scientific strategy of systematically manipulating one or more variables while holding others constant, and thereby forfeit the possibility of establishing precise cause-and-effect relationships.

In the next two chapters of this book, we have focused on the roles of imitation and reinforcement patterns in the development of socially acceptable and socially censured patterns of behavior. Since both the stability of patterns of behavior and the maintenance of social control are highly dependent on the exercise of habitual self-rewarding and self-punitive responses by individual members of society, we have devoted Chapter 4 to a detailed consideration of the manner in which self-control is acquired and maintained; indeed, it is our view that an adequate account of the learning of self-control is crucial for a theory of personality development, as well as for the understanding of psychopathological phenomena. Finally, in Chapter 5, we have attempted to outline procedures that might be employed for the modification of behavior.

It will be evident to the reader that we differ from traditional psychodynamic theorists in our choice of both explanatory concepts and the procedures we recommend for producing behavioral change. While our concepts are more nearly related to those employed in previous learning-theory accounts of personality development, our emphasis on the social aspects of learning constitutes, we believe, a substantial departure from usual learning-theory approaches.

CHAPTER TWO

The Role of Imitation

Imitation plays an important role in the acquisition of deviant, as well as of conforming, behavior. New responses may be learned or the characteristics of existing response hierarchies may be changed as a function of observing the behavior of others and its response consequences without the observer's performing any overt responses himself or receiving any direct reinforcement during the acquisition period. In some cases the amount of learning shown by the observer can, in fact, be as great as that shown by the performer (McBrearty, Marston, and Kanfer, 1961).

THE PREVALENCE OF IMITATIVE LEARNING

Although it is evident from informal observation that models are utilized in all cultures to promote the acquisition of socially sanctioned behavior patterns, the cultural importance of observational learning is especially apparent in accounts given by anthropologists of the process of socialization in societies other than our own. Indeed, in many languages "the word for 'teach' is the same as the word for 'show,' and the synonymity is literal" (Reichard, 1938, p. 471).

The manner in which complex adult-role behavior may sometimes be acquired almost entirely through imitation is illustrated in an account given by Nash (1958) of the social training of children in a Cantelense subculture of Guatemala. The young Cantelense girl is provided with a water jar, a broom, and a grinding stone, which are miniature versions of those used by her mother. Through constantly observing and imitating the domestic activities of the mother, who provides little or no direct tuition, the child readily acquires a repertory of sex-appropriate responses. Similarly, small Cantalense boys ac-

47

company their fathers while the latter are engaged in occupational activities and reproduce their fathers' actions with the aid of smaller versions of adult implements.

North American parents do not provide female children with miniature functioning replicas of the complex appliances that are customarily found in their households, since these would be prohibitively costly, readily damaged, and dangerous for children to operate. They frequently, however, supply their young daughters with a varied array of play materials— toy kitchen ensembles, dolls with complete nursery equipment and wardrobes, cooking utensils, and other junior-size homemaker kits—which foster imitative adult-role behavior. Play materials for male children in our culture are, generally speaking, less likely to be of direct relevance for the acquisition of sex-appropriate, everyday adult-role activities (partly, perhaps, a result, in middle-class families, of the relatively abstract nature of the occupational activities of the adult male), but they nevertheless frequently include building and other construction kits and mechanical gadgets that are associated with male occupational roles. While playing with toys that stimulate imitation of adults, children frequently reproduce not only the appropriate adult-role behavior patterns but also characteristic or idiosyncratic parental patterns of response, including attitudes, mannerisms, gestures, and even voice inflections, which the parents have certainly never attempted directly to teach. As the example taken from the Cantelense society most clearly indicates, children frequently acquire, in the course of imitative role-playing, numerous classes of interrelated responses *in toto,* apparently without proceeding through a gradual and laborious process of response differentiation and extinction or requiring a lengthy period of discrimination training.

Imitative learning is not limited to the adoption of sex-linked vocational and occupational roles. Young children in Lesu are permitted to observe all aspects of adult life (Powdermaker, 1933). They not only accompany adults while the latter perform vocational tasks but they are also present at all adult social gatherings, listening to conversations and witnessing activities that in other cultures would be concealed from children.

They are allowed to listen to obscene stories and to scandal and gossip about the sex life of members of the society and to observe the sex behavior of adults, which they then freely imitate. Similarly, among the Navaho positive training through imitation extends even to eliminative acts. "The mother or an older sister takes the child out when she herself goes to defecate and tells the little one to imitate her position and her actions" (Leighton and Kluckhohn, 1947, p. 35).

In many cultures, then, "children do not do what adults *tell* them to do, but rather what they *see* other adults *do*" (Reichard, 1938, p. 471). While it is evident that much learning in North American society is still fostered through the presentation of real-life models, with advances in technology and written and audiovisual means of communication increasing reliance is placed on the use of symbolic models.

Symbolic models may be presented through oral or written instructions, pictorially, or through a combination of verbal and pictorial devices. Verbal instructions that describe the correct responses and their sequencing constitute one widely prevalent means of providing symbolic models. Indeed, without the guidance of manuals and directives members of technologically advanced societies would be forced to engage in exceedingly tedious and often haphazard trial-and-error experimentation.

Pictorially presented models are provided in films, television, and other audiovisual displays, often without the accompaniment of any direct instructions to the observer. In fact, audiovisual mass media are, at the present time, extremely influential sources of social behavior patterns. Because of the amount of time during which most young people are exposed to pictorially presented models, mainly through television (Himmelweit, Oppenheim, and Vince, 1958; Schramm, Lyle, and Parker, 1961), such models play a major part in shaping behavior and in modifying social norms and thus exert a strong influence on the behavior of children and adolescents. Consequently, parents are in danger of becoming relatively less influential as role models and often are greatly concerned with the problem of regulating their children's television viewing.

Moreover, rate and level of learning may vary as a function of mode of model presentation, since an actual performance is apt to provide substantially more relevant cues with greater clarity than are conveyed by a verbal description. Parents' instructions to children concerning how they are to behave may therefore be far less influential than audiovisual mass media in shaping children's social behavior, unless the parents exhibit modeling behavior that is consonant with the instructions they issue.

In the child-training literature a good deal of attention has been given to parental use of *exemplary models,* which may be presented to the child through verbal description, pictorially, or, if the behavior of the model is already known to the child, simply by reference to the model and one or more of his characteristics. A wide variety of exemplary models, ranging from national heroes or villains to members of the immediate family and neighbors' children, may be utilized by parents. Exemplary modeling may be positive, as when parents point to some child or adult as an example of how their child should behave; in contrast, in negative exemplary modeling the parents select some person as demonstrating undesirable behavior, attitudes, or attributes, often pointing out their consequences for the model, and exhort the child not to follow in his footsteps. The problem with negative modeling is that, in attempting to deter their children from socially undesirable activities, the parents are forced to focus, and sometimes to elaborate, on deviant behavior which otherwise may have received little attention from their children.

Exemplary models often reflect *social norms* and are thus a means of describing or displaying in varying degrees of detail the appropriate conduct for given stimulus situations. The efficacy of normative models in shaping and controlling behavior has been abundantly documented in the research of social psychologists (Berg and Bass, 1961; Biderman and Zimmer, 1961), but few systematic attempts have been made to relate the concepts and principles guiding experimental social psychology to those of current learning theory. The interpretation of normative influences as a special case of modeling may in fact help to bridge the gap between the conceptual frameworks favored by experimental social psychologists and those that predominate among learning theorists.

The importance of social agents as a *source of patterns of behavior* continues to be largely ignored, despite evidence from informal observation and laboratory experimentation that the provision of models in actual or symbolic form is an exceedingly effective procedure for transmitting and controlling behavior. This relative neglect of the *social aspects* of the learning process cannot be attributed entirely to the fact that much learning experimentation has been confined to infrahuman organisms. Numerous studies, extending over the past thirty years, reveal that imitative learning occurs in subhuman species and that the provision of appropriate models can greatly facilitate the acquisition of behavior patterns both by primates (Crawford and Spence, 1939; Warden, Fjeld, and Koch, 1940; Warden and Jackson, 1935) and by animals of lower orders (Bayroff and Lard, 1944; Church, 1957; Herbert and Harsh, 1944). Indeed, earlier failures to demonstrate imitative learning in animals (for example, Thorndike, 1898; Watson, 1908) appear to have been due to the selection of tasks that were too difficult for the animals in question, failure to ensure that the observer attended to the demonstrator's performance, and, an inadequate number of demonstration trials. Given favorable conditions, cats, for example, will relatively quickly master quite complex problems that they have previously observed other cats learning to solve (Herbert and Harsh, 1944).

As might be expected, the most dramatic evidence of the manner in which animals, like humans, acquire novel patterns of behavior through imitative learning comes from observations of chimpanzees reared in human families (Hayes, 1951; Hayes and Hayes, 1952a, 1952b; Kellogg and Kellogg, 1933).

> Each [Donald, the human child, and Gua, the ape] was much interested in typewriters, and during the last few months would go to one whenever it was within reach and pound the keys with his fingers, in this case demonstrating a common tendency for its manipulation. It is impossible to say which of the two first exhibited this behavior, since they were originally observed going to it within a few moments of one another.

Gua would even climb on the typewriter stool and seat herself properly before the machine, moving her hands simultaneously up and down upon the keyboard. According to our records, they first imitated the motions of a typist at the respective ages of 13 and 15 months. At that time they had both seen a typewriter operated from time to time for more than five months (Kellogg and Kellogg, 1933, pp. 140–141).

There is, in fact, considerable descriptive evidence for cross-species imitation, especially in relation to the imitation of human responses by primates. Under most circumstances, of course, humans receive little reward for imitating animals, and it is consequently understandable why an eleven-year-old boy who joined a pack of dogs, and barks and runs on all fours with his canine friends at night, has baffled Washington psychiatrists (*Washington Post,* November 1, 1962). While this boy may have been indiscriminate in his choice of models, he was nevertheless very discreet in his choice of occasions for performing the canine behavior: "I have enough sense not to run around with dogs during the day when people can see me. I only run with them in the alleys at night."

In human societies, the provision of models not only serves to accelerate the learning process but also, in cases where errors are dangerous or costly, becomes an essential means of transmitting behavior patterns. One would not, for example, permit an adolescent to learn to drive a car by means of trial-and-error procedures, nor would one entrust a firearm to an armed services recruit without a demonstration of how it should be handled.

THEORIES OF IMITATION

The concept of imitation in psychological theory has a long history dating back to Lloyd Morgan (1896), Tarde (1903), and McDougall (1908), who regarded imitativeness as an innate, instinctive, or constitutional process or propensity. As the doctrine of instinct fell into disrepute, a number of psychologists, notably Humphrey (1921) and Allport (1924), attempted to account for imitative behavior in terms of Pavlovian conditioning principles. In dealing with language learning, for example,

Allport suggests that a child makes his first approximations to human speech in the course of babbling (which is itself sustained as a conditioned reflex circle) and that these approximations elicit from adults, who perceive the child's utterance as socially significant, the word-sound to which the child's vocalization has approximated, together (on some occasions at least) with a demonstration of the act or object to which this word refers. As a result, the child is classically conditioned to produce the word whenever he hears the adult produce it or whenever the object or event with which it is associated appears in his environment. Allport similarly presents other imitative responses as instances of the classical conditioning of overt acts or emotions to social stimuli with which they have previously been associated.

Holt (1931) has offered an analysis of observational learning that is in many respects similar to Allport's. He notes that when an adult copies a movement made by a child, the latter tends to repeat this movement, and that this sequence may be continued time after time, with the child's imitative response becoming increasingly spontaneous. Holt adds that if, during this interaction sequence, the adult makes a response that is novel for the child, the latter will copy it (pp. 117–119).

Holt's illustration reveals one of the main weaknesses of classical-conditioning theories of imitation: their failure to account satisfactorily for the emergence of *novel* responses during the model–observer sequence. Moreover, demonstrations of observational learning in animal and human subjects do not customarily commence with a model's matching a semi-irrelevant response of the learner. On the contrary, the experimenter selects an already proficient model, or teaches the model in front of an observer, and then provides the observer with an opportunity to match the model's responses.

It is true that young children sometimes initiate an adult–child sequence by making an apparent approximation to adult behavior and that adults frequently respond by giving a demonstration of how the child should, in fact, behave. However, the child's approximation may in many cases represent an outcome of prior, though incomplete, observational learning. Such approximations are undoubtedly sometimes (though not always) acquired, as Mowrer (1952) has suggested in his "autism" theory of language learning, through the association of adult sounds and movements with the rewarding experiences that occur for a child during the course of adult–child interactions.

Classical-conditioning theories rely heavily on the concept of the reflex circle to explain behavior sequences in which the response of one person serves as a stimulus that elicits a second more or less identical response from the same or another person. As Miller and Dollard (1941) have observed, once a reflex circle has been started, it is difficult to account for its stopping, a problem that has not been satisfactorily attacked by exponents of classical-conditioning theories. At the same time, as the preceding paragraphs have indicated, these theories fail to explain the occurrence of novel imitative responses and violate observable facts concerning the sequencing of responses in observational learning.

Although imitation received considerable attention during the earlier part of the present century, it was not until the publication of *Social Learning and Imitation* by Miller and Dollard (1941) that the concept was fully integrated into a behavior-theory framework and the phenomenon of imitative behavior was presented as a major problem confronting learning theorists. Generally speaking, the challenge presented by Miller and Dollard aroused relatively little response among learning theorists, who, with the exception of Mowrer, have dealt with imitation only in a cursory fashion or have neglected the problem entirely. Indeed, in some recent standard texts on learning (for example, Bugelski, 1956; Deese, 1952; Hilgard, 1956; Kimble, 1961) the topic of imitation is barely mentioned and, in some cases, not even listed in the index.

The theory of imitation propounded by Miller and Dollard, has nevertheless been widely accepted during the past twenty years. According to this theory, the necessary conditions for learning through imitation include a motivated subject who is positively reinforced for matching the correct responses of a model during a series of initially random, trial-and-error responses. While Miller and Dollard regard their illustrative experiments as demonstrations of learning by imitation, these in fact represent only the special case of discrimination place learning, in which the behavior of others provides discriminative stimuli for responses that already exist in the subject's behavioral repertory. The theory of Miller and Dollard may account adequately for learning of this kind, but it does not account for the occurrence of imitative behavior in which the observer does not perform the models' responses during the acquisition process and for which reinforcers are not delivered either to the models or the observers. Moreover, it presents imitative learning as contingent on the observer's performing a close approximation to the matching response before he can acquire it imitatively and thus places a severe limitation on the behavioral changes that can be attributed to the influence of a model.

Mowrer (1960b) describes two forms of imitative learning that differ from the matched-dependent learning of Miller and Dollard. In one case, organism A makes a response and at the same time rewards organism B. As a result, A's response takes on secondary reward value for B; consequently, B attempts to reproduce A's response at times when it is not being made by A. An analogous process is assumed in the account given by Whiting and Child (1953) of the development of "identification."

Mowrer also describes another form of imitation, which may be called "empathetic" learning (1960b, p. 115). In this case, A both provides the model and experiences the reinforcement. B, in turn, "both experiences some of the same sensory consequences of A's behavior as A experiences it and also 'intuits' A's satisfactions or dissatisfactions." Imitation of film-mediated aggression could illustrate this process. The observer sees the film model, for example, inflict pain on others and notes the model's verbal and behavioral expressions of satisfaction. As a result, he imitates the pain-producing behavior in the expectation that this behavior will bring satisfaction to him also. This explanation of "higher-order" vicarious learning assumes that the response-correlated stimuli of the model can arouse in the observer an expectation that he too will experience analogous response-correlated stimuli for acting in a similar way to the model.

Mowrer's theory focuses almost exclusively on positively valenced proprioceptive feedback as the crucial process mediating imitative learning. According to Mowrer, imitation occurs only when the observer is directly or vicariously rewarded by the sensory consequences to himself of the model's instrumental responses. Consequently, he regards imitative learning as precisely parallel to habit formation and the two forms of response acquisition as differing only in respect to the origin of the response-correlated stimuli that sustain the learned responses. In the case of habit-formation these stimuli are produced by the acts of the learner, in the case of imitation by the acts of the model; nevertheless, in both cases they take the form of rewarding (motivational or emotional) proprioceptive feedback associated through classical conditioning with the learner's execution of the acts that he performs. It is evident, however, that proprioceptive feedback can account only in part for the acquisition, facilitation, and inhibition of responses that are attributable to the influence of a model. For example, the proprioceptive cues arising from hitting responses directed toward parents and toward peers may differ little, if at all; nevertheless, physically aggressive responses toward parents are generally strongly inhibited, while physical aggression toward peers is much more readily expressed (Bandura, 1960; Bandura and Walters, 1959). Thus, proprioceptive cues constitute only a small portion of the total stimulus complexes that regulate social behavior and it is therefore necessary to take account also of external stimulus elements, which probably play the role of important discriminative cues.

Moreover, behavior is influenced by models even when there are no response-generated cues that have positive or negative valence. Indeed, Mowrer himself has at times laid emphasis on the role of conditioned sensations or images that provide sensory-motor linkage between cognitive and emotional responses. In most cases of observational learning such perceptual or imaginal responses may be the only important mediating processes.

In a recent study of programmed learning from filmed demonstrations, Sheffield (1961) has focused on the role of mediating perceptual and symbolic responses possessing cue properties that are capable of eliciting, some time after a demonstration, overt responses corresponding to those that were demonstrated. Sheffield's theory of imitative learning is congruent with Mowrer's in several important respects. From both points of view learning of this kind is based on the principle of contiguity and is mediated, at least in part, by essentially similar cue-producing cognitive or imaginal responses. Sheffield, however, makes no assumptions concerning the role of mediating conditioned emotional reactions or proprioceptive feedback. This may be due to the fact that Sheffield has addressed himself primarily to the learning of perceptual-motor tasks from filmed demonstrations that do not contain strong positive or aversive stimuli essential for the classical conditioning of emotional responses. Mowrer's theory may be primarily relevant to cases in which the model's responses incur social reward or punishments.

Data from an experiment by Bandura (1962b) strongly suggest that the *acquisition* of imitative responses results primarily from the contiguity of sensory events, whereas response consequences to the model or to the observer have a major influence only on the *performance* of imitatively learned responses. Children observed a film-mediated model who exhibited four novel aggressive responses accompanied by distinctive verbalizations. In one condition of the experiment, the model was severely punished; in a second, the model was generously rewarded with approval and food reinforcers; while the third condition presented no response-consequences to the model. During the acquisition period the children neither performed any overt responses nor received any direct reinforcement and, therefore, any learning that occurred was purely on an observational or vicarious basis.

A post-exposure test of imitative behavior revealed that the differential vicarious reinforcement had produced differential amounts of imitative behavior. Children in the model-punished condition performed significantly fewer imitative responses than children in both the model-rewarded and the no-consequences groups. Moreover, boys reproduced more imitative responses than girls, the differences being particularly marked in the model-punished condition. The study was then extended one step beyond the point where learning experiments are typically terminated. Children in all three groups were offered attractive incentives contingent on their reproducing the model's responses. As shown in Figure 2-1, the introduction of positive incentives completely wiped out the previously observed performance differences, revealing an equivalent amount of learning among the children in the model-rewarded, model-punished, and the no-response-consequences conditions. Similarly, the sex difference was substantially reduced. The fact that some of the

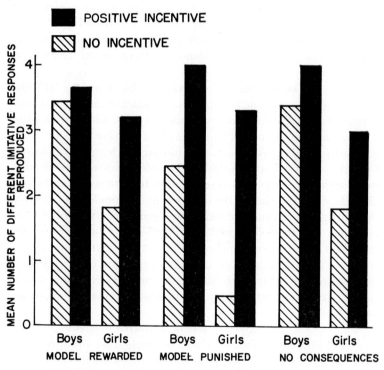

FIG. 2–1. *Mean number of different imitative responses reproduced by children as a function of response consequences to the model and positive incentives.*

children failed to reproduce all of the model's responses indicates that factors other than sensory stimulation undoubtedly influence response acquisition.

Motivational factors or the anticipation of positive or negative reinforcement may augment or reduce the probability of occurrence of observing responses, which is an essential aspect of imitative learning. Conditioning of attention to selected aspects of perceptual configurations has, in fact, been demonstrated by Walters (1958), who trained subjects, through differential reward and punishment, to attend to perceptual stimuli of selected colors and not to attend to differently colored, though otherwise identical, stimulus components. In a subsequent study, designed to obtain confirmation of this conditioning-of-attention effect, Solley and Santos (according to Solley and Murphy [1960]) found that children could be readily trained to direct their attention almost exclusively to some objects in their environment at the expense of others and that, following training, they were able to locate objects associated with rewarding experiences more rapidly than other, just as easily accessible, objects, attention to which had not been previously rewarded. Moreover, findings from animal studies (Lawrence, 1949, 1950) indicate not only that prior learning experiences enhance the distinctiveness of certain cues but also that cues that have been associated with these experiences retain their acquired distinctiveness in new stimulus contexts.

The manner in which direct training in selective observation may result in increased attention to deviant responses is illustrated in a study by Toch and Schulte (1961), who tachistoscopically presented subjects with a "violent" picture to one eye and a matched "neutral" picture to the other. Advanced police administration students, who had completed a three-year course in law enforcement, reported seeing more violent activities than did novices in the same police-training program. Positive reinforcement for attending to violent activities undoubtedly predisposes advanced law-enforcement students to respond to aggressive aspects of the stimuli in their environment and probably also to match real-life aggression with appropriate counter-aggression tactics. It is reasonable to believe that children for whom observation of, or attention to, deviant models has been intentionally or unintentionally associated with pleasurable consequences (as, for example, when they receive attention and interest while listening to parental elaboration of negative models or watch violent TV shows) readily respond to antisocial stimuli and are in this way provided with increased opportunities of learning socially unacceptable modes of behavior.

THREE EFFECTS OF THE OBSERVATION OF MODELS

During recent years, a number of investigators have conducted laboratory-experimental studies in which subjects have been exposed to aggressive real-life or fantasy models. These investigators have differed considerably in their choice of stimulus conditions and of dependent variables. The studies suggest that observation of the behavior of models has three rather different effects, each of which may be reflected in an increase in the number, range, and intensity of the observer's matching responses. In the first place, the observer may acquire new responses that did not previously exist in his repertory. In order to demonstrate this *modeling effect* experimentally, the model must exhibit highly novel responses and the observer must reproduce these responses in a substantially identical form. Second, observation of models may strengthen or weaken inhibitory responses; these *inhibitory and disinhibitory effects* are apparent in studies in which the responses evoked already exist in the subject's repertory. These responses may, of course, not match precisely those made by the model. Third, it is possible that observation of a model sometimes elicits previously learned matching responses in the observer simply because the perceiving of acts of a certain kind serves as a "releaser" for responses of that same class. This *eliciting effect* can be distinguished from disinhibition if we know the past history of our subjects. However, since the classification of a response as deviant implies social censure and since children are generally taught not to make socially censured responses, it is probably safe to assume that the eliciting of previously learned deviant responses through exposure to a deviant model usually, if not always, reflects a disinhibitory process.

TRANSMISSION OF NOVEL RESPONSES

Modeling effects have been demonstrated in a series of experiments by Bandura and his associates (Bandura, 1962a). In a study designed to test for delayed imitation of deviant models in the absence of the models, Bandura, Ross, and Ross (1961) exposed one group of nursery-school children to aggressive adult models and a second group to models who displayed inhibited and nonaggressive behavior. Half the children in each of these conditions observed models of the same sex as themselves, while the remaining children in each group were exposed to models of the opposite sex. For the aggressive-model group the model exhibited unusual forms of physical and verbal aggression toward a large inflated plastic doll. In contrast, the nonaggressive-model group observed an adult who sat very quietly, totally ignoring the doll and the instruments of aggression that had been placed in the room.

Bandura, Ross, and Ross (1963a) extended their investigations in order to compare the effects of real-life models, human film-aggression, and cartoon film-aggression on the aggressive behavior of preschool children. Subjects in the human film-aggression condition saw a movie that showed the adults who had served as the male and female models in the real-life condition portraying aggression toward the inflated doll. Children in the cartoon-aggression condition observed a cartoon character make the same aggressive responses as the human models did in the other two conditions. After exposure to the models, all children were mildly frustrated and measures were then obtained of the amount of imitative and nonimitative aggression they exhibited in a new setting with the model absent.

The children who observed the aggressive models displayed a great number of precisely imitative aggressive responses, whereas such responses rarely occurred in either the nonaggressive-model group or the control group. Moreover, children in the nonaggressive-model group displayed the inhibited behavior characteristic of their model to a greater extent than did the control children. In addition, the results indicated that film-

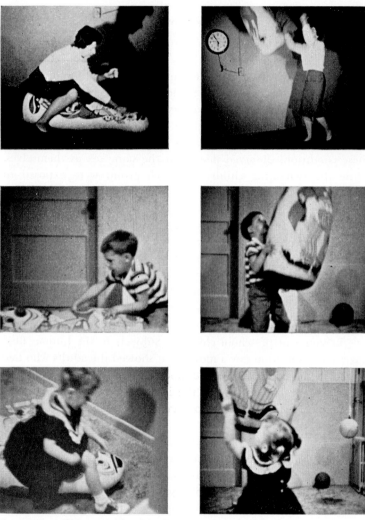

FIG. 2–2. *Photographs of children reproducing the aggressive behavior of the female model they had observed on film (from Bandura, Ross, & Ross, 1963a)*

mediated models are as effective as real-life models in transmitting deviant patterns of behavior.

Illustrations of the way in which children precisely

FIG. 2–2. *(Continued)*

reproduced the models' behavior are provided in Figure 2–2. The top frames show the female model performing four novel aggressive responses; the lower frames depict a boy and a girl reproducing the behavior of the female model.

Experimental demonstrations of modeling effects have so far employed only aggressive behavior as the dependent variable. Anthropological and field-study data suggest, however, that other classes of responses may be readily acquired through the observation of social models. For example, Bandura (1960) compared the behavior patterns of parents of highly aggressive children with those of parents of children who displayed generalized inhibition of social behavior and found that the parents of the inhibited children were generally more inhibited and controlled in their behavior than were the relatively expressive and sometimes impulsive parents of the aggressive boys. A somewhat similar modeling effect seems to be reflected in the finding of Levin and Baldwin (1959) that parents who were socially retiring had children who were shy and inhibited when required to perform in public.

Bandura (1960), in addition, provided evidence that differences between his aggressive and inhibited groups of children in dependency behavior were due, at least in part, to imitative learning. In the first place, the parents of the aggressive boys (who displayed very frequent and direct dependency responses) exhibited much more dependency on other adults than did the parents of the generally inhibited children. Secondly, correlations between ratings of parent behavior obtained from the interview protocols and the ratings of the observations of the boys' behavior suggested that parents who displayed high dependency in their interactions with other adults had children who exhibited frequent and direct dependency behavior in social situations. Conversely, parents who showed generalized response inhibition or specifically inhibited dependency responses had sons who were themselves nondependent or expressed dependency only in attenuated forms. These relationships give some support to the hypothesis that children model themselves after their parents in respect to dependency behavior.

Kagan and Moss (1960), on the basis of carefully collected longitudinal data, have shown that passive-dependent behavior is highly stable and consistent from childhood to early adulthood for females but much less so for males. These investigators attribute this difference in part to environmental pressures that lead to increasing dependency inhibition in the growing boy, in part to the influence of symbolized models in children's books, which generally portray girls as passive and dependent and boys as independent and adventurous (Child, Potter, and Levine, 1946). Bandura's (1960) data suggest that the presence in the home of dependent parent models may retard the usual development of males by counteracting social influences that lead to gradual modifications of boys' dependency responses, while high emotional inhibition in parents may lead to an exaggerated fear of adopting a dependency role in social interactions, a condition that can impede the social-learning process as seriously as failure to develop sex-appropriate task-oriented independence. Because of the more marked changes in social demands for males, the presence in the home of atypical parental models may make adjustment outside the home particularly difficult for boys.

In North American society children have little opportunity to observe adult sex behavior, except sensory stimulation in its more attenuated forms, such as kissing and mild petting. The range of sex behavior that the child has opportunities to observe is thus extremely restricted; moreover, those exploratory activities having sexual implications—for example, curiosity about anatomical differences, fingering of the genital area, and even nudity—are discouraged, left unlabeled or mislabeled, and quickly suppressed (Chapter 3). Thus the child has few opportunities to model his sex behavior after that of his parents; indeed, the limited opportunities for imitation that occur in our culture are more likely to be provided by the mass media, by older children, by members of the peer group, or by "how-to-do-it" marriage manuals. In contrast, some societies are highly permissive of sexual behavior and provide children with ample opportunities to witness all phases of the sexual act, often supplemented with careful and detailed verbal directions. In such societies, a considerable amount of imitative sexual behavior occurs.

> Young Seniang children publicly simulate adult copulation without being reproved; older boys masturbate freely and play sexual games with little girls, but the boys are warned

not to copulate on the grounds that this behavior would weaken them. Lesu children playing on the beach give imitations of adult sexual intercourse, and adults in this society regard this to be a natural and normal game (Ford and Beach, 1951, p. 189).

Even in generally nonpermissive societies, imitative sex behavior will occur if children are given the opportunity of witnessing adult sex responses. For example, case histories of young persons brought up in congested living quarters in which the privacy of adults is restricted show that quite young children may attempt intercourse with peers after they have witnessed this activity occurring among adults in their home or neighborhood. A recent sociological account of life in a Mexican slum district (Lewis, 1961) provides clear examples of imitative sex behavior of this kind in two of the boys of the family that was studied.

Although most North American parents engage in very little public sex behavior that the child could learn imitatively, they transmit to their offspring their own conditioned emotional responses to stimuli that have sexual implications (Bandura and Walters, 1959; Sears, Maccoby, and Levin, 1957). Consequently, one would expect parents who are highly anxious about sexual matters to have children who also display high sex anxiety, an expectation that also obtained some confirmation in Bandura's (1960) study of aggressive and inhibited boys. The correlational data obtained from this study indicated that sex-anxious parents had sons who were both guilty about sex and exhibited anxiety about relating dependently to people. It is probable that the presence of anxiety about sex hinders the formation of close affectional relations. Indeed, the parents of the inhibited boys showed a constellation of presumably inter-related characteristics, including general emotional inhibition, sex anxiety, and relatively infrequent dependency responses directed toward other adults. Their children, in turn, showed a similar behavioral pattern; they were generally inhibited and withdrawn, exhibited guilt about sex, and were especially lacking in dependency responses to others. Undoubtedly, these children had learned to model their behavior after that of their inhibited parents.

Transmission of high sex anxiety from parents to children should lead to a generalized inhibition of the children's sexual responses; consequently, children of parents who are highly anxious about sex might be expected to display relatively little public masturbatory activity, which is perhaps the only unambiguously sexual behavior that children are likely to display in the presence of observers. In Bandura's field study (1960), the correlational analysis indicated that the fathers' modesty was negatively related to the extent to which children could be observed to masturbate in public and that, for the inhibited group of children, the mothers' sex anxiety was also negatively correlated with the boys' masturbatory activities.

THE SHAPING OF FRUSTRATION-REACTIONS
THROUGH MODELING

It is evident that frustration may elicit a wide variety of reactions: for example, aggression, dependency, withdrawal, somatization, regression, apathy, autism, or constructive task-oriented behavior. A widely accepted view is that aggression is the natural, unlearned reaction to frustration and that individual differences in frustration responses are the product of reinforcement histories in which aggressive reactions have been punished or not rewarded, while other modes of response have been progressively strengthened through positive reinforcement. While reinforcement patterns account for some changes in the ordering of responses within frustration-response hierarchies, they provide no explanation of the origin of the responses contained in these hierarchies. Frequently a disease process is invoked as the explanatory factor. For example, a person shows autistic reactions to frustration. The diagnostician labels him as a schizophrenic and attributes the autism to an underlying schizophrenic process. This "explanation" is, of course, completely circular, since the only evidence for the assumed underlying process is the behavior it is called on to "explain." From a social-learning point of view, schizophrenics are persons who show certain characteristic responses to stress and frustration that may be conveniently labeled as "schizoid" or, in the case of children, "atypical" or "autistic."

Learned patterns of response to stress frequently originate from the observation of parental and other models who, during the course of a child's development, usually provide him with ample opportunities to observe their stress reactions and to imitate them. Consequently, when a child encounters a stress situation he is more likely to respond imitatively than to engage in initial trial-and-error behavior. Only when a child has learned aggression as a dominant response to emotional arousal in specific situations will there be a high probability of his displaying aggressive reactions to frustration. For example, in the studies cited earlier, Bandura (1962a) found that children who had observed a model behaving in an aggressive way responded to frustration with kicking, striking with mallets, and other aggressive responses, while equally frustrated children who had watched the nonaggressive model exhibited less aggression than the control group and matched the inhibited behavior of their model (Figure 2–3).

Observations by anthropologists (Bateson, 1936; Whiting, 1941) indicate the importance of models in the cultural transmission of aggressive reactions to frustration. Modeling effects are also apparent in subcultures in which the "delinquent" youth conform to the dominant hostile-aggressive patterns of the subgroup (Cohen, 1955; Whyte, 1937). More specific evidence concerning the role of modeling in the genesis of antisocial aggressive behavior is provided by McCord and McCord (1958), who examined the influence of parent-role models on criminality. These investigators found that children imitated their father's criminality when the mother was also socially deviant, when parental discipline was erratic, or when the parents were rejecting. Since erratic discipline and rejection may, in some families, include the provision of examples of hostile-aggressive behavior, the relative importance of models in the genesis of criminality may be even greater than the McCords' analysis suggests.

Imitation of dissocial aspects of parent behavior among middle-class children has been noted by Bandura and Walters (1959) and by Johnson and Szurek (1952). Usually, however, middle-class parents provide examples of physically aggressive behavior only through the disciplining of their children. In fact, when these parents employ aggressive-punitive methods in

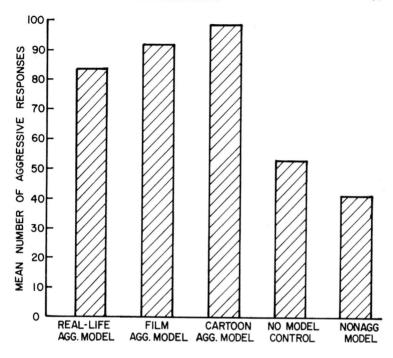

FIG. 2–3. *Mean amount of postfrustration aggression displayed by control children and by those who had been exposed to aggressive and inhibited models*

the control of their children's aggression, their modeling behavior often contravenes their training objectives. For example, if a parent punishes a child physically for having struck a neighbor's child, the intended outcome of the training is that the child should refrain from hitting others. Concurrently with the intentional training, however, the parent is providing a model of the very behavior he is attempting to inhibit in the child. Consequently, when the child is thwarted in subsequent social interactions, he may be more, rather than less, likely to respond in a physically aggressive manner.

Other forms of aggressive behavior are much more frequently displayed by middle-class parents both in their disciplinary procedures and in their personal interactions, and these, too, may be transmitted to the children. Bandura (1960) obtained ratings of aggressive and inhibited boys on a number of scales relating to aggression, some of which were not used for selection purposes. Ratings on the latter scales were correlated with measures of parental aggression, secured from interview data. Bandura found that fathers who expressed much indirect hostility toward their wives had sons who tended to display oppositional behavior. Moreover, within the families of the inhibited boys, the sons of those fathers who expressed direct hostility toward their wives tended to be generally more aggressive. The influence of modeling was reflected also in the correlational data involving the mother's behavior. Mothers who showed indirect hostility and who responded aggressively when instigated had sons who were relatively high in aggression; in addition, inhibition of aggression on the part of the mother was related to a low incidence of aggression in the boy.

Clinical cases provide examples of parents who display extremely deviant behavior which is reproduced by their children. A whole style of life may be transmitted in this manner. Fleck (1960) describes a young schizophrenic whose bizarre hospital behavior evidently paralleled, often in detail, the deviant pattern of home life displayed by his father. The father was pompous and autocratic and ran his household as if he were a divinely sanctioned Messiah. He secluded himself in his bedroom where he spent most of his time in his underclothes reading religious literature. The son was arrogant, withdrawn, and preoccupied with mystical religions, and "a typical daily scene showed him almost naked, sitting on the toilet, studying stock quotations" (p. 337).

Occasionally a parent may not appear deviant in social behavior and yet deliberately provide deviant models for his children. Fleck describes a relatively conforming parent who had encouraged homosexual tendencies in his son by selecting for him homosexual roommates. Whereas in most families the parents expend much energy in ensuring that their sons and daughters are exposed to models who display socioculturally approved behavior, in the case cited by Fleck the father, partly through selection of models, made efforts to promote incestuous and homosexual responses in his son.

Fathers of autistic children have been found to be themselves autistic in certain respects (Eisenberg, 1957). They are frequently obsessive, detached, and humorless and fail to give appropriate emotional responses to people. Even in the case of clinical problems which are generally regarded as constitutional in origin, there is evidence that modeling sometimes plays a major part in establishing the dysfunction. For example, children who suffered from early obesity, which continued into adolescence, were reported by Hammar (1961) as having parents who themselves displayed obesity and preoccupation with food and for whom eating was a preferred frustration or stress reaction.

Deviant response patterns may also arise from parental modeling of denial reactions. A scholarly and fomerly successful lawyer withdrew into obsessive studies that brought him no money. He and his wife for years maintained the pretense to their children that the father was an outstandingly successful man. However, the failure of their father inevitably became apparent to the children. The conflict generated in the daughter of this family arose largely through the mother's displaying of the father-model in a false light (Lidz, Cornelison, Fleck, and Terry, 1957a).

To a certain extent this kind of denial occurs in most families. The model that a parent, usually aided by the spouse, presents to his children rarely faithfully reflects his true attitudes or behavior. Parents often present themselves and one another to their children as more conforming and more socially successful than they are. Later, the children discover that, generally speaking, adults do not behave in as conforming and socially approved ways as they have been led to believe. As a consequence, most children experience the same sort of conflict, though in not such a severe form, as that which was experienced by the children of the lawyer described above.

Another form of model distortion may occur through the deliberate devaluation of the success and social status of a parent, either by himself or by his spouse. One source of such distortion, which may generate conflict in children, is rapid upward social mobility. Thus a parent may, especially in attitudes, retain an identification with lower-class values and practices when through education, income, and area of residence he must appear to his children to belong to a higher social class.

Rapid upward mobility may lead to another kind of model distortion, which is in some respects similar to the deliberate overevaluation already described. A self-made parent may, on the basis of a high income, possess the symbols of a higher social class, yet in his overt behavior, manner of speech, and tastes still remain a lower-class person.

Whenever there is model distortion, the children may themselves learn to distort. They may, of course, largely reject the parent as a model or they may reject the social status to which the parent has aspired. In either case, some of their behavior and attitudes are likely to be regarded as deviant by those with whom they associate.

The manner in which specific behavior patterns may be transmitted from generation to generation through a succession of models has been demonstrated in an experimental study by Jacobs and Campbell (1961). In this experiment confederates of the experimenters established a fictitious group norm concerning the degree of apparent movement in an autokinetic-judgment situation. The original models were then removed one by one from the group, while naive new members were gradually introduced. These new respondents unwittingly became transmitters of the fictitious norm to still newer entrants. Although there was some deviation from the arbitrary norm across successive groups, remnants of the original belief were perpetuated by new members for four or five generations after the total replacement of the original indoctrinators. It is reasonable to suppose that deviant behavior patterns may be similarly passed on within a family, particularly if its members remain in comparative sociocultural isolation.

INHIBITORY AND DISINHIBITORY EFFECTS

The discussion has so far centered on one possible effect of the observation of models, that is, the acquisition of responses that are novel for the observer. Observation of responses of a particular class may also lead the observer to display these or other responses of the same general class when the behavior in question already exists in his repertory. In the studies described in the previous section, Bandura (1962a) demonstrated that children who had been exposed to aggressive models subsequently displayed not only specifically imitative novel responses but also, in comparison to children who had been exposed to non-aggressive models, a relatively large number of aggressive responses which were not actually demonstrated by the models and which therefore could not have been learned during the course of the demonstration.

In a number of studies, children have been shown cartoon films containing aggressive content and then compared to control groups in various play situations. In each case the experimental group showed a relatively high frequency of aggressive responses in, for example, the use of aggressive toys in a free-play situation (Siegel, 1956), the verbal expression of aggressive "impulses" (Mussen and Rutherford, 1961), and the activation of a hitting response in a mechanical toy (Lövaas, 1961a). Lövaas permitted children to play with either of two toys, each of which could be operated by depressing a lever. In one case the lever operated a hitting doll; in the other case it caused a ball to rise within a cage-like structure. Children who had watched an aggressive cartoon gave a greater proportion of responses to the lever that operated the hitting doll than did children who had watched the nonaggressive movie. Larder (1962) used a technique similar to that employed by Lövaas, except that her aggressive stimuli consisted of story material presented by means of a tape-recorder. Again, exposure to the symbolic aggressive model resulted in an increase in children's aggression. In all the above cases, the model appears to have had a disinhibitory effect, one that is especially clear if one compares Lövaas' procedures with those used by Larder. These two latter studies together indicate that both visually presented and verbally presented aggressive content may increase the incidence in observers of a selected non-verbal aggressive response. As the authors suggest, there are times when the presentation of aggressive material may serve simply as a discriminative cue signaling an occasion on which aggressive behavior is unlikely to meet with punishment.

Walters and his associates (Walters and Llewellyn Thomas, 1963; Walters, Llewellyn Thomas, and Acker, 1962) have demonstrated that the disinhibitory effect of exposure to aggressive models is not confined to children. Subjects were requested to participate in a study of memory for witnessed events, a procedure which justified the presentation of filmed material. On their arrival at the laboratory they were asked, in addition, to assist the experimenter in a study of the effects of punishment on learning. In his capacity as the experimenter's assistant, each subject was required to administer electric shocks to a confederate of the experimenter, who was presented as another subject.

The equipment consisted of a three-panel stimulator (Figure 2–4), in some respects similar to an "aggression machine" designed by Buss (1961). The subject's panel contained

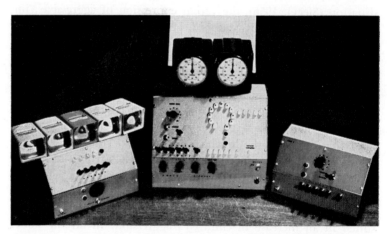

FIG. 2–4. *Stimulator used by Walters and Llewellyn Thomas (1963) for demonstrating the disinhibitory effect of exposure to a film-mediated aggressive model. The confederate's panel is on the left, the experimenter's panel on right. This equipment may also be used for avoidance conditioning or for studies of pain tolerance in which the shocks that the subject administers are monitored through his own body. (Designed and manufactured by Optiscan, Ltd., P.O. Box 302, Station F, Toronto 5.)*

switches for controlling signal lights on the confederate's panel, a rotary switch for selecting shock intensities from one to ten, red and green lights that supposedly signaled errors or correct responses on the part of the confederate (pseudo-subject), and a toggle-switch, which the subject depressed to administer shocks and raised to signal that the confederate had made a correct response. The experimenter's panel was set up in such a way that it enabled him to activate the red or green lights on the subject's panel, so giving the impression that the confederate had made right or wrong responses, and to record the intensity and duration of the shocks the subject administered. Within the context of this experiment, the confederate's panel was a "dummy" unit, used only to show the subject the nature of the task that the confederate (pseudo-subject) was supposed to be mastering.

All subjects, who were themselves given sample shocks to ensure that they were aware of the painful effect, were required to present to the confederate two of four possible light signals, one after the other, on each of thirty trials. The confederate supposedly responded with a correct or incorrect setting of a dial on his panel. On fifteen occasions his settings were "wrong," according to the "feedback" signals on the subject's panel. The subject was, of course, unaware that these signals were under the experimenter's control and in fact entirely unrelated to the confederate's manipulation of his dial. After a pretest series of trials, experimental subjects watched a scene taken from the film *Rebel Without a Cause,* in which two adolescents engaged in a fight with switch-blade knives, while control subjects saw an educational film depicting adolescents engaged in constructive art work. The subject was then again required to present thirty pairs of signals to the confederate and again to shock him on fifteen occasions. The effect of exposure to the film sequences was primarily assessed from pretest-to-posttest changes in the mean intensity of the shocks administered to the subjects.

In different phases of the study, male hospital attendants, high-school boys, and young adult females served as subjects. For the male subjects the filmed material was audiovisually presented; for the female subjects no sound was used, and the presentation was thus purely visual. The effect of exposure to aggressive content was in each case to increase the intensity of the experimental subjects' pain-producing responses. Of course, the confederate in fact received no shocks, since one electrode had been surreptitiously removed from his hand; subjects' remarks during the course of the experiment indicated, however, that they did not doubt that their actions resulted in the infliction of pain on another person. The importance of this procedure arises from the nature of the dependent variable, which quite clearly constituted a measure of the intensity of pain-producing responses in an interpersonal situation.

Other forms of deviant behavior have been shown to be disinhibited following exposure to models who displayed the behavior freely. For example, observers more readily violate prohibitions when they see these violated by others (Freed, Chandler, Blake, and Mouton, 1955; Kimbrell and Blake, 1958; Lefkowitz, Blake, and Mouton, 1955). Moreover, interview data obtained by Bandura and Walters (1959) have suggested that adolescent boys are more likely to engage in sexual intercourse during double or multiple dating than if they were alone with an adolescent girl; presumably, inhibitions are progressively lessened as the boys observe one another's sexual advances.

Disinhibition of sexually significant responses has been experimentally demonstrated by Walters, Bowen, and Parke (1963). Male undergraduates were shown, on a movie film, a series of pictures of nude or almost nude males and females, photographed in poses that were evidently designed to elicit erotic responses. Subjects were told that a moving spot of light on the film indicated the eye movements of a previous subject. For approximately half the subjects the spot of light roved over the bodies of the males and females portrayed in the film and for most of the time appeared in the vicinity of the breast and genital areas. For the remainder of the subjects the spot of light appeared in the background of the picture, thus giving the impression that the observer was avoiding looking at the human bodies. Following exposure to one or the other film, each subject, by means of a remote control button, presented to himself slides made from a series of photographs parallel to those used in the movie sequences. By means of an eye-marker camera (Mackworth and

Llewellyn Thomas, 1962), depicted in Figure 2–5, the subjects' own eye movements were recorded. Subjects who had been exposed to a supposedly sexually uninhibited model spent a significantly longer time looking at the nude and semi-nude bodies, and significantly less time looking at the backgrounds of the pictures, than did subjects who had been exposed to a model who avoided looking at the bodies (Figure 2–6). This study not only provides an objective demonstration of the modeling of sexual behavior but also suggests that *perceptual* responses can be readily influenced by the behavior of others, provided that the observer is

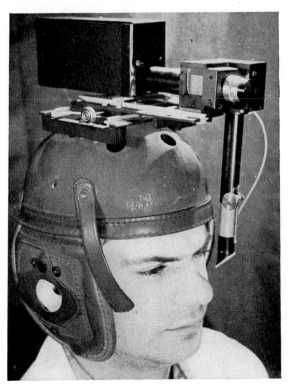

FIG. 2–5. *Eye-marker camera used in study by Walters, Bowen, and Parke (1963). (Designed by Mackworth and Llewellyn Thomas [1962], and manufactured by Optiscan, Ltd., P.O. Box 302, Station F, Toronto 5.)*

Fig. 2–6. *Responses classed as avoidant and nonavoidant in the study by Walters, Bowen, and Parke (1963). During presentation of pictures to the subjects, the eyes of the figures were not masked. A spot of light, seen in the background in the pictures on the left, on the left breast of the female figure on the top right, and in the genital area of the male figure on the bottom right, indicates where the subject is looking.*

supplied with cues that indicate the direction of the model's attention. In every-day life, modeling of perceptual responses is undoubtedly mediated by the sometimes readily observable postural and verbal cues supplied by the model as he directs his attention to various objects in his environment.

Inhibitory and disinhibitory effects of observed consequences to a model will be discussed in a later section. The findings described above seem to reflect disinhibitory effects that result from the nonoccurrence of untoward consequences to an aggressive or otherwise deviant model. Inhibitory effects are more likely to be produced through the observation of painful consequences resulting from a model's behavior or of fearful reactions of the model that the observer has already learned to recognize as danger signals. This latter effect undoubtedly explains in part the tendency for children to exhibit the same fears as those shown by their mothers (Hagman, 1932). Such fears can, of course, be eliminated, provided the mothers later exhibit nonfearful responses to these formerly fear-arousing stimuli (Jersild and Holmes, 1935a).

ELICITING EFFECT

The role of a model as an eliciting stimulus can be most clearly seen when the behavior that is imitated is not likely to have incurred punishment. Socially approved behavior, such as volunteering services or monetary contributions (Blake, Rosenbaum, and Duryea, 1955; Rosenbaum, 1956; Rosenbaum and Blake, 1955; Schachter and Hall, 1952), pledging oneself to a course of action (Blake, Mouton, and Hain, 1956; Helson, Blake, Mouton, and Olmstead, 1956), and eating food substances not ordinarily selected (Duncker, 1938), can be readily elicited if appropriate models are provided.

An obvious eliciting effect may be observed in cases in which an adult, who has lost the idioms and pronunciation of the local dialect of the district in which he was raised, returns for a visit to his home. The original speech and pronunciation patterns, which would take a stranger years to acquire, may be quickly reinstated.

In a discussion of the imitative behavior of animals, Thorpe (1956), the British ethologist, maintains that most eliciting and disinhibitory effects should not be regarded as instances of imitation, since they do not involve "the copying of a novel or otherwise improbable act or utterance, or some act for which there is clearly no instinctive tendency" (p. 122). Instead, Thorpe attributes the majority of such effects either to "social facilitation" or to "local enhancement," phenomena for which there are parallels in our account of human social learning. Social facilitation is said to occur when "the performance of a more or less instinctive pattern of behavior by one [member of a species] will tend to act as a releaser for the same behavior in another or in others, and so initiate the same lines of action in the whole group" (p. 120). Thorpe uses the contagion of yawning responses as an example of social facilitation in humans; more precise analogies to the "mimetic" behavior of birds and subhuman mammals are, however, provided by human crowd behavior, in which (undoubtedly learned) responses are "released" through "behavioral contagion," a term applied by Thorpe to the phenomenon he is discussing.

The analogy between social facilitation and human group behavior is even more apparent from Thorpe's account of "local enhancement," which he regards as "a special form of social facilitation" (p. 121), one which results from the directing of an animal's attention to a particular object or part of its environment. As an example of local enhancement, Thorpe cites Lorenz's (1935) observation that the successful escape of a duck from a pen was followed by similar escape behavior on the part of other members of a flock of confined ducks *only if* one duck happened to be near another at the time of the latter's escape and so had its attention directed to the successful escape response. It is evident that occurrence of local enhancement, as this term is employed by Thorpe, does not preclude the occurrence of imitative responses, in the sense in which imitation has been employed in this book. Indeed, as we have pointed out, rather careful attention to a model's responses to the environment seems to be a prerequisite for precise matching of these responses by the observer.

Thorpe's examples of eliciting and disinhibitory effects of animal models leave no doubt that such effects do occur; his refusal to classify them as instances of imitative behavior springs from his conviction that imitation must involve "self-consciousness," "ideation," and the production of "novel responses." To infer the presence or absence of such elusive processes as "self-consciousness" and "ideation" is an extremely hazardous undertaking, since no clearly defined referents for these concepts have as yet been established; to limit imitative behavior to "modeling effects" (to use our terminology) restricts the concept of imitation unnecessarily and involves a radical departure from common sense usage.

Modeling effects are possible only if the model exhibits responses that the observer has not yet learned to make, while disinhibitory effects can occur only if inhibitions have already been set up. However, in many cases of deviant behavior the model acts in ways which are both novel for the observer and socially disapproved; in such cases it is possible for the modeling, disinhibitory, and eliciting effects to occur simultaneously, and it is therefore virtually impossible to identify their relative contribution to the genesis of deviation.

INFLUENCE OF RESPONSE CONSEQUENCES
TO THE MODEL

Imitation is not independent of the response consequences to the model. These consequences are sometimes specific to the behavior which is being observed, as when reward or punishment immediately follows the performance of the model's acts. At other times, the model may not receive rewards in the observer's presence, but the latter's behavior may nevertheless be influenced by his knowledge that the model has during his life-history amassed rewarding resources or has been generally punished for his style of life. In the relevant literature, the influence of long-term rewarding and punishing consequences to models is usually dealt with in terms of personality characteristics such as prestige, competence, high status, and power.

The influence of immediate response consequences to the model has rarely been studied in experimental situations.

Bandura, Ross, and Ross (1963b) assigned nursery-school children randomly to one of the following groups: aggressive model rewarded; aggressive model punished; a control group which had no exposure to the models; and a second control group shown highly expressive but nonaggressive models. The models were two adult males presented to the children on film. In the aggression-rewarded condition the model employed considerable physical and verbal aggression for the amassing of the possessions of the other adult. The film shown to the children in the aggression-punished condition was identical with that shown to the aggression-rewarded group, except that the sequence was rearranged so that the aggressive behavior shown by the model resulted in his being severely punished. After observing the models, the children were tested in a different experimental situation designed to assess the incidence of postexposure aggressive responses.

Children who witnessed the aggressive model rewarded showed more imitative physical and verbal aggression than children who saw the model punished; the latter group did not, in fact, differ significantly from the control groups in their use of responses that could be regarded as precisely imitative. Moreover, exposure to the punished model effectively inhibited the boys' aggressive responses that were not precisely imitative, whereas observation of highly expressive or rewarded aggressive models produced substantial disinhibitory effects. Postexperimental interviews indicated that although children in the model-rewarded condition expressed disapproval of the model's behavior, they nevertheless preferred to emulate the aggressor than to emulate the object of the aggression. Thus the consequences to the agent outweighed the acquired value systems of the observers. On the other hand, children in the aggressive-model-punished group both failed to reproduce his behavior and rejected him as a model for emulation.

Consequences to a deviant model who violates a prohibition influence in a similar manner the extent to which his deviant behavior will be imitated. Walters, Leat, and Mezei (1963) assigned kindergarten children to one of three groups: model rewarded for deviation, model punished for deviation, and a control group to whom no model was presented. The children were first shown an assortment of attractive toys with which they were forbidden to play. The model-rewarded group then saw a film in which a child was playing with the forbidden toys and was subsequently rewarded through his mother's nurturant interaction. In the case of the model-punished group, the mother rebuked the child for playing with the toys. Children in all three groups were tested for "resistance to temptation" by being left in the room with toys for a period of fifteen minutes with nothing else to occupy their attention except a dictionary. Children who saw the model rewarded deviated more readily and more often than children who saw the model punished, while control children showed an intermediate degree of resistance to temptation. This study indicates that consequences to a model, according to their nature, may have either inhibitory or disinhibitory effects.

Inhibition or disinhibition of imitative responses may be mediated by vicariously learned conditioned emotional reactions. A series of experiments by Berger (1962) demonstrates that when a model is punished in the presence of an observer, the latter will display conditioned fear responses. In each study one group of observers was informed that the performing model would receive a shock whenever a light dimmed, the dimming of the light being in each trial preceded by a buzzer. Another group of observers was instructed that the performer would make a voluntary arm movement whenever the light dimmed but that the performer was receiving no aversive stimulation. Additional groups were included in which the model was supposedly shocked but refrained from making arm movements, and in which the model was neither shocked nor exhibited arm movement responses. The measure of vicarious conditioning was the frequency of observers' galvanic skin responses to the buzzer. Observers who were instructed that the model was receiving aversive stimulation and saw the model make avoidance responses displayed vicariously conditioned emotional reactions to a greater extent than did observers in the other three groups. Had the models provided additional nonverbal and vocal pain cues resulting from actual aversive stimulation, the vicarious conditioning effects would probably have been even more marked.

Berger's studies demonstrate that fear responses may be acquired even when the observer himself receives no punishment; it is plausible also to assume that if a model gives free expression to, and is rewarded for, responses for which the observer has been punished, counterconditioning or extinction of anxiety will occur and disinhibitory effects will be apparent.

While sometimes the observer sees the consequences of the model's behavior, at other times he can only infer probable consequences on the basis of tangible evidence of the model's past successes. For example, the model may possess material resources, such as money or fashion-book clothing, which are symbols of socioeconomic success (Lefkowitz, Blake, and Mouton, 1955). Or he may be customarily the recipient of social reinforcers such as praise and admiration (Hovland, Janis, and Kelley, 1953). He may demonstrate attributes and skills that are known to be successful in earning material rewards or social approval (Gelfand, 1962; Kanareff and Lanzetta, 1960; Lanzetta and Kanareff, 1959; Mausner, 1953, 1954a, 1954b; Mausner and Bloch, 1957; Rosenbaum and Tucker, 1962), or he may occupy a place in a seniority or occupational hierarchy that could increase his probabilities of current success (Bandura and Kupers, 1963; Jakubczak and Walters, 1959; Miller and Dollard, 1941). In such cases, the reinforcement contingencies that have given the model his status position may not be clear to the observer, who is consequently likely to imitate the model in an indiscriminate and sometimes unrewarding manner.

There is evidence, then, that social response patterns, both deviant and conforming, can be readily transmitted through the influence of a model and that imitation is facilitated if the model receives rewards. On the other hand, if the model is known to receive punishments, the observer may refrain from making novel deviant responses or even be restrained from performing deviant acts that he has already learned.

INFLUENCE OF OBSERVER CHARACTERISTICS

Characteristics of the observers, deriving from their previous reinforcement histories, also influence the extent to which imitative behavior occurs. Persons who have received insufficient rewards, such as those who are lacking in self-esteem (deCharms and Rosenbaum, 1960; Gelfand, 1962; Lesser and Abelson, 1959) or who are incompetent (Kanareff and Lanzetta, 1960), and those who have been previously rewarded for displaying matching responses (Lanzetta and Kanareff, 1959; Miller and Dollard, 1941; Schein, 1954) are especially prone to imitate a successful model. So too are highly dependent individuals (Jakubczak and Walters, 1959; Kagan and Mussen, 1956; D. Ross, 1962), who are probably also persons who have frequently been rewarded for conforming behavior. Moreover, observers who believe themselves to be similar to models in some attributes are more likely to match other classes of responses of the models than are observers who believe themselves to be dissimilar (Burnstein, Stotland, and Zander, 1961; Stotland and Dunn, 1963).

Jakubczak and Walters (1959) conducted a social-influence study in which the degree of dependency of the subjects and the age-status of the model were both varied. Nine-year-old boys were divided into a low-dependency group, who had indicated unwillingness to accept help on tasks they were unable to accomplish themselves, and a high-dependency group, who were willing to accept help even when they required none. All subjects were twice exposed to the autokinetic effect; on one occasion an adult served as the confederate of the experimenter, while on the other occasion the confederate was a child only a little senior to the subjects. Generally speaking, the results indicated that adults were more effective than peers in modifying the responses of the subjects and that high-dependent children were more readily influenced by models, both adult and peer, than were low-dependent children. The latter difference, however, was quickly obliterated when the models began systematically to make explicit judgments that were contrary to those previously made by the observers. This study thus indicates how both model characteristics and observer characteristics may under some circumstances enhance the efficacy of a model for inducing imitative responses.

Generalized matching behavior can occur to some degree even when the model exhibits responses that usually incur social disapproval. Stotland and Patchen (1961) administered a measure of anti-Negro prejudice to female students. Approximately a month later, these students read a case history of a person who was highly prejudiced. Half the students were led to believe that they had objective characteristics in common with the bigoted model, while the remaining students were told that the model had characteristics which they did not themselves possess. A second administration of the prejudice scale three weeks later revealed that students who were initially low on anti-Negro prejudice became more prejudiced if the bigoted model in the case history had been presented as similar to themselves, whereas students who conceived of themselves as dissimilar in background and personal characteristics to the model did not alter their attitudes.

Hypnotic suggestion, presumably because it increases the dependency of deeply hypnotizable subjects, can be effectively used to modify attitudes concerning social issues and even to induce attitudes of which the subjects formerly disapproved. While under hypnosis, subjects are in effect presented with symbolized models of how they should behave during the posthypnotic period. An interesting and important finding is that under these circumstances the modeling of one segment of an expressed attitude can lead to a marked change in other attitudinal components that are not directly manipulated (Rosenberg and Gardner, 1958). This technique deserves wider application in the study of social-influence procedures, particularly in investigations of the effects of real-life and symbolic models on social behavior. One may suspect that hypnotic techniques would be particularly effective in inducing imitative responses both because of the prestige-model–dependent-observer relationship that can be established and because of the restriction and focusing of attention that occurs in the hypnotized subject.

Transient emotional states, as well as stable characteristics, of an observer may modify the extent to which he is influenced by a model. There is some evidence that emotional arousal, at least of moderate intensity, may increase the probability of matching behavior. Walters, Marshall, and Shooter (1960) reported that high-school boys who had been placed in a stress situation, and whose self-reports indicated that they had been emotionally aroused, modeled their autokinetic judgments after fictitious arbitrary judgments made by the experimenter to a greater extent than did boys who had experienced no stress. In a subsequent study, McNulty and Walters (1962) found that high-school boys, whose electromyograms indicated that they had been emotionally aroused by an experimental manipulation, showed greater attitude change in directions specified by the responses of two adult confederates of the experimenter than did more relaxed subjects.

Physiologically induced arousal can also increase the incidence and degree of matching behavior. Schachter and Singer (1962) gave college students one of three treatments before placing them in a room with a confederate of the experimenter, who behaved in an aggressive manner. All students were told that they would be given an injection of a harmless substance, "Suproxin," whose effects on vision were under investigation. One group of subjects was injected with adrenalin and was at the same time informed that the drug would have some harmless temporary side-effects—palpitations, trembling, and flushing—which are characteristically produced by the drug. A second group of subjects was also administered adrenalin but was told nothing concerning its side-effects, while other students were injected only with an ineffective saline solution. Following the experimental treatment, all subjects were required to go to a waiting room while the injection took effect. Here they were exposed to the experimenter's confederate, supposedly another subject, who consistently criticized and attacked the experimental procedure in an angry and sometimes vehement manner. In comparison to the placebo group, the subjects who were injected with adrenalin, and who were not informed of its physiological side-effects, showed a considerable amount of aggressive behavior, whereas subjects who were injected with adrenalin, and who were correctly informed of its side-effects, showed very little precisely or nonspecifically imitative aggression. In another phase of this study, four treatments were employed, the three already described and one in which subjects were injected with adrenalin and deliberately misinformed concerning its side-effects. The confederate in this phase behaved in an age-inappropriate euphoric manner, for example, by making and flying paper airplanes and playing hula-hoop and basketball with materials, furniture, and equipment that were placed within the room. Subjects who were misinformed or uninformed concerning the true effects of adrenalin followed the confederate's example and behaved in an euphoric manner to a greater extent than did subjects who were given correct information concerning the drug. These results suggest that the influence of models may be most potent when the observers are emotionally aroused and cannot rationally attribute their feelings to stimuli other than the model's behavior. The aggressive behavior of a punitive parent may produce precisely this stimulus condition for the children in his family.

The social influence exerted by film-mediated models appears also to be a function of the degree of emotional arousal of the observers. Schachter and Wheeler (1962) compared the responses of three groups of subjects to a slapstick comedy film. Before watching the movie, one group was injected with adrenalin, a second group was injected with chlorpromazine, and the third with a placebo. Adrenalin-injected subjects showed a greater amount of amusement, assessed both by self-reports and by observations of behavior, than did placebo subjects, while chlorpromazine-injected subjects were least affected by the slapstick movie.

There is thus considerable evidence that emotional arousal, whether induced by stressful external situations or by the use of drugs, can increase the probability and degree of changes in social behavior, and that the direction which such changes take may often be specified by the cues provided by a model. Behavioral contagion (Lippitt, Polansky, Redl, and Rosen, 1952; Redl and Wineman, 1951) and other forms of deviant crowd behavior (Brown, 1954) undoubtedly reflect augmented mutual modeling, eliciting, and disinhibitory effects under conditions in which the participant observers are emotionally aroused.

Emotional arousal may alter perceptual thresholds and in other ways facilitate, impede, and channel observing responses. Evidence from studies of nonsocial behavior suggests that observers under a moderate degree of arousal are more vigilant of environmental cues, but that intense arousal results in a restriction of the range of cues to which an observer will attend (Bindra,

1959; Eastabrook, 1959; Kausler and Trapp, 1960). It is reasonable to suppose that emotional arousal influences observation of social cues in a similar manner, so that imitation is facilitated by moderate arousal but becomes more and more limited and fragmentary as the level of arousal further increases. However, one might predict that under conditions of behavioral homogeneity, exemplified by some crowd phenomena, a very high degree of arousal will not impede imitation, since there are relatively few conflicting cues to which the observer can attend.

IMITATION, IDENTIFICATION, AND ROLE PLAYING

Observational learning is generally labeled "imitation" in experimental psychology and "identification" in theories of personality. Both concepts, however, encompass the same behavioral phenomenon, namely, the tendency for a person to reproduce the actions, attitudes, or emotional responses exhibited by real-life or symbolized models. Numerous distinctions have been proposed, of course, at one time or another. Some writers, for example, reserve the term "identification" for matching behavior involving a class of responses defined as "meanings," and "imitation" for highly specific acts (Lazowick, 1955; Osgood, Suci, and Tannenbaum, 1957). Similarly, Parsons (1951) contrasts imitation with identification in terms of specificity and generality of learning, with the additional qualification that a "generalized cathectic attachment" is an essential antecedent of identification but unnecessary or absent in the case of imitation. Others define imitation as matching behavior occurring in the presence of the model, while regarding identification as involving the performance of the model's behavior in the latter's absence (Mowrer, 1950).

The diversity in the definitions of imitation and identification also springs in part from the fact that some writers apply these terms primarily to response-defined variables, others apply them to antecedent or process variables which are stimulus-defined, while still others assign to imitation the status of a dependent variable and treat identification as an independent variable, and vice versa.

It is possible to draw distinctions between these and other related terms—for example, introjection and incorporation

—based on certain stimulus, mediating, or terminal-response variables. However, one might question whether it is meaningful to do so, since essentially the same learning process is involved regardless of the content of what is learned, the object from whom it is learned, or the stimulus situations in which the relevant behavior is emitted. Therefore, it is in the interest of clarity, precision, and parsimony to employ the single term, imitation, to refer to the occurrence of matching responses.

Role playing and role behavior have received considerable attention from social psychologists, psychiatrists, and sociologists (Cameron, 1947; Cameron and Magaret, 1951; Goffman, 1959; Mead, 1934; Moreno, 1934; Newcomb, 1950; Sarbin, 1954) in relation to problems of socialization, social adjustment, psychopathology, and psychotherapy. As used by social psychologists, role behavior usually refers to the occurrence of complex adult responses that are guided by social norms or similar forms of symbolic models. Analogously, in developmental psychology (for example, Maccoby, 1959) role playing refers to a process whereby, through imitating adult activities, the child gains mastery of behavior patterns that he will be *expected* to display as an adult. Generally speaking, the imitative behavior involved in role playing and role behavior, as these terms are used by developmental and social psychologists, occurs in the absence of explicit instructions of how the observer should behave, though of course they may be aided by descriptions of positive exemplary models.

In contrast, role playing as an experimental or therapeutic technique ordinarily involves instructions to the subject or patient to reproduce the behavior of a real-life or a generalized symbolic model (for example, Buss and Foliart, 1958). The imitator is then required to practice his assigned role and from this point on supplies for himself further examples of how he is required to behave. The forms of response that the agent displays in his assigned and accepted role may then be transferred to stimulus situations other than those in which they were learned and, as a study by Rosenberg and Abelson (1960) demonstrates, may induce concomitant responses that the original model did not in fact display. Role-playing may be a particularly effective means of producing behavior change, since (at least in most experimental situations) the role player dependently accepts the assigned role and then is usually reinforced by approval for reproducing the behavior of the model. Indeed, during the role-playing process, when his own previous activities become a model for his own further behavior, the agent may be receiving reinforcement both in his capacity as a model and in his capacity of observer and imitator.

From the discussion presented above it is evident that a variety of antecedent conditions may result in the occurrence of matching responses on the part of an observer. Sometimes, as in the case of role playing when used as an experimental technique, the antecedents may include explicit instructions to the observer to reproduce a set of demonstrated or described activities. Such an instruction may also accompany the presentation of positive exemplary models by parents, but is in any case by no means a necessary antecedent of imitation. Indeed, when children assume parent or adult roles in play, an activity which according to Sears (1957) is a crucial step in the "identification" process, such instructions are usually absent, as they are when an adult adopts role behavior in the sense in which this latter term is used by social psychologists such as Newcomb (1950). In all cases, however, the essential learning process consists of the presentation of a model, symbolic or real-life, whose behavior the observer matches. Any distinctions that are made between role playing and role behavior, on the one hand, and imitation and imitative behavior, on the other, should therefore be based on antecedent conditions or on the nature of the model that is involved. Unfortunately, up to the present time, role theorists have, generally speaking, failed to relate their concepts in any systematic matter to the principles and processes of observational learning, and the labeling of certain types of matching behavior as instances of role playing or role enactment therefore remains, in many instances, a completely arbitrary matter.

THEORIES OF IDENTIFICATION AND EXPOSURE
TO MULTIPLE MODELS

The studies to which reference has so far been made have generally involved a single model. However, during their life history children are exposed to a series of models, the relative strength of whose influence depends on their availability, their homogeneity or heterogeneity, their interrelationships, and the extent to which each of them has received rewarding or punishing consequences for his behavior.

During the child's early years the family constitutes the child's basic reference group; at this stage, the range of available real-life models is restricted to family members, particularly the parents, who serve as the source of biological and conditioned rewards for the child. Consequently, theoreticians who accept the psychoanalytic view that a child's early experiences are crucial for determining his future development and behavior have focused on the role of intrafamily dynamics in determining the direction and extent of a child's imitation of the same-sex and opposite-sex parent, a topic which is customarily labeled as the problem of "identification."

Psychoanalytic theory has provided the most widely accepted explanation of the identification process. According to Freud, there are two quite different sets of antecedent conditions, both fear-inducing, that result in a child's identification with a parent. *Anaclitic identification* (Freud, 1925 [1917]) occurs when a nurturant adult, usually the mother, to whom the child has developed a nonsexual dependent attachment, commences to withhold rewards that she has previously freely dispensed; the resulting threat of loss of the loved object then motivates the child to "introject" her behavior and qualities. *Defensive or aggressive identification* (Freud, 1924b [1912], 1949 [1945]), which received increasing emphasis in Freud's later writings, occurs only for boys. The mechanism of identification with the aggressor depicts introjection as the outcome of the resolution of the Oedipus complex in which the child adopts the characteristics of the rivalrous like-sex parent, thereby reducing anxiety over anticipated punishment by castration for his incestuous wishes toward his mother and at the same time vicariously gaining the affectional gratifications of the opposite-sex parent. Fear of punishment, rather than fear of loss of love, thus provides the primary incentive for a boy to identify with his father.

Different aspects of Freud's identification theory have been emphasized by subsequent writers on the topic, several of whom have attempted reinterpretations in terms of learning-theory concepts. Mowrer (1950) describes two forms of identification, developmental and defensive, parallel to those outlined by Freud. However, Mowrer focuses on the developmental form in both his theoretical elaboration and his laboratory analogues of the identification process. According to Mowrer, developmental identification occurs because the caretaking adult, ordinarily the mother, mediates the young child's biological and social rewards and thus her behavior and attributes take on secondary reward value. On the basis of stimulus generalization, responses that parallel those of the caretaker attain reward value for the child in proportion to their similarity to those made by the caretaking adult. Consequently, the child can administer positively conditioned reinforcers to himself simply by matching as closely as possible the caretaker's positively valenced behavior.

This process is well illustrated by Mowrer's account of the acquisition of language responses (1950, 1958). For example, in the first step of training a bird to talk, the trainer emits words in conjunction with the presentation of food, water, physical contact, and other primary reinforcers. As the formerly neutral word stimuli take on secondary reward value, the bird is motivated to reproduce them. However, in later expositions of the process of learning by observation, including language acquisition, Mowrer (1960a, 1960b) has placed more emphasis on the role of positively conditioned proprioceptive feedback and imaginal mediating responses in the facilitation of imitative behavior.

Sears (1957) has, like Mowrer, placed most emphasis on anaclitic identification and regards a nurturant interaction between a caretaking adult and a child as a necessary precondition of identification. Through this interaction the child learns to want and value his mother's presence and nurturant activities and by the end of the first year of life acquires a dependency drive. However, the mother cannot always be present to mediate the child's rewards; moreover, she may at times withhold or withdraw her attention and affection as a disciplinary or training technique. The consequent dependency frustration and insecurity concerning parental affection and approval leads the child to adopt the method of role practice as a means of reinstating the parent's nurturant responses. Imitative responses may bring direct rewards from parents, who are likely to be pleased, and even flattered, when the child emulates their behavior. Moreover, through role-playing in fantasy the child can perform the parent's nurturant acts himself and thus vicariously obtain rewards that the parent is at the time unable or unwilling to bestow. Thus, through the repeated association of imitation with direct or self-administered reward, identification becomes an acquired drive for which the satisfying goal response is acting like another person. A similar account of identification is offered by Whiting and Child (1953).

More recently, Whiting (1959, 1960) has proposed a theory of identification that places primary emphasis on the defensive aspects of the process. His status-envy theory represents an extension of the Freudian hypothesis that identification is the outcome of a rivalrous interaction between the child and the parent who occupies an envied status. While Freud presents the child as in competition with the father only for the mother's sexual and affectional attention, Whiting regards any forms of reward, material or social, as valued resources around which rivalry may develop. He further assumes that the more a child envies the status of another person in respect to the consumption of resources of which he feels himself to be deprived, the more he will play the role of that person in fantasy. Thus, when a child competes unsuccessfully with an adult for affection, attention, food, and care, he will envy the adult consumer and consequently identify with him.

In contrast to Whiting, other writers (Maccoby, 1959; Mussen and Distler, 1959; Parsons, 1955) appear to assume that the controller, rather than the consumer, of resources will be the primary model for children's imitative role-playing. This power theory of social influence has received considerable attention in social psychology, though not in the context of theories of identification.

Social power has been defined as the ability of a person to influence the behavior of others by controlling or mediating their positive and negative reinforcements. French and Raven (1959) have distinguished five types of power, based on expertness, attractiveness, legitimacy, coerciveness, and rewarding power, each of which is believed to have somewhat differential effects on the social-influence process. For example, the use of coercion, in which the controller derives power from his ability to administer punishments, not only creates and supports avoidance behavior toward the controller but also decreases his attractiveness and hence his effectiveness in altering the behavior of others beyond the immediate social-influence setting (French, Morrison, and Levinger, 1960; Zipf, 1960). The use of reward power, in contrast, tends to elicit and strengthen approach responses toward the power figure and to increase his attractiveness or secondary-reward value through the repeated association of his attributes with positive reinforcement. Attractiveness is assumed also to extend the controller's power influence over a wide range of behavior (French and Raven, 1959).

Relevant data are available concerning two issues raised by theories of identification, since both the role of nurturance and the role of power in facilitating imitation and determining the source of imitative behavior have been subjects of investigation. Research cited in earlier sections demonstrates that a wide range of imitative responses, deviant and conforming, social and nonsocial, in the presence or absence of the model, may be elicited without the necessity of first establishing a nurturant-dependent relationship between the model and the observer. Although this research indicates that nurturance is not a necessary antecedent of imitative learning, other studies provide some evidence that it can foster imitation.

In an experiment by Bandura and Huston (1961), one group of nursery-school children experienced a highly nurturant and rewarding interaction with a female model, whereas for a second group of children the same model behaved in a distant, nonrewarding manner. Following the social-interaction sessions, the model and the child played a game, the object of which was to guess which of two boxes contained a picture sticker. In executing each trial, the model exhibited relatively novel verbal, motor, and aggressive responses that were totally irrelevant to the game to which the child's attention was directed. A measure was obtained of the number of imitative responses the child reproduced while performing his trials. Except for aggressive responses, which were readily imitated regardless of the nurturant quality of the model, children who experienced the rewarding interaction with the model imitated her behavior to a substantially greater extent than did children with whom the same model had reacted in a distant and nonrewarding way. Moreover, the children in the model-rewarding condition also displayed more behavior that was only partially imitative of the model's social responses. This study indicates that exposure to a model possessing rewarding qualities not only facilitates precise imitation but also increases the probability of the occurrence of responses falling within the same class as those made by the model but which the model does not in fact emit.

The association between rewarding parental characteristics and imitative behavior has been demonstrated in a number of studies in which reward and punishment have been assessed from interview material or thematic responses. Mussen and Distler (1959) selected two groups of kindergarten boys, one displaying a high degree of male-role preference and the other a low degree of male-role preference, on the basis of their responses to a projective test (Brown, 1956). The boys were then required to complete nine incomplete stories, involving parent-child relations, during the course of individual doll-play sessions. In comparison to the boys who received low male-role-preference scores, the children with strong masculine-role preferences perceived their fathers as relatively powerful sources of both reward and punishment, a finding which the authors interpret as primarily supporting a social-power theory of imitative learning. In a later study, Mussen (1961) compared senior high-school boys who displayed strongly masculine vocational interests with boys of the same age who obtained strongly feminine vocational-interest scores. As in the Mussen and Distler study, boys with strong masculine interests were more likely than boys with weak masculine interests to depict their fathers as rewarding and positive in their attitudes toward them; however, the strongly masculine adolescents also tended to portray their fathers as nonpunitive and nonrestrictive, a discrepancy between this and the earlier study which could be attributable to the age difference between the subjects. However, since the relationship between punitive power and sex-role preference that was found in the earlier study was of borderline significance, it is perhaps not surprising that this result was not replicated. Mussen's findings for adolescents indirectly corroborate results previously reported by Payne and Mussen (1956), in whose study boys with high and low father-son similarity in responding to items on a personality inventory were required to construct story endings involving father-son relationships. Analysis of the data revealed that boys with high father-identification perceived their fathers as highly rewarding and affectionate persons.

Further evidence of an association between parental characteristics and children's imitative behavior is provided by P. S. Sears (1953), who found that boys of warm affectionate fathers tended to assume the father role in doll-play activities more frequently than did boys of fathers who were relatively cold. Sears' study also revealed the importance of the quality of interactions between models when more than one model is involved, since boys who more strongly adopted the mother role had mothers who were both warm and affectionate toward their children and devaluated their husbands.

Bandura and Walters (1959) reported that nonaggressive boys exhibited greater father-preference and more frequently perceived themselves as thinking and acting like their fathers than did aggressive boys. Comparisons based on parent interviews revealed that the fathers of the aggressive boys were relatively nonnurturant and nonrewarding of their sons' behavior in the home. Moreover, the aggressive boys' fathers were much more punitive than those of the nonaggressive boys, a finding that suggests that the punitive coercion favored by the former group of fathers had in most respects decreased their effectiveness as models for their sons to emulate.

In a comparative study of the status envy, social-power, and secondary-reinforcement theories of imitative learning, Bandura, Ross, and Ross (1963c) utilized three-person groups, representing prototypes of the nuclear family. In one condition of the experiment an adult assumed the role of controller of resources and positive reinforcers. Another adult was the consumer or recipient of these resources, while the child, a participant observer in the triad, was essentially ignored. In a second treatment condition, one adult controlled the resources; the child, however, was the recipient of the positive reinforcers, while the other adult was assigned a subordinate and powerless role. An adult male and female served as models in each of the triads. For half the boys and girls in each condition the male model controlled and dispensed the rewarding resources, simulating the husband-dominant family; for the remaining children, the female model mediated the positive resources as in the wife-dominant home. Thus, the experimental design permitted a test of whether power inversions would promote cross-sex imitation. Following the experimental social interactions the two adult models exhibited divergent patterns of behavior in the presence of the child, and a measure was obtained of the degree to which the child patterned his behavior after that of the models.

In both experimental treatments, regardless of whether the rival adult or the children themselves were the recipients of the rewarding resources, the model who possessed rewarding power was imitated, when the models were subsequently absent, to a greater extent than was the competitor or the ignored model. To the extent that the imitative behavior elicited in this experiment may be considered an elementary prototype of identification within a nuclear family group, the data fail to support the interpretation of the identification process as a child-initiated defensive maneuver. Children clearly identified with the source of rewarding power rather than with the competitor for the rewards. Moreover, power inversions on the part of the male and female models produced cross-sex imitation, particularly in girls. Compared to boys, the girls showed a greater readiness to imitate the behavior exhibited by an opposite-sex model. This difference probably reflects both the differential cultural tolerance for cross-sex behavior displayed by males and females and the relatively greater positive reinforcement of masculine-role behavior in our society.

Failure to develop sex-appropriate behavior has received considerable attention in clinical psychology and psychiatry and has customarily been interpreted as a manifestation of underlying psychodynamic processes, especially latent homosexuality. To present these processes as internal causal factors does little to clarify the genesis of sex-inappropriate behavior. On the other hand, to identify the influence of external social-learning variables, such as the distribution of rewarding power within the family, on the formation of deviant sex-role behavior both assists in the understanding of the development of deviant sexuality and directs attention to the manner in which culturally approved patterns may be formed.

Theories of identification have usually assumed that within the family setting the child's initial identification is confined to his mother, and that boys during early childhood are forced to reject the mother as the primary model and to turn to the father as the main source of imitative learning. However, throughout the course of development most children are provided with ample opportunities to observe the behavior of both parents.

When a child is exposed to a variety of models, he may select one or more of them as the primary source of behavior, but he rarely reproduces all the elements of a single model's repertory or confines his imitation to that model. In the experiment by Bandura, Ross, and Ross (1963c), although children adopted many of the characteristics of the model who possessed rewarding power, they also reproduced some of the elements of behavior exhibited by the model who occupied the subordinate role. Consequently, the children were not simply junior-size replicas of one or the other model; rather, they exhibited a relatively novel pattern of behavior representing an amalgam of elements from both models. Thus, within one family even same-sex siblings may exhibit quite different patterns of behavior, owing to their having selected for imitation different elements of their father's and mother's response repertories.

Innovation of social behavior may also occur, as the child gets older, through increasing contact with models provided by the peer group and adults other than parents. The degree of innovation, however, is likely to be a function of the diversity of modeling agents. In highly homogeneous social groups, for example, where all models display essentially the same pattern of behavior, imitative responses may undergo little or no change across successive models. Even within a heterogeneous subgroup, behavior and values transmitted from the home may govern the selection and rejection of extrafamilial models (Newcomb, 1943), thus reducing the possibility of marked changes in behavior patterns that are established during earlier stages of development.

Deviant patterns of behavior are likely to elicit rejection from other group members (Schachter, 1951) and, in turn, to be accompanied by suspicion and hostility directed toward other members of the community. In some cases a deviant parent may raise his family in almost complete sociocultural isolation. Studies by Lidz *et al.* (1957a, 1957b, 1958) and Fleck (1960) indicate that parents of schizophrenics may not only model bizarre and idiosyncratic behavior but also so greatly restrict the range of their families' social contacts that their children are given little opportunity for exposure to extrafamilial models who could exert a corrective influence. Moreover, it is not unusual for the most deviant parent to occupy a high power position in the family and to strive to reduce the power of the other members.

In less extreme cases, when parents are rejected by the majority of members of their own socioeconomic group, they form friendship alliances with similarly deviant individuals. They thus create a relatively homogeneous and mutually nurturant and supportive circle of deviant adult models who are likely not only to preserve the deviant culture but also to transmit it to their offspring. This phenomenon is clearly evident both in delinquent subcultures (Shaw and McKay, 1942) and in deviant religious and nonreligious cults (Festinger, Riecken, and Schachter, 1956; Zubek and Solberg, 1952).

IDENTIFICATION WITH THE AGGRESSOR AND THE SEX-TYPING OF AGGRESSION

Identification with the aggressor, whereby a person is presumed to transform himself from the object to the agent of aggression by adopting the attributes of an aggressive threatening model in order to reduce fear of attack, is widely accepted as an explanation of the imitative learning of aggression. The main evidence in support of this mechanism consists of the case material presented by Anna Freud (1946 [1936]). However, in some of Anna Freud's examples, the model in fact exhibits no aggression and the therapist simply assumes that the child who aggresses is anticipating attack. If the therapist's assumption is correct in these cases, the child's aggression could constitute a defensive maneuver, designed to ward off attack, but could hardly represent identification with the aggressor. In other of Freud's examples in which a child is hurt accidentally or without malice (for example, in the course of dental care) and subsequently exhibits aggressively demanding or destructive behavior in the presence of the therapist, no evidence is provided to show that the child's response was contingent on his previously being hurt. Moreover, even if a contingency were involved, the child's aggression could be merely a direct response to an emotionally arousing experience. The clearest example that Freud gives of imitative behavior involves the case of a boy who reproduced his teacher's grimaces while the latter was punishing or reproving him. Freud's interpretation that the boy "through his grimaces was assimilating himself to, or identifying himself with, the dreaded external object" (p. 118) is complicated by the fact that during his performance his classmates burst out laughing, thus providing strong reinforcement for the boy's imitative response. It is therefore doubtful, even in this case, that the imitative behavior was maintained by fear-reducing mechanisms.

Bettelheim's (1943) account of prisoners' reactions in a Nazi concentration camp is also frequently cited as evidence for the occurrence of identification with the aggressor. Bettelheim describes the responses of prisoners to the guards as frequently infantile and submissive and gives examples of how "old" prisoners, those who had spent more than a year in the camp, often copied the guards' behavior. For example, they were verbally and physically aggressive toward other prisoners, sometimes acting more aggressively than their guards when they were placed in charge of others; they inflicted tortures and suffering on newcomers to the prison population; they enforced nonsensical rules that the Gestapo had already discarded; they even modified their uniforms after those of the guards and boasted that they could be as tough as the Nazi officers.

While Bettelheim's account makes it evident that the old prisoners often imposed on their fellow prisoners the same kind of control through aversive stimulation that they themselves had endured, it by no means follows that their behavior provides conclusive evidence for defensive identification with the aggressor, in the sense that this concept is employed within the context of Freudian theories. For example, the Gestapo officers are said by Bettelheim to have imposed group-oriented punishment, the offenses of individuals often resulting in suffering for their fellow prisoners. Since the group punishments were frequently severe and the responses of the guards highly capricious, it is not surprising that, in order to escape suffering themselves, experienced prisoners enforced demands that were intermittently, or had been formerly, made by the Gestapo officers. By thus enforcing rules, even when the Gestapo had abandoned their consistent observance, the old prisoners produced conformity within the camp, a condition that might be expected to forestall the occurrence of group punishments, provided the conformity pattern thus established did not contravene the Gestapo demands.

Moreover, the mechanisms involved in the prisoners' behaving as aggressively as the guards were undoubtedly diverse. In the case of enforcement of rules, imitative behavior may have served to reduce anxiety concerning possible aversive consequences to the enforcers arising from the nonconforming behavior of others. However, antagonism toward persons who were seemingly the prisoners' friends and allies in the eyes of outsiders (for example, foreign correspondents and former fellow-prisoners who had publicly reported camp conditions), also interpreted by Bettelheim as an example of identification with the aggressor, may have been due simply to the fact that the newspaper accounts written by these persons in fact brought severe punishment on the prisoners.

Undoubtedly, Bettelheim provides evidence for direct matching of the guards' behavior. The prisoners, for example, collected old pieces of the guards' uniforms and sewed their own uniforms in such a way that they resembled those of the guards. Such matching behavior was a source of punishment for the imitators and therefore could hardly have served an anxiety-reducing defensive purpose. Indeed, since this particular behavior persisted in spite of punishment, it seems to provide evidence against the defensive-identification hypothesis and perhaps to suggest that the prisoners were, in accordance with the social-power hypothesis, imitating powerful controllers of resources.

Moreover, the fact that only a small minority of prisoners directly matched the guards' behavior, through copying their manner of dress and behavior, suggests that these prisoners may have developed authoritarian attitudes and modes of response before their imprisonment and thus would be predisposed to admire and imitate these attributes in the guards. Striving to match the behavior of the elite who possess control over rewarding resources is a characteristic also of upwardly mobile persons, who, like the prisoners in question, tend to persist in their matching behavior in spite of the social disapproval they incur from their peers and admired models.

There is considerable evidence that aggressive-punitive parents tend to have aggressive children (Bandura, 1960; Bandura and Walters, 1959; Glueck and Glueck, 1950; Jenkins and Hewitt, 1944; Lewis, 1954; McCord, McCord, and Zola, 1959). However, this does not necessarily mean that the children's aggression is the outcome of a fear-motivated process of identification. In fact, it has been demonstrated in a number of experimental studies that both children and adults readily imitate aggressive models that constitute no threat whatsoever (Bandura, Ross, and Ross, 1961, 1963a; Lövaas, 1961a; Mussen and Rutherford, 1961; Walters and Llewellyn Thomas, 1963). Moreover, the data from studies by Bandura (1962b) and Bandura, Ross, and Ross (1963b), in which models were rewarded and punished for aggression, demonstrate that the success of the model's behavior is a crucial factor in determining the degree to which an aggressive pattern of behavior will be reproduced by the observer. On the basis of the response-consequences interpretation of modeling effects (Bandura, Ross, and Ross, 1963b; Walters, Leat, and Mezei, 1963), it would be predicted that if the behavior of an aggressive model is highly successful in producing social and material rewards, the child will identify with the aggressor, even though he may dislike the attributes of the model (Bandura, Ross, and Ross, 1963b). If, on the other hand, the aggressor's behavior fails to gain power and control over important resources or actually brings punishment, identification with the aggressor will not occur. It is probable, therefore, that fear of a punitive agent is usually an irrelevant, rather than an instigating, factor in the identification process.

The influence which the presence in the home of an aggressive masculine model has on the development of aggression has been inferred from doll-play studies. Bach (1946) found that six- and ten-year-old children, both boys and girls, whose fathers were absent from home showed less doll-play aggression than those whose fathers were present. On the other hand, P. S. Sears (1951) found that while the presence or absence of the father influenced the doll-play aggression of boys of nursery-school age, this variable had no influence on the doll-play aggression of nursery-school girls. In both the above studies, the fathers were absent from the home during the period that observations of the children were made, and it is probable that the observed differences between father-present and father-absent children reflected only temporary modifications of behavior. Indeed, Stolz (1954) reported that war-born children whose fathers had been absent from home during the first two years following the child's birth showed no more doll-play aggression at the nursery-school stage than did children whose fathers had been continually present.

Levin and Sears (1956) secured measures of the punitiveness of parents, and of the degree of "identification" with the same-sex parent shown by their preschool children, from ratings of mother interviews. Strongly masculine-identified boys showed significantly more doll-play aggression than weakly masculine-identified boys, especially when their fathers were the agents of punishment. On the other hand, the severity of the fathers' punishments had no influence on the children's aggression. Granted that the father is generally the more aggressive parent, both this study and studies of the effects of the absence of the father support previously provided evidence that children imitate parental aggression. However, they provide no support for the assumption that this imitative aggression reflects a defensive process.

Bandura, Ross, and Ross (1961) examined the influence of the sex of the model and the sex of the child on the imitation of aggression. Boys showed significantly more imitative aggression than girls, but the sexes did not differ in the extent to which they reproduced the model's verbal aggression. These findings are consistent with the doll-play sex differences reported by Johnson (1951), who found that girls displayed more "prosocial" aggression, for example, verbal rebukes and reprimands, than boys, and less "contrasocial" physical aggression. These findings are not surprising for children brought up in a society in which aggression is much more tolerated in boys and in which the socially approved physically aggressive models—for example, in sports, movies, and television—are males. Bandura, Ross, and Ross (1961) reported, in addition, that the male model was a more potent influence on male subjects than was the female model. Boys who were exposed to an aggressive male model exhibited significantly more physical and verbal imitative aggression, more nonimitative aggression, and more aggressive gun play than did girls who were exposed to the male model. Moreover, while children exposed to a nonaggressive female model did not differ from control subjects on any measure of aggression, those exposed to a nonaggressive male model performed significantly less imitative and nonimitative physical and verbal aggression than children in the control group. In a second study by Bandura, Ross, and Ross (1963a), boys again displayed significantly more aggression than girls, and again an aggressive male model was a more powerful stimulus for aggression than an agressive female model.

The relative potency of male and female models for eliciting imitative responses may be a function of the extent to which the behavior in question is sex-typed. As doll-play and real-life observations indicate (Goodenough, 1931; P. S. Sears, 1951), physical aggression is a characteristically masculine response for which sex differences are established within the first three years of life, undoubtedly through the joint influence of social models and social-reinforcement patterns. Once these differences are established, this kind of behavior is apparently more easily disinhibited by observation of models for whom it is sex-appropriate than by observation of models for whom it is not sex-appropriate. Obviously, appropriateness of a particular class of responses could be a function of variables other than sex, for example, the age or social role of the aggressor.

Summary

In this chapter the influence of the behavior of models in transmitting prosocial and deviant response patterns has been discussed in relation to data provided by both field studies and laboratory experimentation. Three possible effects of exposure to a model were distinguished: (1) a modeling effect, involving the transmission of precisely imitative response patterns not previously present in the observer's repertory; (2) an inhibitory or disinhibitory effect, reflected in an increase or decrease in the frequency, latency, or intensity of previously acquired observer responses that are more or less similar to those exhibited by the model; and (3) a possible eliciting effect, in which the observation of a model's responses serves as a cue for "releasing" similar observer responses that are neither entirely novel nor inhibited as a result of prior learning.

Relevant research demonstrates that when a model is provided, patterns of behavior are typically acquired in large segments or in their entirety rather than through a slow, gradual process based on differential reinforcement. Following demonstrations by a model, or (though to a lesser extent) following verbal descriptions of desired behavior, the learner generally reproduces more or less the entire response pattern, even though he may perform no overt response, and consequently receive no reinforcement, throughout the demonstration period. Under such circumstances, the acquisition process is quite clearly not as piecemeal as is customarily depicted in modern behavior systems.

The role of models in the transmission of novel social responses has been demonstrated most extensively in laboratory studies of aggression. Children who have been exposed to aggressive models respond to subsequent frustration with considerable aggression, much of which is precisely imitative, whereas equally frustrated children who have observed models displaying inhibited behavior are relatively nonaggressive and tend to match the behavior of the inhibited model. There is some evidence from field studies that dependency responses and anxiety about sexual behavior can also be transmitted from parents to children. Moreover, cross-cultural and clinical observations provide examples of the shaping of antisocial, autistic, and other forms of grossly deviant response patterns through modeling.

In addition to teaching observers entirely novel patterns of response, the presentation of models may have inhibitory and disinhibitory or eliciting effects. For example, exposure to an aggressive model may result in the observer's displaying pain-producing responses, which, although not precisely imitative, have social effects that are in some respects similar to those that result from the model's behavior. Nonspecific imitation of this kind is perhaps most likely when the responses involved are already present in the observer's behavioral repertoire but are infrequently manifested because of the social disapproval they elicit.

The influence that the behavior of a model will exert on an observer is partly contingent on the response consequences to the model. Children who observe an aggressive model rewarded display more imitative aggression than children who see a model punished for aggression. Similarly, rewarding and punishing consequences to a model who violates a prohibition influence the extent to which his transgression will be imitated. In addition, models who are rewarding, prestigeful, or competent, who possess high status, and who have control over rewarding resources are more readily imitated than are models who lack these qualities. Such factors also determine in part which models will be selected as major sources of exemplary social behavior patterns. While immediate or inferred response consequences to the model have an important influence on the observers' *performance* of imitative responses, the *acquisition* of these responses appears to result primarily from contiguous sensory stimulation.

Characteristics of observers—for example, the degree to which they have previously been rewarded or punished for compliant behavior—also influence the extent to which imitative responses will occur. Moreover, susceptibility to the social influence of models is increased by temporary or transient states of the observer, such as emotional arousal of a moderate degree of intensity or the intensified dependency that can be induced through hypnotic procedures.

The same classes of events and the same model and observer characteristics that enhance or reduce the extent to which a model influences an observer contribute to the development of adult-child similarities of behavior, which in psychodynamic theories have usually been categorized as instances of identification. Since, however, this latter term is highly elusive and carries many surplus meanings, the behavioral phenomena to which it refers were conceptualized in terms of social-learning principles. It was consequently possible to apply a large body of research concerning observational learning to the understanding of the development of parent-child similarities and to suggest alternative interpretations of the genesis of certain forms of matching behavior that, in psychodynamic theories, have usually been considered to be the outcome of defensive processes.

It is evident, however, that the social-influence process cannot be accounted for entirely in terms of the effects of the presentation of parent and other models. Once imitative responses occur, the consequences to the agent will largely determine whether these responses are strengthened, weakened, or inhibited. Direct training through reward, aversive stimulation, and other disciplinary procedures undoubtedly play a large part in shaping and in maintaining patterns of social behavior. This issue is discussed in the next chapter.

CHAPTER THREE

Reinforcement Patterns and Social Behavior

The effects of different kinds of patterns of reinforcement were outlined briefly in Chapter 1. This topic has received considerable attention from investigators of theoretical problems in learning, but relatively little systematic investigation in relation to problems of social behavior. Generally speaking, it has been assumed, rather than demonstrated, that reinforcement principles apply within complex social settings and that they govern the social behavior of human beings in precisely the same manner as they regulate the responses of human and animal subjects in highly structured nonsocial laboratory experiments. In this chapter we have attempted to review and evaluate findings relating to the effects on specific classes of social responses both of reward and punishment and of the omission and cessation of these possible outcomes. The majority of relevant investigations, including the data obtained from the authors' own laboratory and field studies, relate primarily to the fostering, regulation, and control of aggression; consequently, most attention is given to the problem of how aggressive responses are acquired, maintained, and modified through reinforcement patterns, although the influence of reinforcement variables on dependency and sexual behavior also will be discussed in some detail.

Aggression

Deviant response patterns of an aggressive kind have received considerable attention from workers in many disciplines. The thinking and practice in mental-health professions have been considerably influenced, directly or indirectly, by Freud's early theory of aggression, according to which aggression is a "primordial reaction" to the thwarting of pleasure-seeking or pain-avoiding responses (Freud, 1920 [1917]; 1925 [1917]). For Freud, frustration consisted primarily of the blocking of libidinal forces; subsequent expositors of the frustration-aggression hypothesis have specified a wide range of frustration events, including almost any form of withholding or delay of gratification. Thus aggression has been considered to be a product of broken homes, adverse socioeconomic conditions, urbanization, frustrated mobility strivings due to ethnic or class barriers, physique-related limitations, and intrapsychic tensions. Freud's theorizing about aggression has also shaped much of the thinking and research in the area of developmental psychology, particularly since the formulation of the frustration-aggression hypothesis by members of the Yale Institute of Human Relations (Dollard, Doob, Miller, Mowrer, and Sears, 1939).

THE FRUSTRATION-AGGRESSION HYPOTHESIS

In the form in which it was originally propounded, the frustration-aggression hypothesis presented aggression as a natural and inevitable consequence of frustration. In later modifications of the hypothesis (Dollard *et al.,* 1944; Miller, 1941), aggression was regarded as a natural, though not an inevitable, consequence of frustration, since nonaggressive responses to frustration could be learned. Nevertheless, *aggression* was still considered the *naturally dominant* response to frustration, and a nonaggressive response as likely to occur only if aggressive responses had previously met with nonreward or punishment. While some members of the Yale group (for example, Sears, 1941; Whiting, 1944) were willing to discard the notion that aggression is the only unlearned reaction to frustration, *frustration* continued to be regarded as an *inevitable antecedent* of aggression; in other words, whenever an aggressive act occurred, it was assumed that it was instigated by frustration.

In spite of the emphasis on the role of instigators in the frustration-aggression hypothesis, relatively little research has been conducted on the effects of the three factors that were considered to be responsible for the amount of frustration: the strength of instigation to the frustrated response, the degree of interference with the frustrated response, and the number of frustrated response sequences. Instead, research has been concentrated on inhibition, object displacement and response displacement, and the occurrence of catharsis. The crucial problems of how aggressive responses are originally learned, of the form that aggressive responses initially take, and the role of factors other than interference with an ongoing response sequence (or of operations labeled as "frustrative" and thought to be equivalent to interference) in the shaping and maintaining of aggressive behavior were largely ignored. In effect, in spite of its avowed relationship to reinforcement-learning principles (Hull, 1943), *Frustration and Aggression* failed to provide an adequate starting point for a social-learning approach to aggression. Probably the book's main contribution was, through specifying certain antecedent conditions that might elicit or inhibit the performance of aggressive acts, to stimulate studies of aggression in which antecedent events were manipulated.

Criticism of the frustration-aggression hypothesis focused at first on the nature of responses to frustration. Bateson (1941) pointed out that in some cultures (for example, that of the Balinese) aggression was by no means a typical response to frustration. Barker, Dembo, and Lewin (1941) and Wright (1942, 1943) demonstrated that nursery-school children may regress when frustrated, a reaction that was observed also in rats in an ingenious experiment by Mowrer (1940). Other critics have argued that only some kinds of frustration evoke an aggressive response and that other kinds do not. Maslow (1941), Rosenzweig (1944), and, more recently, Buss (1961) have noted that attack or threat is more likely to elicit aggressive reactions than the blocking of ongoing sequences, although attack and blocking are, of course, not totally unrelated. Pastore (1952) emphasized the role of the arbitrariness of the frustration in determining whether or not an aggressive response will occur and suggested that arbitrary frustration involved interference with the attainment of an expected goal. Obviously, one of the major sources of controversy is the ambiguity in the definition of frustration. A search for antecedents of aggression other than ones that have been categorized as frustration has only recently begun.

DEFINITION OF AGGRESSION

In the development of a social-learning theory of aggression, the first requirement is a definition of what constitutes an aggressive response. The authors of *Frustration and Aggression* define aggression as a sequence of behavior "the goal-response to which is the injury of the person toward whom it is directed" (p. 9). With few exceptions, subsequent theory and research have adopted *intentionality* as an essential aspect in the definition of aggression (for example, Bandura and Walters, 1959; Sears, Maccoby, and Levin, 1957). The main problem with such a definition is that intentionality is not a property of behavior but refers to antecedent conditions which frequently have to be inferred from the behavior of which they are supposedly an essential ingredient. Let us suppose that each of two individuals is observed in the act of vigorously chopping down a tree. In one case he is chopping a tree down because his supply of firewood is running dangerously low; in the other case, the tree, which belongs to a neighbor, is dropping leaves and dead branches into his driveway, which he is forced continually to clean up. Or suppose that some children are standing in a ring playing catch-ball. In one case, Child A throws the ball to Child B; B suddenly turns away and is hit in the face. In the other case, B has continuously ignored A in the game; when A gets the ball, he waits until B is looking away, throws the ball, and hits B in the face. In both situations the children are hurt, cry, and require first aid. In this pair of examples, the behavior described is identical; yet, on the basis of the intentionality criterion, one act in each pair would be labeled "aggression" and the other would not.

A complex set of criteria—some relating to the form of the response, some to its antecedents, and still others relating to its intensity—determine whether or not a response will be labeled as aggressive. The fact that the intensity of a response often influences its labeling as aggressive is often overlooked. It is true that mild responses—for example, nagging or gentle sarcasm—are sometimes regarded as aggressive. On the other hand, responses of high magnitude, even relatively acceptable ones, are rarely thought of as nonaggressive. For example, the efforts of upper-mobile families to obtain entry into a social group that represents the status level to which they are aspiring are, in many circles, regarded as aggressive. Since the intensity of response is an important factor in determining whether or not it will produce pain or damage, research into the learning of high-magnitude responses may throw considerable light on the problem of aggression.

A definition of aggression that supposedly avoids the intentionality criterion has been proposed by Buss (1961), who regards aggression as "a response that delivers noxious stimuli to another object" (p. 1). Buss further stipulates that the response must be made in an interpersonal situation. Such a definition may be preferable to that used by Dollard *et al.* (1939) but has one major limitation. Responses generally labeled as aggressive may be learned and performed in situations in which no noxious stimulus is, in fact, delivered, because there is no object to injure or because the object is inanimate and consequently cannot be hurt.

It is, indeed, difficult to define aggression in such a way as to exclude the concept of intent and at the same time to avoid placing in this category responses that, on the basis of common-sense criteria, would certainly not be regarded as aggressive. Undoubtedly for this reason, Buss surreptitiously reintroduces the intentionality criterion in a discussion in which he excludes some pain-producing responses from the category of aggression. According to Buss, an individual who delivers a noxious stimulus in a "clearly recognized social role," for example, that of a parent as a disciplinarian, is not acting in an aggressive manner. The classification of responses as aggressive or nonaggressive certainly involves a social judgment, but this does not form the basis for Buss' social-role exception. "To the extent that the child's pain or discomfort is *a source of satisfaction* to the parent, the parent's punishing response *is aggressive* (p. 3; italics not in original). This qualification quite clearly presupposes the arousal of some motive, need, or "intent" to produce pain. There are additional covert references to intent in Buss' treatment of "accidental" responses, which he also excludes from the category of aggression. "Older children and adults are capable of *disguising* aggression behind a *facade* of accidents" (p. 4; italics not in original). Buss, in effect, vacillates between a definition of aggression solely in terms of response variables and a definition that also involves reference to complex stimulus-response sequences.

As Buss has pointed out, the term "aggression" usually has an interpersonal reference. When aggression is said to be expressed toward an inanimate object, it is frequently implied that some person or persons will suffer on account of the damage that is caused. However, the suffering to individual human beings is often so indirect or hypothetical (as, for example, when a youngster is said to be aggressive on account of petty vandalism) that there seems little reason for including any reference to interpersonal situations in the *definition* of aggression. Such a reference may, in fact, distract attention from some important non-interpersonal situations, such as playing with a punchball, under which aggressive responses may be learned. Strictly speaking, of course, it is not "aggressive" responses that are learned, but only classes of responses that are labeled as aggression on the basis of social judgments that themselves must be learned. An adequate learning approach to the problem of aggression must consider both how responses usually labeled as aggressive are acquired and maintained and how a child learns to make the social judgments that enable him to discriminate an aggressive from a non-aggressive response. Unfortunately, in spite of their number, psychological studies of aggression throw surprisingly little light on either of these problems.

There are two possible approaches to the problem of defining and studying aggression. One may define aggression solely by reference to observable characteristics and effects of responses and without reference to goals the responses supposedly mediate; for example, aggression may be defined as the class of pain-producing or damage-producing responses or as responses that *could* injure or damage *if* aimed at a vulnerable object. Since the consequences of a single response may depend on circumstances that are irrelevant to the understanding of the development of a habit, the latter definition seems preferable. Children learn derogation partly through imitating the use of derogatory epithets and statements that are uttered in their presence by parents or other adults (Allport, 1954); these responses are aggressive, according to the definition in terms of the potential effects of the response, though during acquisition they may not produce injury or damage.

Alternatively, one may include in the definition of aggression references to complex stimulus events, for example, the social context of the act or the recent or more remote past of the agent. In such a case, intent may be inferred, though not solely on the basis of response variables.

If the first alternative is selected, it is possible to study the manner in which aggressive responses are acquired, strengthened, maintained, extinguished, and inhibited, and the conditions under which generalization and discrimination occur. This approach avoids the subjectivity and value judgments involved in studies of aggression in which the intent of the agent is taken into consideration. At the same time, it can generate conceptual confusion because the responses under study are often displayed in circumstances in which they would not be socially judged as aggressive.

Introducing the concept of intentionality, on the other hand, fosters an approach to socially significant problems and facilitates communication among students of social behavior. An investigator who uses the intentionality criterion may study the antecedents of vandalism but will not study the manner in which a lumberjack learns to chop down a tree. In defining his variable, however, this investigator must realize that he is basing his definition on stimulus events and social values and not solely on the characteristics of the responses he is studying.

Definition of frustration

The task of establishing a serviceable definition of frustration is, if anything, more complex than that of defining aggression. A multitude of experimental operations have been employed in "inducing" the condition of "frustration." These range over simple nonreward, the withdrawing or withholding of positive reinforcements, and the introduction of negative reinforcers. It has been well documented in research involving both human and animal subjects that these operations have very diverse effects, ranging from the elimination to the intensification of the behavior, interference with which, according to the frustration-aggression theory, should result in aggression. Moreover, the term "frustration" has been used both for the experimental operations themselves and for internal responses of the organism that supposedly result from operations of these kinds (Marx, 1956). In this chapter, all operations or conditions that prevent or delay reinforcement are regarded as frustrative. Since prevention or omission of reinforcement is equivalent to indefinitely prolonged or infinite delay, *frustration may be simply defined as delay of reinforcement*. However, in presenting certain points of view, for the sake of brevity, "frustration" will be used also for hypothetical or inferred states or responses of the organism, which are in other places more consistently regarded as "frustration-induced."

Delay of reinforcement may arise from the existence or creation of environmental barriers, physical or social; for example, famine, isolation, laws restricting sexual behavior, or conditions under which an excessive amount of work is required for obtaining the necessities of life. Personal limitations, physiological or psychological, genetic or learned, are other potential sources of frustration. Fears and conflicts, which may result from attack or punishment, fall into this category. Thus the presentation of noxious stimuli may, but need not, result in frustration.

Many of the operations designed to induce frustration have this in common, that they are likely to elicit responses of high magnitude. It should be noted that responses of high magnitude (for example, the vigorous chopping of a tree, or throwing of a ball, or the hard punching or kicking of an object) are frequently learned under conditions that are in no way frustrative. In military training, soldiers are taught to use guns, bayonets, and grenades in the absence of frustration, in the expectation that under appropriate instigation they will use these weapons for destructive purposes. Once learned, such responses can, of course, be elicited under frustrative conditions and presumably will be elicited if the appropriate stimuli are present, stimuli that may include instruments of injury or destruction and the presence of the agent thought responsible for the frustration. A boy who has learned how to use a switch-blade knife through solitary play or through seeing the knife used to produce injury (either in real-life or in fantasy productions, such as movies or televised shows) is more likely to injure another child with a switch-blade knife than if he had never learned to use a knife or had never observed a knife used as an injurious weapon. Given the appropriate stimulus conditions, including one of the forms of frustration, this child is likely to utilize his past learning to perform an act that would undoubtedly be labeled as aggressive.

DISCRIMINATION LEARNING

Let us now consider a father who devotes some of his time to playing punchball with his young son. He punches the ball himself and then, with or without verbal encouragement, elicits a similar response in the boy. He responds to the boy's punching with approval. The boy punches harder and is again positively reinforced. Indeed, a competition in prowess is likely to develop. In the course of the play, the father both provides the model for the hitting response and reinforces the response when it is made. In fact, the father is likely to provide differential reinforcement for intense responses, since weak hitting responses are frequently interpreted as a sign of lack of virility. Once the intense hitting response has been established, it can be elicited in various situations, some frustrative and some nonfrustrative.

In the course of development, then, a child is provided with many opportunities to acquire responses of high magnitude in nonfrustrative situations; these responses may remain relatively high in his response hierarchies and can thus be readily mobilized to cope with the various situations that have been classed as frustrating. While the fact that these responses are not elicited more frequently may be in part due to expectations of punishment, it is probably due just as much, if not more, to good discrimination learning, which results from differential reinforcement and requires more than simple inhibition.

POSITIVE REINFORCEMENT OF AGGRESSION

Training in interpersonal aggression has, for ethical and practical reasons, rarely been attempted in a controlled laboratory setting. There is considerable evidence, however, from cross-cultural and field studies that aggressive habits are acquired largely through the direct reinforcement of aggressive responses. In the culture of the head-hunting Iatmul (Bateson, 1936) the scalping of enemies is reinforced not only by the prestige that accrues to the possessor of the scalp but also, more immediately and tangibly, by the dances and celebrations that follow the decapitation. The success of the hero-killer is, however, only a climax in a series of experiences of inflicting and receiving pain and humiliation in situations in which the agent of injury is acclaimed for his acts. During their own initiation ceremonies the adolescents of this society suffer bullying and humiliation, then later, as young adults, inflict socially approved suffering on fresh batches of novices. Bateson regards the aggression of the Iatmul male as a form of overcompensation; a more obvious and parsimonious explanation is that the child and adolescent in this society are constantly surrounded by aggressive models and that when the occasion comes for them to reproduce the aggressive behavior of the adults, their imitative responses are socially approved, while failure to behave aggressively is negatively reinforced.

> In the first week of their seclusion, the novices are subjected to a great variety of cruel and harsh tricks of this kind [jabbing a crocodile bone against the novice's gums] and for every trick there is some ritual pretext. And it is still more significant of the ethos of the culture that the bullying of the novices is used as a context in which the different groups of the initiators can make pride points against each other. One moiety of the initiators decided that the novices had been bullied as much as they could stand and were for omitting one of the ritual episodes. The other moiety than began to brag that the lenient ones were afraid of the fine fashion in which *they* would carry out the bullying; and the lenient party hardened their hearts and performed the episode with some extra savagery (p. 131).

In contrast, among the Hutterites (Eaton and Weil, 1955) who stress pacifism as a style of life, aggressive behavior goes consistently unrewarded. Despite the fact that children in this subculture are subjected to relatively severe and presumably frustrating socialization pressures, they show virtually no interpersonal aggression.

Social class and ethnic differences in amount of overt agression appear to be, at least in part, a function of the extent to which members of a particular social group tolerate and show approval of aggressive actions. Lower-class parents were reported by Davis and Havighurst (Davis, 1943; Davis and Havighurst, 1947) to encourage and reward aggression to a greater extent than middle-class parents and at the same time to impose fewer frustrations on their children's "impulses." While these two findings are not independent, since aggression is one of the forms of behavior under consideration, together they suggest that reward of aggression, and not frustration, was the more potent determinant of the relatively high degree of aggression found among the lower-class children.

This interpretation is indirectly supported by the outcome of a study by Bandura and Walters (1959) of the child-training practices of parents of aggressive and nonaggressive boys. Bandura and Walters found that the parents of the aggressive boys were more inclined to encourage actively and to condone aggression than were the parents of the nonaggressive boys. The difference between the two groups of fathers was particularly marked. A very similar finding emerged from Bandura's (1960) comparison of the child-training procedures of aggressive and inhibited boys. The data indicated that the parents of the inhibited boys exhibited a generalized nonpermissive and nonpunitive attitude toward aggression, thus affording little opportunity for aggression to be learned either through direct reinforcement or through imitation. By contrast, the parents of the aggressive boys, particularly the mothers, while nonpermissive and punitive for aggression toward themselves, permitted a great deal of sibling aggression and encouraged and rewarded their son's aggressive behavior when this was directed toward other children.

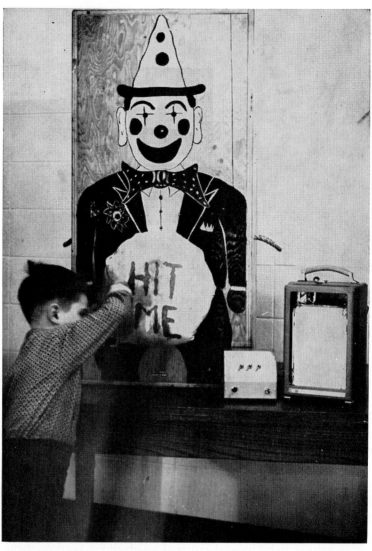

FIG. 3–1. *"Bobo" clown for studying influence of reinforcement patterns on the acquisition and maintenance of aggressive responses. The left-hand photograph presents the front view of the clown, the experimenter's panel for controlling reinforcements, and the recording equipment. The right-hand photograph shows the interior of the box on which the clown is painted; at the top left is the dispenser; at the top right is a series of microswitches by means of which intensities of hitting responses are recorded;*

FIG. 3–1   (Continued)

in the lower center is a shaft which is moved inwards by the child's punches. (Designed and assembled by W. G. Clark, Department of Psychology, University of Toronto, and Optiscan, Ltd., P.O. Box 302, Station F, Toronto 5.)

The effects of parental discriminative training in aggression were reflected in the boys' social behavior and responses to pictorial aggression-eliciting stimuli. The aggressive boys expressed considerably more physical and verbal aggression toward their peers, more oppositional behavior toward their teachers, and less inhibition of aggression than the inhibited boys. In contrast, they displayed no more aggression toward their parents, which is not surprising in view of the parents' nonpermissiveness and punitiveness for aggression toward themselves. In response to pictorial stimuli the differential patterning of aggression was again apparent. The groups did not differ in the extent to which they directed physical aggression toward their parents, although the aggressive boys expressed more verbal and indirect forms of aggression. In peer interactions, the aggressive boys displayed more physical aggression than the inhibited boys, but no more verbal aggression. However, when hostile feelings toward peers were considered, the inhibited boys described the agent as feeling considerably more anger that was not translated into overt motoric forms. A similar discriminative patterning of parental reinforcement of aggression, on the one hand, and discriminative aggressive responses by the children, on the other, was revealed in the earlier field study of adolescent boys (Bandura and Walters, 1959).

The influence of positive reinforcement on the development of aggressive behavior has been demonstrated in a number of controlled laboratory experiments. Patterson, Ludwig, and Sonoda (1961) found that children who had been verbally reinforced for hitting an inflated doll gave more hitting responses during a subsequent session with the doll than did children who had not received training in aggression. The importance of schedules of reinforcement is apparent from a study by Cowan and Walters (1963), who placed children under one of three reinforcement conditions: continuous reinforcement, reinforcement on a fixed-ratio 1:3 schedule, and reinforcement on a fixed-ratio 1:6 schedule. The equipment consisted of a specially constructed "Bobo" clown (Figure 3–1), which permitted the automatic recording of the children's responses on an Esterline-Angus recorder. Following a baseline period the experimenter dispensed marbles according to a predetermined schedule until eighteen hitting responses had been elicited. During this period rates of aggressive responses increased for the total group of children, though typical individual acquisition curves were rarely obtained. Unlike most responses studied in learning experiments, hitting the doll was an initially dominant response to the stimulus situation, and many children commenced responding at rates (more than one response a second) that were probably close to their physiological limit. These findings indicated that the intensity, as well as the frequency, of aggressive responses should be studied, especially when the experimental setting provides little opportunity for the children to engage in alternative nonaggressive responses. The modified equipment illustrated in Figure 3–1 permits intensity of hitting to be employed as a dependent variable.

After eighteen responses had been reinforced, no more marbles were dispensed, but the children were permitted to continue responding. During this extinction period there were significant effects attributable to scheduling, with continuously reinforced subjects giving the smallest number of aggressive responses before extinction and children reinforced on a fixed-ratio 1:6 schedule giving the largest number.

Evidence that intermittently reinforced aggressive responses not only are more persistent but also tend to generalize to new situations was provided by Walters and Brown (1963). Two groups of seven-year-old boys received two training sessions in which they were reinforced with marbles for hitting, with at least moderate intensity, an automated Bobo doll. One of the experimental groups was reinforced on a fixed-ratio 1:6 schedule, the other on a continuous schedule. Two control groups were included in the study; one of these was given two play sessions with the Bobo doll but was not reinforced, while the other group was given no experience with the doll. In the testing session each child was matched against another child in competitive physical-contact games and in a free-play session. One competitor in each pair had been randomly assigned to one of the four comparison groups; his opponent was randomly selected from the remainder of the seven-year-old boys available in the school in which the test was conducted. Children reinforced on the fixed-ratio 1:6 schedule gave significantly more physically aggressive responses in the testing situation than did children in the other three groups, among which there were no reliable differences. This study demonstrates that aggressive responses that are acquired through intermittent reinforcement in a noninterpersonal, nonfrustrating situation may be subsequently utilized to overcome blocking or thwarting in interpersonal situations.

A further indication that aggressive responses, if reinforced, increase in frequency and generalize is provided by Lövaas (1961b). Preschool children were initially tested on two pieces of equipment, each operated by a lever. In one case, the lever caused a doll to strike another doll on the head with a stick; in the other case, the lever propelled a ball to the top of a cage. The children then participated in a verbal conditioning session, in which they were requested to speak into a "talk-box," on which were seated a dirty doll and a clean doll. During the training session, half the children were reinforced for making the responses, "bad doll," "dirty doll," and "doll should be spanked," while the remainder were reinforced for nonaggressive verbal responses such as "good doll" and "clean doll." Children who were reinforced for aggressive verbal responses showed a marked increase in the incidence of responses of this kind during the training period, while children who were reinforced for nonaggressive verbal responses gave an increasing number of responses of this class (Figure 3–2). Moreover, in a posttest free-play session with the striking doll and the ball-cage equipment, the children who had been reinforced for *verbal* aggression showed a significantly greater amount of *nonverbal* aggression than the children who had been reinforced for making nonaggressive verbal responses. Lövaas' study thus demonstrates that reinforcement effects generalize from one class of aggressive responses to another.

The effects of reinforcement of aggression may be dependent on the initial strength of the subjects' aggression inhibition. Staples and Walters (1963), using the equipment designed by Walters and Llewellyn Thomas (Figure 2–2), measured the level of intensity of shock that adult female subjects delivered

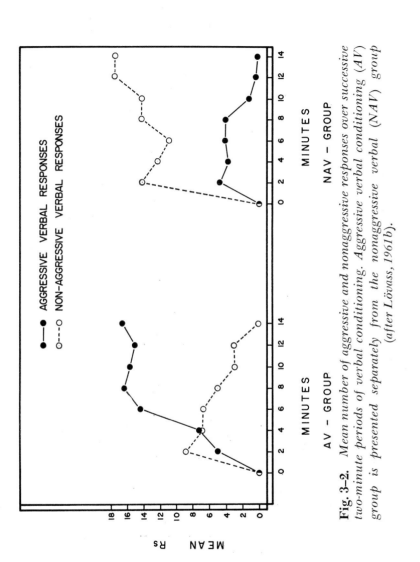

Fig. 3-2. *Mean number of aggressive and nonaggressive responses over successive two-minute periods of verbal conditioning. Aggressive verbal conditioning (AV) group is presented separately from the nonaggressive verbal (NAV) group (after Lövass, 1961b).*

to a confederate of the experimenter in a feigned conditioning study. The subjects were then assigned to experimental and control conditions in such a way that the two groups were approximately matched on the basis of the initial mean shock levels selected by the subjects in a pretest set of trials. Experimental subjects were given a training session in which they were verbally reinforced for administering shocks of relatively high intensity, while the control subjects received no reinforcements. For the analysis of results both experimental and control subjects were divided into three subgroups, one of which had initially administered shocks of high intensity, another shocks of low intensity, and the third shocks of intermediate intensity. A significant interaction effect involving initial intensity level and effect of reinforcement revealed that subjects who used initially high levels of shock increased their shock levels under reinforcement to a greater extent than either of the other two groups. Indeed, subjects who used initially low levels of shock intensity and were subsequently reinforced for relatively intense responses showed no more change in response level than comparable subjects who received no reinforcements. These differences persisted throughout a subsequent series of trials during which none of the subjects, experimental or control, received reinforcements. If initial level of shock is taken as an index of strength of aggression inhibition, it may be concluded that reinforcement of aggressive responses is more likely to increase aggression among subjects with low aggression inhibition than among subjects with high aggression inhibition. Such "personality" variables, which undoubtedly reflect the influence of prior modeling and reinforcement patterns, may have an important, though frequently ignored, influence on the outcome of reinforcement procedures.

Transitory states of the organism may also modify the effectiveness of reinforcers for establishing and maintaining behavior patterns. In the study by Cowan and Walters (1963) both institutionalized and noninstitutionalized children served as subjects. The institutionalized children made many more aggressive responses following the withdrawal of reinforcers, a finding that Cowan and Walters attributed to these children's greater emotionality, which presumably facilitated the learning of the aggressive response pattern.

Confirmatory evidence that positive reinforcement of aggressive responses is more effective if children are under moderately high emotional arousal was secured from a study by Hops and Walters (1963), which employed experimentally induced stress as an antecedent variable. In this study Grade I and Grade II children were assigned to one of four experimental treatments, three of which were designed to be to some degree emotionally arousing. Immediately afterwards, the children were presented with the automated Bobo toy described earlier, and their responses under reinforcement and subsequent nonreinforcement conditions were recorded. While the arousal manipulations influenced the responses of the older Grade II children very little, Grade I children who had been placed under emotionally arousing conditions maintained higher rates of hitting responses for a longer period of time following withdrawal of reinforcers than did children whom the experimenter's procedures and instructions were designed to relax. One role of frustration in the acquisition of aggression may be to increase emotionality and thus to make the frustrated individual more attentive to positive reinforcements that accrue from aggressive behavior.

Except for the study by Lövaas (1961b), investigations of the effects of positive reinforcement of hostile verbal responses have been carried out with adult subjects. In a number of these (Binder, McConnell, and Sjoholm, 1957; Buss and Durkee, 1958; Simkins, 1961; Zadek, 1959) operant conditioning methods have been employed to increase the frequency with which subjects emit hostile statements or expressions. Reinforcers have consisted of verbal tokens of approval and of material rewards. In addition, analysis of response-reinforcement contingencies, as they occur naturally in psychotherapeutic interactions, reveals that positive reinforcement by the therapist of patients' hostile verbal responses greatly increases the probability of occurrence of responses of this class, whereas negative reinforcement substantially decreases the incidence of verbal aggression (Bandura, Lipsher, and Miller, 1960; Goldman, 1961).

PUNISHMENT AND INHIBITION OF AGGRESSION

Much theorizing concerning aggression has leaned heavily on the assumption that the relatively severe socialization of aggression in North American society (Whiting and Child, 1953) leads to an early and fairly generalized inhibition and attenuation of aggressive responses. Developmental studies of the incidence of aggression in the home (Goodenough, 1931), in nursery school (for example, Appel, 1942; Muste and Sharpe, 1947; Walters, Pearce, and Dahms, 1957), and in doll-play (for example, P. S. Sears, 1951) do not entirely support this belief. The assumption is, however, so firmly rooted that increases in aggression are generally explained in terms of decreases of inhibition. It is, therefore, somewhat surprising to find that there has been only one study with children in which punishments have been dispensed for aggressive behavior and the effects of this procedure systematically recorded.

Hollenberg and Sperry (1951) gave four sessions of doll-play to two groups of nursery-school children. Children in the experimental group were verbally rebuked for aggressive behavior during the second of the two sessions. In all other sessions with both experimental and control subjects, the experimenter adopted the customary permissive role. For the control group aggressive responses steadily increased from session to session, a typical finding and one that is usually interpreted in terms of weakening of inhibitions. The experimental group, in contrast, showed no increase in aggressive responses from the first to the second session and a fairly marked decrease in aggression during the third session. The effect of verbal punishment was, however, only temporary, since differences between the experimental and control groups had largely disappeared by the fourth session.

Sears and his collaborators (Sears, 1961; Sears, Maccoby, and Levin, 1957; Sears, Whiting, Nowlis, and Sears, 1953) have studied relationships between parental punishment for aggression and aggressive responses in preschool and grade-school children. In the first of these studies (Sears *et al.*, 1953), the investigators obtained a positive correlation between maternal punitiveness for aggression and the incidence of boys' aggressive behavior in nursery school, a finding that was confirmed by Sears, Maccoby, and Levin (1957), who also found a similar relationship for girls. However, in a follow-up study, Sears (1961) reported only small and mostly nonsignificant relationships between parental punitiveness for aggression in the first five years of a child's life and the antisocial aggression, assessed from a questionnaire, of twelve-year-old children.

The authors (Bandura, 1960; Bandura and Walters, 1959) have reported that aggressive boys whose parents use punitive methods of discipline display little direct aggression toward their parents but are highly aggressive in interactions with peers and adults outside the home. A similar relationship between parental punitiveness and children's aggression was noted by Eron, Walder, Toigo, and Lefkowitz (1963), who found that punitive parents had children who were rated by peers as high in aggression.

Verbal rebuke, insult, or attack has been used as an experimental variable in a number of studies with adults, usually college students, However, the behavior attacked has not been the aggressive response that constituted the dependent variable. Under these conditions, verbal insult or attack appears to increase, rather than decrease, the incidence of aggression (Cox, 1952; McClelland and Apicella, 1945; Walters and Zaks, 1959). These studies have usually introduced simultaneously two variables, experimentally induced failure (or feelings of failure) and verbal attack; consequently, it is difficult to assess which of these variables is primarily responsible for the increase in aggression— which has, in any case, not usually been displayed directly toward the experimenter.

Graham, Charwat, Honig, and Weltz (1951), who used an incomplete-sentences technique, found that adolescents were more likely to counteraggress when they were the objects of a strong attack than when the attack made on them was weak. However, when the attacker was a parent or an authority figure, counteraggression was considerably reduced and increased relatively little as a function of increasing severity of attack. Since there were positive correlations between measures of magnitude of counteraggression in response to five classes of instigators and hence no evidence for displacement, this study provides a neat demonstration of the effects of discrimination learning.

Generally speaking, punishment by an authority figure seems to inhibit direct aggression in the presence of the punitive agent, but to be associated with high aggression toward other possible targets. However, it is obvious that no firm statements can be made concerning the relationship of punishment and aggression unless the agent of punishment, the recipient of aggression, and the nature of both the punitive and aggressive responses are taken into account. This point is further discussed in Chapter 4, where it is made evident that the effects of punishment are far more complex than those of reward and, as recent discussions of some of the relevant literature by Mowrer (1960a) and Hall (1961) have already indicated, much less well understood.

Theorizing and experimentation on the inhibition of aggression have focused exclusively on the inhibitory influence of anxiety or guilt, on the assumption that response inhibition is necessarily a consequence of pairing responses with some form of aversive stimulation. The development of aggression inhibition through the strengthening of incompatible positive responses, on the other hand, has been entirely ignored, despite the fact that the social control of aggression is probably achieved to a greater extent on this basis than by means of aversive stimulation.

PERMISSIVENESS

Permissiveness refers to the willingness of a socializing agent to allow a given form of behavior to occur or to continue once it has commenced. Other concepts used in literature relevant to child-training practices, for example, *lax* or *indulgent* discipline (for example, Baldwin, Kalhorn, and Breeze, 1945; Glueck and Glueck, 1950) and *laissez-faire* leadership, home atmosphere, or methods of control (for example, Lewin, Lippitt, and White, 1939) overlap with the concept of permissiveness without being precisely equivalent. The problem with these latter concepts is that they have usually been defined in too vague, global, or complex a fashion for the reader to be sure what aspects of adult behavior they encompass.

The effects of maternal permissiveness for aggression have received a good deal of attention in the studies by Sears and his collaborators (Sears *et al.*, 1953; Sears, Maccoby, and Levin, 1957). A mother who expects and accepts aggressive behavior is providing opportunities for aggression to occur and consequently to be positively or negatively reinforced. Positive correlations between maternal permissiveness for aggression during the child's first five years of life and the amount of aggression the child displayed in the home during this period was reported for both boys and girls by Sears, Maccoby, and Levin (1957). However, the correlations were small, and for the follow-up sample Sears (1961) failed to find significant relationships between earlier maternal permissiveness and the amount of antisocial aggression shown by the children at age twelve.

Bandura and Walters (1959) found that mothers of aggressive boys were somewhat more permissive for aggression directed toward themselves than were mothers of nonaggressive boys. These mothers did not, however, differ in respect to permissiveness for aggression toward other adults, siblings, or peers, nor were there any differences between the two groups of fathers.

The effects of parental permissiveness are not independent of the consequences that follow the performance of the permitted act. Presumably, parents who permit and reward aggression will develop aggressive habits in their children. On the other hand, parents who both permit and punish aggression appear also to produce highly aggressive children (Sears, Maccoby, and Levin, 1957; Bandura, 1960; Bandura and Walters, 1959). This aggression may, however, as a result of discrimination learning, be mainly directed at persons other than the primary frustrating agents.

The effects of permissiveness have also been noted in studies of doll-play aggression. With a permissive adult present, children's doll-play aggression has been shown to increase within a session (Hartup and Himeno, 1959) and over two to four consecutive sessions when the experimenter and the experimental setting have remained the same (Bach, 1945; Hollenberg and Sperry, 1951; P. S. Sears, 1951). An increase in children's aggression when the child's mother was introduced into the second of two doll-play sessions has been reported by Levin and Turgeon (1957); however, they found no increase if an adult stranger, instead of the mother, was present. Subsequently, Siegel and Kohn (1959) found an increase in children's aggression over two free-play sessions when a permissive, but not strange, adult was present only during the second of the sessions. Since adult permissiveness, under some circumstances, may be construed as tacit approval, these increases in aggression have been attributed to positive reinforcement (Buss, 1961). Alternatively, they may reflect a weakening of inhibitions that seem to occur when activities that have formerly been disapproved or punished are followed by neither reward nor punishment, a phenomenon discussed in Chapter 4. Indeed, Yarrow (1948) found that nonaggressive, as well as aggressive, responses increased in frequency over two sessions of permissive doll-play, a finding that suggests that adult permissiveness has a general reinforcing or disinhibitory influence on children's play activities rather than a specifice influence on aggression. The introduction of a stranger in the study by Levin and Turgeon creates, of course, a somewhat different situation, since for a number of reasons—for example, arousal of curiosity and thus of competing responses, and lack of knowledge of how the stranger will respond—the presence of a strange adult frequently has a general inhibitory effect on children's play activities.

Nonpermissiveness for aggression in the form of early intervention when an aggressive act is anticipated involves the blocking of an instrumental act and presumably should be frustrative. Thus, nonpermissiveness should, according to the frustration-aggression hypothesis, increase the incidence of aggressive activities. However, there is no evidence that nonpermissiveness consistently influences performance in this manner.

One of the major problems in investigations of child-training antecedents of aggression is that the parents, although perhaps the most important, are not the only socializing agents. Nonpermissiveness for aggression in schools may increase aggression in children whose parents have permitted aggressive habits to be established. On the other hand, consistent nonpermissiveness in the home may prevent aggressive habits from developing. Thus, like punishment, permissiveness may have a number of outcomes, its effects being primarily a function of the previous reinforcement history of the child whose behavior is being modified or controlled.

Role of Frustration

The role of frustration can be best understood by considering its effect on both aggressive and nonaggressive responses. In many studies, of which one by Miller and Stevenson (1936) was the forerunner, frustration has consisted of withholding rewards previously dispensed for a response, removing some of the stimulus objects essential for the performance of the instrumental act, or eliciting responses incompatible with the frustrated behavior (Brown, 1961), while the dependent variable has been the intensity or strength of the response under investigation.

The frustration-drive hypothesis, which has developed from, and has guided, the majority of these studies, has recently been stated by Brown in the following manner: "When stimuli normally capable of eliciting a response are present, but the response is prevented from running its usual course, behavior may be affected as though a motivational variable had been introduced" (1961, p. 195). The basic assumption, which is also crucial for the conflict-drive theory of Whiting and Sears (Sears et al., 1953; Whiting and Child, 1953), is that frustration, or conflict between expectancy of reward and nonreward, increases the motivational level of the organism through the addition of conflict-produced, frustration-produced, or "irrelevant" drive (Amsel, 1951, 1958, 1962; Brown and Farber, 1951; Lawrence and Festinger, 1962; Lawson and Marx, 1958).

A study by Haner and Brown (1955) is frequently regarded as supporting a frustration-drive theory. These investigators set out to test the hypothesis that the strength of an aggressive response varies with strength of frustration, the latter being defined in terms of the point in the response sequence at which blocking occurred. In their study, grade-school children were given the task of inserting thirty-six marbles in holes in a board and were promised a prize if they were successful on four trials. At the end of each trial, the experimenter sounded a buzzer, which the children turned off by depressing a plunger. On different trials children were failed at varying distances from a goal and a record was obtained of the amount of pressure they exerted on the plunger. Haner and Brown found that children who were near to completing a task when blocked made more intense responses than children who were farther from reaching their goal.

In a somewhat similar study, Holton (1961) demonstrated that children who were near to reaching a goal when frustrated, and in whom the frustrated response was well established, gave more vigorous responses when a reward was withheld than did children who were far from the goal and whose instrumental responses had received relatively little prior reinforcement.

Haner and Brown showed that blocking may result in the intensification of a response which is not a component of, but immediately succeeds, the frustrated response sequence. Confirmation of this finding is provided by Penney (1960), who trained children to manipulate a lever to receive a marble, then to manipulate a second lever and receive another marble. For the experimental groups the first reward was omitted on two thirds of the test trials. Speed of moving the second lever increased when the first lever-moving response was not rewarded, provided that this latter response had acquired sufficient habit strength from previously dispensed rewards.

Holton's study, in contrast to those by Haner and Brown and by Penney, demonstrated an increase in vigor of the frustrated instrumental response following the introduction of nonrewarded trials. Parallel increases in the strength of children's instrumental responses at the commencement of extinction procedures have been noted by Screven (1954) and Longstreth (1960).

The vigor of instrumental responses may be increased by delay as well as by omission of reward—which may, in fact, be conceptualized as infinite or indefinite delay. Olds (1953, 1956) carried out a series of experiments with children in which the subjects' task was to crank a token machine for poker chips, which were then exchangeable for toys. The force children exerted on the crank increased with increasing delay of reward and decreased with decreasing delay.

It is well established that learning is less efficient when reward is delayed than when reward is immediate (Hock-

man and Lipsitt, 1961; Lipsitt and Castaneda, 1948; Lipsitt, Castaneda, and Kemble, 1959; Setterington and Walters, 1963). Prolonged omission or delay of reward, of course, results in the
weakening of a response or the emergence of alternative responses. The prolonged omission of a wide range of basic reinforcements may, however, lead to apathy (Lazarsfeld and Zeisl,
1933).

SHAPING FRUSTRATION REACTIONS

The relationship between frustration and aggression can now be conceptualized as follows. Frustration may produce a temporary increase in motivation and thus lead to more
vigorous responding. The dominant response to stimuli present
before frustration may be one that when mild is not classed as
aggressive, but when strong is so categorized. Frustration also
changes the stimulus situation and consequently changes in the
kind, as well as in the intensity, of responses may be expected.
Interference with a response sequence may be a stimulus for
eliciting response hierarchies in which, because of past learning,
pain-producing responses tend to be dominant. Modification of
the associative strength of responses through stimulus change
can thus, independently of changes in the motivational level of
the subject, lead to the occurrence of aggressive behavior. Prior
experiences of frustrated subjects, and particularly their "personality characteristics" (that is, the response patterns that are
dominant in many of their response hierarchies), should consequently determine to a large extent the nature of their responses to frustration.

An experimental study by Davitz (1952) demonstrates the inadequacy of the frustration-aggression hypothesis
and also the importance of direct training in the development of
aggressive modes of response. Davitz first observed ten groups of
four children between the ages of seven and nine in a free-play
situation and recorded their responses on film. Half the groups
were now given seven brief training sessions in which they were
rewarded by praise and approval for making competitive and
aggressive responses. The remaining groups of children were rewarded during four training sessions for constructive and co-

operative behavior. In the final phase of the experiment, all groups of children were led to believe that they would be shown a series of movies. After the first reel, the experimenter handed each child a bar of candy. Frustration was induced by interrupting the second reel just as the movie approached its climax and at the same time taking away the candy. Immediately after this interruption, the groups of children were filmed for a second time in a free-play situation. Children who had been trained to behave aggressively in competitive games responded more aggressively to frustration than the groups trained in constructive activities. Moreover, children who had received training in constructiveness responded more constructively to frustration than did the children who had been trained in aggression. This study provides a neat demonstration that most "frustration" situations are simply stressful stimuli that will elicit, according to the character of the stimuli that are present, the response pattern that is currently dominant in the subjects' response hierarchy.

In the above study, the prosocial responses of one group of children were strengthened through experimental manipulation. Wright (1943) selected for study pairs of children who exhibited strong or weak affiliative behavior and observed changes in their social behavior toward each other and toward the experimenter from prefrustration to postfrustration sessions. Strong friends *increased* cooperativeness and *decreased* conflict behavior toward each other under frustration, whereas weak friends showed little change in behavior. In addition, intergroup comparisons revealed that although the two groups of children did not differ in their behavior during the prefrustration session, the strong friends exhibited significantly more cooperative behavior and less conflict under frustration than did the weak friends. Not only did frustration elicit affiliative peer behavior in the strong friends, but the resulting mutual support counteracted the inhibition over aggression toward the adult experimenter who was the agent of frustration. Thus the strong friends displayed toward the adult considerably more aggression than the weak friends, the difference being particularly marked in the expression of physical aggression.

Evidence that personality characteristics influence responses to frustration is provided in studies by Otis and Mc-Candless (1955), who observed more dominant-aggressive reactions to frustration in children with a dominant "need for power" than in children with a dominant "need for love-affection," and by Block and Martin (1955), who found that undercontrolling children gave predominantly aggressive responses to frustration whereas overcontrolling children exhibited constructive behavior. Moreover, Bandura's (1960) finding that aggressive boys experienced no more, and in all probability less, frustration of dependency behavior than had inhibited boys suggests that these two groups of boys had acquired contrasting patterns of response to frustration as a result of different learning histories and not because of differences in the magnitude of the frustrations they had experienced.

Several investigators have failed to find differences in aggression between frustrated and nonfrustrated children (Jegard and Walters, 1960; Mussen and Rutherford, 1961; Walters and Brown, 1963; Yarrow, 1948). These negative findings, occurring in studies in which other predictions were confirmed, cast further doubt on the utility of the frustration-aggression hypothesis.

Dependency

In the psychological literature such responses as seeking proximity and physical contact, help, attention, reassurance, and approval have been categorized as dependent (Beller, 1955). Since the human infant is almost totally helpless and remains relatively incapable of caring for himself for a number of years, dependent responses receive a considerable amount of positive reinforcement in most societies (Whiting and Child, 1953). Although independence training in North America is usually initiated in early childhood, this training is primarily focused on the mastery of developmental tasks. For example, the child is taught to clothe, feed, and occupy himself, and later on to master certain instrumental social and occupational skills that will permit him in adulthood to maintain an independent socio-vocational adjustment.

While there are very marked changes in *task-oriented* dependent responses from infancy to adulthood, *person-oriented* dependency is expected and reinforced throughout all stages of development. Some changes in the form of person-oriented dependency occur, but these are largely attributable to the acquisition of instrumental skills. On the other hand, there are major changes in the objects to which this kind of dependency is expressed. Seeking proximity and physical contact, for example, is not merely permitted but actually expected at all stages of an individual's life, and particularly during adolescent and adult years as he increasingly engages in heterosexual behavior. Eventually, dependent responses of this kind become focused primarily on a single object, the marriage partner, although in attenuated forms they may still be expressed toward other persons. Indeed, it is culturally expected that within the marriage partnership husband and wife will engage in physical manifestations of dependency that do not differ greatly from those that occur in the parent-child relationship.

Other forms of person-oriented dependency—for example, the seeking of approval and help—are expected to be shown toward a wide variety of persons, such as friends, colleagues, and members of one's reference groups.

Failure to develop task-oriented independent responses is usually attributed to a lack of such factors as motivation, initiative, or achievement drive, to limitations of capacity, social resources, or opportunity, or to just plain laziness, but is rarely, in and of itself, regarded as indicative of psychopathology. Failure to develop and maintain appropriate person-oriented dependency is, in contrast, one of the main criteria for identifying certain forms of behavior disorder. It should be noted that over-developed person-oriented dependency does not usually constitute, nor become labeled as, a serious form of deviation. In fact, overdependent individuals are usually regarded as self-indulgent, egocentric, or "spoiled," but not as emotionally disturbed. This perhaps accounts for the paucity of studies of over-dependency in the clinical literature. By contrast, deficits in person-oriented dependency have received a great deal of attention, for example, in studies of autism, of the effects of prolonged institutionalization, and of children who have been deprived of a normal family life.

Certain classes of patients, such as psychopaths, are usually regarded as incapable of forming person-oriented dependent relationships; on the other hand, they are also described as possessing highly developed manipulatory skills designed to secure person-oriented dependency gratifications. In fact, in most cases, their deviant behavior is characterized not by an absence of such dependency, but by the transience of the dependency relationships into which they enter. Such failures to maintain appropriate dependency attachments have been of considerable concern to workers in the mental health field.

DEFINITION OF DEPENDENCY

Dependency may be defined as a class of responses that are capable of eliciting positive attending and ministering responses from others. Since dependency responses are prosocial in nature, the presence of intent can perhaps be more readily established than in the case of aggression. These responses, however, do not inevitably elicit positive reactions from others, particularly when they are of high frequency or inappropriately timed. Under these circumstances, the agent may wittingly or unwittingly feign states of disability, lack of capacity, or illness in order to ensure positive rather than negative counter-responses. If the agent does not actively seek attention or care, but simply presents himself as relatively helpless or suffering, the object of dependency may appear not to be the initiator of the interaction sequence, and the problem of intent then arises.

The problem of intent also occurs in the case of high magnitude responses. For example, a young child kicks his mother's leg, when he has failed to obtain a desired toy that is placed beyond his reach, and the mother has not attended to his verbal requests for assistance. If the kick is mild, there is a good chance that the child's response will be regarded as dependent; if the kick is strongly administered, it is more likely that the response will be labeled "aggressive." The covert assumption, of course, is that a hard kick is *intended* to hurt. But in the case cited, it may be argued that the hard, as well as the mild, kick is intended to procure the mother's attention and so can be categorized as dependent. The intentionality criterion can thus lead to categorization of a single response sequence as both dependent and aggressive. Indeed, negative attention-seeking behavior provides a good example of a response pattern the categorization of which consistently baffles research workers (Bandura and Walters, 1959; Sears, Whiting, Nowlis, and Sears, 1953).

POSITIVE TRAINING IN DEPENDENCY

There have been relatively few observational and interview studies of direct training in dependency and still fewer experimental investigations; research into children's dependency has instead been focused on identifying changes in dependency objects and on the development of independence, on the assumption that independence emerges from dependency. Moreover, greater attention has been given to generalized parental variables such as acceptance, affection, child-centeredness, and indulgence, than to specific aspects of dependency training.

It has generally been assumed that adult nurturance is a critical factor in the establishing of dependency in children. Nurturance involves positive reinforcement of dependency, the active eliciting of dependency responses, and the conditioning of positive emotional responses to the nurturant adult. The occurrence of nurturant behavior, itself complex, has usually been inferred from such parent characteristics as affectional demonstrativeness and warmth that may, but need not, involve all three facets of nurturance and certainly involve many other facets of parent behavior.

Positive relationships between parental demonstrativeness and warmth and the dependency of children have emerged from a number of field studies. Sears, Maccoby, and Levin (1957) found that mothers who were affectionately demonstrative responded positively to their children's dependent behavior and described them as high in dependency. Bandura and Walters (1959) reported that mothers of nonaggressive adolescent boys who were relatively high in dependency showed more warmth than mothers of relatively nondependent aggressive boys; the fathers of the high-dependent boys were both warmer and more affectionately demonstrative than the fathers of the low-dependent group. Moreover, a correlational analysis of data from families of aggressive and inhibited children indicated that parents who were warm, affectionate, rewarded dependency, and had spent a good deal of time in caring for their sons had children who tended to display a high degree of dependency behavior (Bandura, 1960).

Rheingold (1956) carried out an experimental study of "mothering" in which she performed caretaking acts toward institutionalized children for a period of eight weeks. A control group of children remained in the usual hospital routine. An assessment of the children's social behavior at the end of the eight-week period indicated that the infants who had received the nurturant care of the experimenter were more socially responsive both to the experimenter and to an examiner than were the control children. Clinical case material suggests that an extreme degree of "mothering" may create very strong dependency habits in children. For example, Levy (1943) found that highly indulgent mothers who were extremely solicitous in caring for their children's needs and were constantly rewarding dependency responses had highly dependent children.

Additional indirect evidence that maternal permissiveness for, and reward of, dependency increases children's dependency behavior was obtained by Heathers (1953). Six- to twelve-year-old children were blindfolded and then requested to walk along a narrow unstable plank, which was balanced on springs and raised eight inches from the floor. As the child stood on the starting end of the plank, the experimenter touched the back of the child's hand and waited for him to accept or reject the implied offer of help. Parent-training measures, in the form of ratings previously secured by means of the Fels Parent Behavior Scales (Baldwin, Kalhorn, and Breeze, 1945), were available to the experimenter and were related to the performance of the children. The analysis showed that children who accepted the experimenter's hand on the initial trial of the Walk-the-Plank Test tended to have child-centered parents who encouraged their children to lean on others rather than to take care of themselves and who held their children back from developing age-appropriate skills.

Unlike aggression and sex, dependency is generally regarded as a prosocial form of behavior. Consequently, parents are usually reluctant to acknowledge any failure to reward, or any punishment of, their children's dependency. It is therefore not surprising that field studies in which parental handling of dependency has been directly investigated have generally failed to reveal any strong relationships between the parent behavior and the dependency responses of children. In Bandura's (1960) study, however, thematic interview material secured from aggressive and inhibited boys revealed that the former group of boys, who displayed a great deal of dependency behavior, depicted parents as providing a considerable amount of intermittent reward for their son's dependency responses.

The reward of dependency responses has rarely been used as an antecedent variable within experimental studies. Nelsen (1960) investigated the effects of both reward and punishment of dependency on the incidence of children's dependent responses in a subsequent social-interaction situation. During training half the children were shown approval for dependency, while the remaining children received mild verbal rebukes for acting in a dependent manner. Pretest-to-posttest changes indicated that reward for dependency resulted in an increase in dependency responses toward the rewarding agent, while punishment for dependency resulted in a decrease of such responses. The effects of reward were more marked for girls than for boys.

Cairns (1962) reported that prior reward for dependency facilitated children's learning when correct responses were reinforced by verbal approval. Grade-school children were first shown some toys in a cabinet and were told that they could play with a new toy each time a bell rang. For two groups of children the doors of the cabinet were closed, and the toys were therefore accessible only through the help of the experimenter. The children in one of these groups were rewarded, through the experimenter's compliance, for asking help or seeking attention in response to the signal that another toy might be taken from the cupboard; similar behavior from the children in the other group was consistently ignored. The children in a third group were given free access to the toys and experienced rewarding responses from the experimenter that were not contingent upon their exhibiting dependency behavior. Following the experimental treatments, all children were set a discrimination task by a second experimenter, who said "Good" each time a child made a correct response. Children who had been previously reinforced for dependent responses learned more rapidly than children in either of the other two groups. Cairns' results suggest that children in whom dependency habits are strongly developed are more responsive to social reinforcers. Support for this interpretation is provided by Ferguson (1961), who used Beller's (1955) scale to select high-dependent and low-dependent children and then compared their performance on a task similar to that used in Cairns' study. The results indicated that high-dependent children, when rewarded by approval, learned more rapidly than low-dependent children.

Parents who encourage and reward dependency also serve as nurturant models for their children. Consequently, parental reward of dependency should be one antecedent of strongly developed affiliative patterns in children. This joint reinforcement and modeling effect appears to be reflected in the finding of Hartup and Keller (1960) that nursery-school children who sought help and affection relatively often tended also to give frequent attentive, affectionate, protective, and reassuring responses in their interactions with their peers.

Punishment and inhibition of dependency

Warmth, affectional demonstrativeness, and "mothering" have been selected for study as possible antecedents of the development of dependency habits; similarly, rejection, another nonspecific parent characteristic, has been made the focus of attention in studies of the negative conditioning of dependency. One important component of severe rejection is probably the punishment of dependency behavior; however, if rejection is not extreme, both reward and punishment may occur, and the effects of rejection will then depend on the extent to which one or other of these types of parental responses predominate.

The effects of punishment on dependency are inevitably modified by the effects of the rewards that are dispensed for dependency from time to time, particularly during the child's early years, in almost every family situation. Thus dependency training contrasts strongly with sex training, during which rewards are rarely, if ever, dispensed, and with aggression training, which in most homes involves only intermittent, highly selective, and relatively infrequent dispensing of rewards. Moreover, especially in early childhood, dependency behavior cannot be relinquished as readily as sexual or aggressive behavior, since a child's immediate needs must receive some attention from even reluctant adults. Consequently, initial discouragement of dependency is likely to intensify a child's efforts to obtain dependency rewards. Indeed, Sears, Maccoby, and Levin (1957) found rejection to have little relationship to dependency if there was, at other times, little reward for dependency, but to have a positive relationship to dependency if the mother had also rewarded this kind of behavior.

In the case of the more severe forms of rejection, one would expect inhibition of dependency behavior, an outcome that is reflected in the finding of Bandura and Walters (1959) that aggressive boys who had experienced a good deal of parental rejection showed much less dependent behavior than more accepted nonaggressive boys. In this study parents who expressed rejection of their children were found to have punished dependency to a greater extent than those who were more accepting; moreover, ratings of the boys' dependency made from interviews with the boys were negatively correlated with ratings of paternal rejection made from father interviews. Finally, boys who felt rejected by their parents showed a low incidence of dependency responses toward parents, teachers, and peers.

When rejection involves primarily the withholding of positive reinforcers, rather than the presentation of negative reinforcers, its effect may be to intensify the dependency toward the frustrating agent. Hartup (1958), in an experimental study of nurturance withdrawal, found that children who had experienced delay of reward for dependency exhibited more dependent behavior than children whose dependency had been consistently rewarded. Similarly, Gewirtz (1954) demonstrated that children displayed more attention-seeking behavior in the presence of a nonresponsive adult than in the presence of an adult who centered his attention on the child. Withholding of positive reinforcers appears to produce more sustained increases in dependency behavior in children whose past social-learning experiences have made them highly dependent than in children in whom dependency habits are weakly established (Baer, 1962; Beller and Haeberle, 1961a, 1961b). Thus, the occurrence of a dependent response to frustration is more likely if dependent responses are dominant in children's response hierarchies.

In the study by Nelsen (1960) children who were negatively reinforced for dependency showed a subsequent decrease in dependency responses; in this case the effect was more pronounced for boys. An analysis of patient-therapist interaction sequences by Winder, Ahmad, Bandura, and Rau (1962) indicated that whereas positive reinforcement of dependency responses greatly increased the extent to which these were emitted in therapy sessions, negative reinforcement resulted in a marked decrease in their frequency. Thus, even with adults, relatively consistent punishment of dependency appears to have an inhibitory effect.

When active punishment is combined with reward, its effects on dependency behavior may under some circumstances be the same as when rewards are intermittently withheld. Fisher (1955) compared the social responses of two groups of puppies. One of these was consistently petted and fondled by the experimenter for approach responses, while the second group of puppies was administered the same kind of reward treatment with the addition of training sessions in which the puppies were handled roughly and on occasions electrically shocked for approach responses. Tests of dependency behavior conducted toward the end of, and following, thirteen weeks' training indicated that the puppies which had received both reward and punishment exhibited greater dependency behavior in the form of remaining close to a human than did the puppies in the reward-only group.

While the withholding of rewards for dependency seems to produce an increase in dependency behavior, active punishment appears to reduce its incidence unless there is relatively frequent concurrent reward. Consequently, since withholding of reward is generally regarded as a less severe disciplinary technique than punishment, it is understandable that Sears, Whiting, Nowlis, and Sears (1953) found some support for the hypothesis that there is a curvilinear relationship between the complex variable of maternal frustration-and-punishment of dependency and the incidence of dependency in preschool children.

The correlational data from Bandura's (1960) investigation into the child-training antecedents of aggressive and inhibited behavior indicated that punishment for dependency behavior decreased its directness, but that significant relationships between punitiveness for dependency and its frequency were largely absent. The only exceptions were found in the case of the aggressive boys, for whom maternal punishment for dependency seemed to have the effect of *increasing* dependency responses to adults. This outcome was also reflected in the boys' thematic interview responses, which strongly suggested that differential reinforcement histories had led the aggressive and inhibited boys to respond to dependency frustration in quite different ways.

In the first place, the mothers of aggressive boys tended to ignore mild forms of dependency behavior, whereas more intense forms secured their attention. If more vigorous responses are thus differentially reinforced, one would expect these responses, which might well be labeled as aggressive, to become strongly established. Rewarding of responses of this kind in order temporarily to terminate their occurrence could, as we noted in Chapter 1, be one means of establishing troublesome behavior. Indeed, teachers were beginning to complain that the dependency behavior of the aggressive boys had become burdensome.

In the case of the inhibited boys, nonaggressive withdrawal reactions occupied a dominant position in the hierarchy of responses elicited by situations in which dependency was frustrated. When the mother punished dependency, inhibited boys depicted the frustrated child as giving up the goal of gaining the mother's nurturance and attention and making dependency responses to other persons. In addition, they reported more withdrawal behavior following frustration of dependency by peers; since there was no indication that they had been greatly punished by peers for exhibiting dependency behavior, it is reasonable to conclude that the withdrawal response had generalized from the home situation to peer interactions.

There was one notable difference between the findings of Bandura's investigation and the authors' earlier study of aggressive adolescent boys (Bandura and Walters, 1959). In contrast to the adolescents, who showed relatively little dependency behavior and a marked inhibition of dependency responses, Bandura's aggressive preadolescent boys exhibited a great deal of dependency behavior toward their parents, teachers, and peers. This difference seems in part to reflect a developmental process, and in part the influence of differential reinforcement histories. In the first place, preadolescents are necessarily more dependent than adolescents; in fact, a number of the parents of the aggressive adolescents had commented on the strength of their sons' dependency behavior during preadolescent years. When the preadolescents expressed dependency, they tended to do so in forms that elicited mild punishment from others, and such forms of dependency had apparently also predominated in the earlier histories of the delinquent adolescents. With increasing age, the aggressive preadolescents would be expected to show a marked decrease in dependency behavior, assuming that their dependency responses continued to be ignored and to elicit punishment.

Moreover, once boys begin to exhibit serious antisocial behavior, as many of the delinquent adolescents had already done, they tend to be openly rejected by parents, teachers, and the majority of peers, and this consequence inevitably promotes dependency inhibition. In addition, there were some differences between the two groups of families, for example, a difference in socioeconomic status, which could have influenced parents' child-training practices and consequently further increased the difference between the two groups of boys in their readiness to express dependency behavior.

Investigations into the effects of maternal privation have shown that institutionalized and other maternally deprived children are socially nonresponsive and nondependent

(Bowlby, 1952; Freud and Burlingham, 1944; Gewirtz, 1961; Goldfarb, 1943; Lowrey, 1940; Spitz, 1945; Yarrow, 1961). However, they have also incidentally noted the occurrence of frequent, direct, and intense dependency responses in some children presumably deprived of maternal care. This differential effect would be expected if the children under investigation had experienced differential amounts of reward, nonreward, and punishment for dependency behavior.

Sex Behavior

Long before they reach sexual maturity, children exhibit forms of behavior that are regarded, in North American society, as having sexual implications. For example, fingering of genitals, exposing the genital organs, or looking at the genital organs of others are labeled as sexual responses. In contrast, parents in some societies regard actions of these kinds as having no sexual significance and may provide conditions that foster the occurrence of such behavior. When climatic conditions permit, they do not insist on the use of clothes by children; consequently, nudity does not acquire sexual significance during the child's early years. Moreover, parents in some societies not only permit their children to masturbate openly but actually instigate this behavior by themselves fondling their children's genitals during the course of caretaking activities.

In North American society the mammary region is a culturally conditioned sexual object, the sexual implications of which become increasingly apparent to children, especially in later childhood years; accentuation, partial exposure, and concealment are some of the means by which its sexual significance is developed. Looking at, fondling, and manipulating the breast consequently become a highly significant sexual activity for males. In other cultures the breast has no unique sexual significance; exposure is normal, and breast stimulation may not form a part of sex play (Ford and Beach, 1951).

In the same way as certain parts of the body become culturally conditioned sexual stimuli, certain patterns of behavior acquire sexual significance either as foreplay or as part of the sexual act itself. Whereas in North American society inflicting pain on the sexual partner is regarded at best as a perverted derivative of sexual behavior, in other societies—for example, among the Trobriand Islanders (Malinowski, 1929)—the inflicting of severe pain through biting and scratching is a normal accompaniment of coitus. There is also wide cultural variation in the selection of sensory stimulants, such as perfumes and adornments, that are used as means of erotic arousal.

It is thus apparent from cross-cultural data that the regions of the body, the social acts, and the extrinsic sensory cues utilized for arousal all vary considerably from society to society and that what is considered highly attractive in one society may be neutral or highly repulsive to the members of another social group.

Social training of sex in North American society is accomplished mainly through the transmission to children of parental anxiety reactions to the exploratory, manipulative, and curiosity behavior that inevitably occur during childhood (Chapter 3). Parents insist that certain parts of the body be concealed even from other family members and react to exposure with evident concern. When children manipulate their genitals or touch parts of adults' bodies that for them have sexual significance, parents induce responses incompatible with the manipulative act by removing the child's hands and presenting distracting stimuli. Usually the maneuver is executed in a manner that is designed not to call attention to the potential sexual significance of the act to which the parent is responding. Children thus learn that certain regions of the body and certain curiosity and exploratory acts are taboo, but since much of this negative conditioning occurs before children have mastered verbal skills, it is evident that the avoidance learning commences before the sexual significance of the prohibitions can be fully apparent to the child.

Children are encouraged to seek information about most topics; curiosity is, in fact, regarded as an indication of an alert inquiring mind and usually elicits positive responses from adults. In contrast, when children seek information about sex differences and the reproductive process, many parents give the minimum amount of information, exhibit considerable anxiety, give nonhuman examples, and attempt to postpone presenting facts on the grounds that the child is too young to understand (Bandura and Walters, 1959; Sears, Maccoby, and Levin, 1957). In this way, the basic sexual processes become a focus for anxiety and are consequently associated with the negatively conditioned parts of the body and curiosity-exploratory behavior by virtue of also being taboo.

Even after children can understand and engage in verbal communications, parents fail to label, and often mislabel, the exploratory and manipulative behavior that they were attempting to control during infancy. For these reasons, it is only later in childhood that children learn clearly to identify much of the behavior in question as sexual; in the present age, the mass media, especially television, may be the main source from which children learn this identification, though older playmates and peers also aid in the process.

Indirect methods such as distraction without labeling are frequently used to circumvent the continuance of behavior that more closely approximates to adult sexuality, such as sex play with other children. However, in handling such behavior many parents also impose more direct negative sanctions in the form of verbal rebuke, isolation, and discouraging association with the playmates involved (Sears, Maccoby, and Levin, 1957).

In infrahuman species sexual behavior is mainly under hormonal control. In contrast, human sex behavior is predominantly the outcome of social learning, and thus nonhormonal factors largely determine the timing, incidence, and nature of the sexual activities of human males and females. For example, in North American society, the marked increase in heterosexual behavior in middle and late adolescence is certainly due less to hormonal changes than to cultural expectations. North American parents at this stage of their children's development actively encourage dating and permit mild forms of necking; in contrast, in other cultures the fostering of heterosexual interaction takes place at earlier, and sometimes at later, stages of a child's development, and consequently no marked changes in sexual behavior occur during adolescence.

Sex training in Wogeo (Hogbin, 1945), a New Guinea island, though not entirely permissive, contrasts in many ways with that which prevails in North America. For example, the male adolescent in this society is expected to form a homoerotic relationship with a youth of his own age. The bond friends engage in socially approved public expressions of affection that are not permitted to other members of the society, including spouses. The youths walk arm in arm, hold hands, sleep together, and engage in mutual masturbation, a practice that is socially sanctioned for Wogeo adolescents. Though at a later stage the bond friends act as intermediaries for one another in arranging affairs with women, the friendship may continue beyond marriage and be a source of friction between spouses.

Since premarital intercourse is approved for Wogeo males only after they have completed puberty rites, a stage that is not reached until the nineteenth year or later, direct avoidance training is utilized to make boys refrain from too early heterosexual experiences. Male children are taught that intercourse may result in physical defect, illness, or even death, and consequently youths suffer severe fears when they break the "taboo" on pre-initiation intercourse. In contrast, Wogeo girls receive no avoidance training; indeed, since they are usually rewarded with presents when they engage in premarital affairs, their heterosexual behavior is both materially and socially reinforced. As a consequence, Wogeo youths ordinarily gain their first experiences of intercourse as a result of active and forceful seduction by a female. Wogeo culture thus differs markedly from that of North America both in its provision of more lenient sex training for girls than for boys and in its encouragement and reinforcement of homoerotic relationships among males during their adolescent and early manhood years. It also differs in its clear labeling and freer discussion of sexual organs and functions, and in the directness of the avoidance training it provides for its youths. In contrast, as we have noted earlier, North American sex training is characterized by an absence of labeling, or by mislabeling, of sex organs and functions and by the indirectness of its avoidance-training procedures.

In North American society, cultural expectations that are fostered and maintained by the mass media are playing an increasingly important role in the patterning of sexual behavior and can force changes in parental wishes and attitudes. For example, the authors' studies of the families of preadolescent and adolescent boys (Bandura, 1960; Bandura and Walters, 1959) suggest that many parents are not entirely happy about the formation of steady dating patterns during early adolescence and that the participants in most respects do not obtain major satisfactions from them. Nevertheless, because parents fear that their children may deviate from a social norm that is propagated by the mass media, they feel that they should arrange social events which involve a child's being with an opposite-sex partner and thus foster early steady dating.

Parents are even less accepting of the cultural expectation, again largely attributable to the influence of mass media, that adolescents should engage in heavy petting, and they refuse to entertain the possibility that their children are likely to engage in premarital intercourse. In fact, they resort to fear- and guilt-provoking appeals, designed to serve as inhibiting forces against sexual transgression. However, the cultural expectation concerning petting is propagated and maintained within the peer group. Consequently, there are pressures for adolescents to engage in heavy petting, which for the majority of males and a fair proportion of females culminates in premarital intercourse during late adolescence or very early adulthood (Ehrmann, 1959; Kinsey, Pomeroy, and Martin, 1948; Kinsey, Pomeroy, Martin, and Gebhart, 1953). These pressures are quite strong, since the popularity of girls may be highly dependent on their willingness to engage in petting, while for boys this activity is often regarded as proof of masculinity.

Because of prolonged negative conditioning at home, the majority of young people respond to their initial heterosexual experiences with anxiety and guilt and in particular fear that their parents will learn of their activities. Parental failure to engage in adaptive, discriminative training in sexual behavior and attitudes is thus a source both of ignorance and misinformation, so increasing the dangers of the pregnancies that the parents are especially concerned to prevent and of persisting conflict concerning sexual activities and physical intimacy. In fact, due to the discontinuity of cultural demands and conditioning, the more successfully parents inhibit their children's sexual behavior, the more likely is conflict-ridden sexual behavior to occur in adulthood.

Experimental studies of most forms of sex behavior are practically nonexistent; consequently, the available research data come largely from interview and questionnaire studies. Kinsey and his coworkers (1948, 1953) have noted the influence of demographic variables, which are presumably correlated with specific child-training factors, on the incidence of sexual behavior and on the form which it takes. Similarly, Ehrmann (1959) found that such variables as socioeconomic status and religious affiliation influenced behavior at all stages of the dating and mating process. Ehrmann also reported some relationships between child-training factors (such as types of parental discipline) and court-ship and sex responses; however, his child-training factors were in most cases not specifically enough defined to indicate with any certainty the precise manner in which they could have influenced the social learning of patterns of sex behavior. Nevertheless, Ehrmann's results suffice to show that the sex behavior of male college students is more influenced by home-background and child-training factors than is that of female college students. This sex difference may arise largely from the more uniformly inhibitory training that females receive in North American society, resulting, as Ehrmann himself notes, in the male's being the initiator of most premarital heterosexual interactions.

Some evidence that parental permissiveness for heterosexual behavior results in intercourse in early adolescent years was obtained by Bandura and Walters (1959). Fathers of aggressive boys not only were relatively permissive of heterosexual behavior during adolescence but also on occasions instigated and positively reinforced their sons' heterosexual advances. Their adolescent boys both showed less anxiety, and had engaged in intercourse more frequently, than the sons of fathers who were less permissive in their attitudes. However, the relative frequency of sexual intercourse among the aggressive boys was probably also in part due to the influence of child-training variables that fostered general deviant behavior. The effect of parental permissiveness on the sexual responses of preadolescent boys is reflected in correlations between parent and child variables secured by Bandura (1960). Children whose fathers were permissive for nudity, permissive and nonpunitive for sex play with other children, and willing to give information concerning sex matters tended to express little anxiety and guilt about sex; in addition, children tended to exhibit relatively little sex guilt if their mothers were nonpunitive for sex play and readily provided sex information.

Deviant sexual responses appear to be sometimes the result of parental encouragement and reinforcement of inappropriate sexual behavior. Litin, Giffin, and Johnson (1956) describe a case of extreme transvestism in a five-year-old boy, who almost continuously dressed up in his mother's clothes, including cosmetics and jewelry, exhibited almost complete feminine role behavior, and had even adopted a girl's name, suggested to him by his mother. The mother encouraged and rewarded the sex-inappropriate behavior with affectional demonstrativeness and verbal approval, while the grandmother and neighbors supported the mother's training by supplying the boy with generous quantities of female apparel. The same authors present the case of a thirteen-year-old boy whose mother had actively fostered voyeuristic behavior toward herself by sleeping with the boy, by being physically and verbally seductive, and at the same time appearing in the nude before him. When the patient was six years of age, the mother had shown him her vagina a number of times at the boy's request, but had responded with disapproval when he suggested intercourse and from that time had discontinued her physically seductive behavior. The boy's strongly established voyeuristic habit had generalized to persons other than the mother and had eventually led to his being brought for clinic treatment. Generalization of strongly reinforced homosexual responses was apparent in the case of a sixteen-year-old girl whose mother had throughout the girl's lifetime encouraged mutual stroking of the breasts and other erotic play. The mother sought psychiatric advice when the daughter formed a homosexual attachment to a teacher, of whom the mother was evidently jealous.

A mother's active reinforcement of inappropriate sexual behavior is again evident in the case of a seventeen-year-old exhibitionist described by Giffin, Johnson, and Litin (1954). This mother took showers with her son, enjoyed exhibiting herself to him and in looking at his nude body, and described her anatomical attributes to him in great detail and commented on his, while at the same time demonstrating affection to him during these interactions.

The above cases are only a small sample of those documented in the papers to which reference has been made. With few exceptions, the deviant behavior appears to be the result of pairing positive reinforcement in the form of close physical intimacy with sexual responses that are inappropriate for the sex or age of the child. For example, one would expect permissiveness for nudity in and of itself to result only in decreased sexual inhibition and decreased sexual curiosity; on the other hand, coupling exposure with strong positive reinforcements, such as affectional demonstrativeness expressed in a seductive manner, would be likely to endow nudity with both exaggerated sexual significance and strong positive valence. Indeed, for many of the children sexual cues and responses had acquired very strong reward value and in some cases had led to very well developed patterns of heterosexual behavior, long before the onset of the hormonal changes of adolescence. Moreover, the mothers maintained the sexual responses over a long period of time both through direct and—though the experimental evidence is meager—through vicarious reinforcement. As Johnson and Szurek (1952) have pointed out, the parents may also receive vicarious reinforcement from the deviant behavior of their children.

Studies of verbal sex responses to pictorial stimuli have bearing on the role of inhibitory factors in the expression of sex behavior. Clark and Sensibar (1955) found a decrease in students' sexual responses to pictorial test items following exposure to sexually arousing stimuli; when the experiment was replicated during a fraternity drinking party, an event likely to reduce inhibitions, there was an increase in sexual verbalizations to the same pictorial stimuli. Inhibitory and disinhibitory effects are also apparent in a study by Mussen and Scodel (1955), who reported that college students gave fewer verbal sex responses to thematic stimulus items in the presence of a nonpermissive older examiner than when the examiner was younger and more permissive. The more liberal attitudes toward sex that students express following the reading and discussion of books on human sex behavior (for example, the Kinsey report) (Giedt, 1951), undoubtedly reflect an analogous disinhibitory process achieved through a permissive atmosphere and direct or tacit social approval of verbal sex behavior.

A study by Leiman and Epstein (1961) seems to provide a further example of the manner in which social training may considerably modify the sex behavior of human subjects. The experimenters first selected male subjects whose responses to an inventory indicated that they were high or low in guilt over sex. A deprivation index was then obtained for each subject on the basis of self-reported data concerning his sex behavior. At the same time, thematic stimuli were presented and the incidence of the subject's sexual responses was recorded. High-deprivation subjects gave more sexual responses than low-deprivation subjects, provided they were low in guilt; in the case of high-guilt subjects, however, this relationship was reversed. On the basis of the results for high-guilt subjects, one may infer that biological cues associated with sex deprivation can motivate avoidance responses in subjects who anticipate self-punitive reactions when they express themselves sexually.

Inhibition of verbal sexual responses has similarly been demonstrated in studies in which subjects have been required to identify and report sexually significant words (Cowen and Beier, 1954; McGinnies, 1949). Moreover, disinhibition has been experimentally produced by repeated exposure to sexual stimuli in a permissive setting (Bitterman and Kniffin, 1953) and by permissive and encouraging instructions (Postman, Bronson, and Gropper, 1953).

The disinhibitory effect of direct positive reinforcement of verbal sex responses has been demonstrated in two studies. Banks and Walters (1959) verbally reinforced a group of nurses and hospital attendants for saying sexually significant words in a two-choice guessing situation. These subjects more readily reported other words of sexual significance in a subsequent tachistoscopic "recognition" task than did other hospital staff members whose prior training had involved only the reporting of nonsexual words. Evidence that the incidence of sexual responses is modified through both positive and negative reinforcement is provided by Goldman (1961), who found that patients gave an increasing number of sexual responses in therapy if these were encouraged and approved by the therapist and a decreasing number of responses if the therapist were nonresponsive or disapproving.

There is some evidence that conditioned avoidance responses aroused by sexual stimuli generalize to other adjacent stimuli. McGinnies and Sherman (1952) found that tachistoscopically presented nonsexual words were less readily reported if they followed the presentation of a word having sexual implications. A similar generalization effect was obtained by Walters, Banks, and Ryder (1959) in a study that supported predictions based on a social-learning interpretation of perceptual-defense phenomena.

The influence of discrimination learning on verbal sex behavior is readily apparent, though sometimes overlooked. In some social contexts sexual words, even of a taboo kind, are permitted or even approved. Thus, while a student may hesitate to pronounce a taboo sexual word in the presence of a female experimenter (McGinnies, 1949), he may freely use much "dirtier" words in the presence of his peers. In perceptual defense studies, the disinhibitory effects of instructions that lead subjects to expect sexual words (Freeman, 1954; Lacy, Lewinger, and Adamson, 1953) can be explained in terms of discrimination learning, since the creation of a "set" or "expectancy" of this kind involves the partial restructuring of the social context. Though the experimental evidence is meager, it is quite apparent that nonverbal sex responses are equally influenced by discrimination learning. Indeed, the patterns of sexual behavior shown by some male students in Ehrmann's (1959) study indicated that they had learned to seek out girls of a lower social class when they wanted sexual intercourse but to attempt only the more socially approved forms of physical contact with girls who were of the same class as themselves.

It thus appears from cross-cultural data, clinical case material, and available experimental evidence that direct training variables influence sex behavior in much the same way as they affect the expression of dependency and aggression. However, experimental studies of sexual responses other than verbal ones are undoubtedly needed in order to demonstrate more precisely the influence of reinforcement patterns.

Summary

In this chapter, the role of reinforcement patterns in the establishing and maintaining of aggressive, dependency, and sexual behavior were discussed in relation to findings from both experimental and field studies.

The influence of positive reinforcement on the acquisition and maintenance of aggressive behavior has been investigated in a number of controlled laboratory experiments. It has been demonstrated that positive reinforcement in the form of verbal approval or material rewards will increase the frequency of children's aggressive responses; that reinforcement of one class of aggressive responses may result in an increment in another class of aggressive responses; and that the effects of rewarding aggression in relatively impersonal play situations are transferred to new social situations in which interpersonal aggression may be displayed.

There have been few studies of the effects of punishment on aggressive behavior. The available data suggest that verbal or physical punishment by an authority figure tends to inhibit aggression in the presence of the punitive agent; on the other hand, children who have received a great deal of aversive training tend to display much aggression toward objects other than the agent of punishment. This latter outcome undoubtedly reflects the modeling of aggressive behavior, which was discussed in Chapter 2. We were forced to conclude that no firm statements could be made concerning the effects of punishment for aggression on the subsequent expression of aggression unless the previous reinforcement history of the recipient of punishment, the type and patterning of punishment administered, and the status both of the agent of punishment and of possible recipients of aggression were taken into account.

Since parental permissiveness has frequently been regarded as an antecedent of aggression, the relevant literature was briefly reviewed. Permissiveness seems to have a general disinhibitory effect on activities of children that have previously been discouraged or punished, but there is little reason to believe that it is specifically a reinforcer for aggression.

The over-all results from studies of direct reinforcement and modeling of aggression call for important revisions in the frustration-aggression hypothesis, which has, over the past half century, guided much of the theorizing and research on aggression. This hypothesis depicts frustration as an inevitable antecedent of aggression and regards aggression as the dominant unlearned response to frustration. The bulk of the research data indicates that frustration, or the withholding of positive reinforcement, is associated with an increase in motivation, which may be reflected in a temporary intensification of a response. However, the nature of the response to frustration will depend on the prior social training of the frustrated subject, or, more specifically, on the reinforcement and modeling procedures which he has previously experienced. Thus, according to the social-learning theory presented in this book, one can readily produce a highly aggressive child by merely exposing him to successful aggressive models and rewarding the child intermittently for aggressive behavior, while keeping frustration at a very low level. Nevertheless, in accordance with our high-magnitude criterion of aggression, the increased vigor of a response that follows frustration may transform a response not usually regarded as aggressive into one that would almost inevitably be classed as an instance of aggression.

Research evidence concerning the influence of reinforcement patterns on dependency and sex behavior, though somewhat meager, suggest that reinforcement variables modify these classes of responses in much the same manner as they modify aggression. The reward of dependency responses increases dependency behavior, whereas the punishment of dependency behavior appears to reduce its incidence, except when intermittent rewards are also supplied. Indeed, there is some evidence that a combination of aversive stimulation and reward for dependency behavior may increase dependency to a greater extent than when only rewards are given. The withholding of positive reinforcers for dependency temporarily increases the incidence of dependency responses in children whose past reinforcement histories have made them highly dependent—an effect which would be predicted on the basis of frustration theory. On the other hand, prolonged withholding of rewards for dependency leads to a decrease in dependency behavior. The consequences of both nonreward and punishment of dependency behavior are thus contingent on the frequency with which concurrent positive reward for dependency is supplied.

     Because of the strongly inhibitory sex training that predominates in North American society, experimental studies of sex have been largely confined to investigations of verbal responses. Disinhibition of verbal sex responses has been achieved through the exposure of subjects to sexually significant pictorial or written stimuli in a permissive setting and by the provision of positive reinforcement. Experiments in which subjects have been required to report words with sexual connotations have, in addition, provided evidence that conditioned emotional responses aroused by sexual stimuli generalize to adjacent nonsexual stimuli. The results of other studies of this same general kind demonstrate the influence of discrimination learning on the readiness with which verbal sexual responses are emitted in different social contexts.

     Evidence concerning the effects of reinforcement patterns on nonverbal sexual behavior comes mainly from interview and clinical studies. These studies, however, provide ample evidence that deviant sex behavior often results from the reinforcement of socially disapproved sexual responses, often in conjunction with parental modeling of atypical patterns of sexual behavior.

The part that reinforcement patterns play in the shaping and maintenance of prosocial and deviant patterns of response is thus apparent both from investigations into the antecedents and correlates of selected areas of behavior in laboratory and field studies and from clinical case histories. Reinforcement patterns also play an important part in the development of self-control responses, the presence and absence of which have received considerable attention in accounts of moral development and in theories of psychopathology. In the next chapter, which deals with the topic of self-control, the role of negative reinforcement is considered in some detail, though attention is also given to the part played by observational learning and positive reinforcement of prosocial responses in the socialization of behavior. Chapter 4 thus represents primarily an attempt to apply the social-learning principles set forth in the three preceding chapters to the crucial problem of how self-control is acquired and maintained.

CHAPTER FOUR

The Development of Self-control

So far attention has been focused on the presentation of external stimuli, in the form of behavioral examples and patterns of reinforcement, for the guidance and modification of the social responses of children. As the child becomes physically more mobile and his range of social contacts increases, he spends less and less time in the company of his parents, whose opportunities of directly influencing his behavior consequently decrease. Nevertheless, most children, even in the absence of reinforcement from external agents, maintain many of the response patterns they have acquired through parental training. At this stage, self-generated stimuli may outweigh the influence of external stimuli in governing behavior.

SELF-REACTIONS AS DETERMINANTS OF SOCIAL CONTROL

The process of acquiring self-control has usually been described as one in which parental standards are incorporated, introjected, or internalized, a "superego" is formed, or some inner moral agent that is a facsimile of the parents is developed to hold in check impulses that are "ego-alien." These descriptions are replete with terms that have considerable surplus meaning and that frequently personify the controlling forces. The superfluous character of the constructs becomes evident when one examines laboratory studies in which animals are trained not to exhibit behavior that the experimenter has arbitrarily selected as deviant. For example, Whiting and Mowrer (1943), using a socialization paradigm, taught rats, as a result of punishment, to take a circuitous route to a food reward instead of a considerably shorter and more direct one; the rats maintained this behavior for some time after punishments were withdrawn. The substitution of less direct, more effortful, and more complicated ways of obtaining reward exhibited by the animals parallels changes in children's behavior that result from social training and are ordinarily regarded as indices of the development of self- or impulse-control. However, no one would say that the rats in the Whiting and Mowrer study had internalized the superego of the experimenters or had introjected their standards.

Numerous attempts have been made to identify differences among fear, guilt, and shame as determinants of social control and even to characterize cultures in terms of the modal inhibitory forces that maintain social conformity (Benedict, 1946; Mead, 1950; Piers and Singer, 1953; Whiting, 1959). Two criteria have been advanced for distinguishing guilt from shame. The first of these assumes a dichotomy between external and internal sanctions and regards shame as a reaction to actual or anticipated disapproval by an audience and guilt as a negative self-evaluation resulting from a deviation from an internalized moral standard. Somewhat similar bases for distinction are Riesman's (1950) contrast between inner-directed and outer-directed persons and the public-private dimension of Levin and Baldwin (1959).

It is reasonable to believe that both external and internal sanctions are instrumental in maintaining social control in almost every society and individual (Ausubel, 1955). Indeed, the requirement that in case of guilt the intrapsychic self-evaluative response should occur without reference to any actual or fantasied reactions of external agents is probably very rarely, if ever, met. This requirement presupposes that guilt is mediated by an internal moral agent, which originated and developed from sanctions imposed by the parents or other primary socializing agents, but which is now completely independent of an individual's current social experiences. To the extent that a person selects a reference group whose members have standards that are similar to his own, his self-evaluations undoubtedly involve an assessment of how these members would react to his behavior. The size of the group by reference to which a particular person evaluates his behavior may vary considerably; when a person's immediate reference group is small and select and does not share the values of the majority of persons of his social class, it may sometimes appear that he is making an independent self-evaluation and displaying "inner-directed" behavior, whereas he may be, in fact, highly dependent on the actual or fantasied approval or disapproval of a few individuals whose judgments he values highly.

A second criterion that has been proposed as a basis for distinguishing guilt and shame assumes that these are a function of degree of responsibility or voluntariness, which may be thought of in terms of a dichotomy between a transgression and a defect (Levin and Baldwin, 1959) or between a motive and an attribute (Piers and Singer, 1953). From this point of view, a person has little or no responsibility for a personal limitation and consequently can feel no guilt, but only shame, on account of his defect. It is true that persons may attempt to conceal intellectual and physical shortcomings in order to avoid negative reactions from others, but these do not necessarily involve a negative self-evaluation that could be described either as guilt or as shame. Let us imagine that a keen swimmer, as a result of an accident, acquires an unsightly scar that invokes reactions, such as staring, from others. He may forego swimming, thereby avoiding displaying his defect in public, but his giving up swimming would in this case be a means of avoiding aversive stimulation and not necessarily a shame, or a self-punitive guilt, reaction. This example highlights the difficulty of distinguishing between shame and fear of aversive responses from others. Of course, the former swimmer could negatively evaluate himself for concealing the defect, or attribute to himself responsibility for the injury.

It is evident that sharp distinctions such as those considered above give rise to semantic difficulties and do little to further the understanding of the acquisition and maintenance of self-control responses, which are undoubtedly a function both of fear of anticipated aversive reactions from others and of self-generated aversive stimulation. On the other hand, it is profitable to attempt to identify social influences that generate or intensify fear of others' disapproval or self-punitive responses for transgressions and defects, and factors that affect the size and nature of the groups that persons permit to influence their behavior.

Social restrictions and demands

In all cultures there are social demands, customs, and taboos that require a member to exhibit self-control. Biological gratifications must be regulated in relation to the time schedules of the culture and to prescribed routines. Feeding, elimination, and sleep routines are rigorously imposed by parents and involve delay of gratification of biological needs or interference with other rewarding activities. In conforming to these schedules and demands, the child has often to relinquish behavior that has previously led to immediate and direct reinforcement and to replace this by responses that are less efficient for obtaining immediate reinforcement for the agent. Thus, even the basic socialization processes involve the acquisition of a certain degree of self-control and the observing of social prohibitions and requirements.

Self-control of this kind is demanded for the convenience and well-being of other members of society. Although conformity to schedules involves some delay of reward, gratifications are freely permitted once this is achieved; moreover, since the scheduled gratifications are initially mediated by other family members, they occur in the context of social reinforcements and thus themselves acquire reward value. For example, while enforcing a bedtime routine, most parents give children their undivided attention and associate the observation of the time schedule with events such as story reading or participation in some highly rewarding play activity. Consequently, when children have adapted to such schedules, they have little incentive to deviate.

The situation is different in cases in which attractive rewards are denied to some members of society but are freely available to others. In this case, the problem of maintaining self-control extends beyond childhood years and for most individuals persists throughout their lifetime. Some highly valued rewards are permitted only to those members of society who have attained a certain social status by reason of age, social position, rank, or ethnic background. Barriers to obtaining such rewards may arise from personal limitations, intellectual or physical, and other fortuitous factors, over which the individual has little or no control. They may arise also from a lack of socio-vocational skills, possession of which gives access to the financial resources that are, for the majority of people, the primary means of obtaining highly rewarding goal-objects. Since proficiency in such skills is often dependent on an early commencement of training, which must then continue over a lengthy period of time, persons not infrequently find that lack of opportunities or guidance during their childhood and adolescent years has, in effect, imposed a life-time barrier to their legitimately acquiring possessions and status, or participating in activities that for other persons are evident sources of enjoyment and means for obtaining additional social and material rewards. Thus, both genetic and early-experience factors may create conditions under which persons are tempted to acquire socially acceptable rewards by socially unacceptable means. In fact, many theories of delinquency and crime portray the deviator as one who is oriented toward obtaining rewards that are very highly valued in the culture, but who lacks the opportunities of learning the means of obtaining them in a legitimate way (Cloward and Ohlin, 1960; Merton, 1957).

Social restrictions are not, however, aimed solely at the regulation of means for attaining culturally approved goals. In most, if not all, societies there are certain goals that are strongly prohibited, no matter what means are used to achieve them; yet, for some individuals, the attainment of these goals is a highly effective reinforcer. Sexual perversion and the use of drugs are examples of goals of this kind.

In the generally competitive atmosphere of North American society, achievement demands are made on the majority of children. Cultural achievement norms include the attainment of a level of academic or vocational proficiency that is likely to lead to economic self-sufficiency, and the establishing and maintaining of a home in which a family may be raised. Achievement demands are highly variable among social-class, ethnic, and other subcultural groups; nevertheless, in a society in which upper-mobility is a cultural ideal, parents and other adults in the family usually exert pressures on young people to surpass, or at least equal, the attainments of the previous generation. Nevertheless, as we have already noted, even in competitive societies restrictions are customarily placed on the means by which achievements may be attained. Thus a high degree of social approval in North American society is contingent both on achievement striving and on the observance of social restrictions designed to prevent this striving from having socially harmful consequences.

DISCRIMINATIVE TRAINING IN SELF-CONTROL

Compliance with regulatory social schedules, to which reference was made in an earlier paragraph, involves a considerable amount of discrimination learning in the exercise of self-control. Children must also be taught to discriminate circumstances under which certain classes of behavior may be exhibited from those under which they are not socially acceptable, and to utilize only those forms of response that are appropriate for the occasion. For example, children are expected to refrain from showing physical aggression toward adults or initiating physical attacks on peers; yet, at the same time, boys are expected to relax controls if first attacked by peers and to make efforts to defend themselves, though usually with the restrictions that they do not employ implements that could result in serious injury or use defensive physical aggression against younger or weaker opponents. Moreover, in certain well-defined social contexts, particularly in competitive physical-contact sports, boys are expected not only to defend themselves from attack but also to initiate and maintain physically aggressive behavior. Similar kinds of discrimination are also required in adulthood. For the majority of the population exercise of self-control involves refraining from injurious forms of attack, even in the face of persistent instigation, and the attenuation of the more noxious forms of aggression. However, disciplinary agents, such as parents, police, and armed servicemen, are permitted much freer and more direct expression of aggression in certain well-defined social contexts.

Restraints placed on the expression of sex behavior illustrate demands for self-control which are quite age- and status-specific. A child is required to maintain generalized self-control of sex responses until adolescent years, when some attenuated forms of sexuality are expected toward carefully selected sex objects. When adulthood is reached, demands for self-control are considerably relaxed; indeed, in the case of marital partners, overcontrol is regarded as a symptom of psychosexual maladjustment. Thus, in the case of sexuality the discriminations that are involved are primarily temporal.

There are other response systems over which individuals are expected to develop discriminative self-control, for example, dependency and cooperative–competitive behavior. In these and most of the other cases discussed so far, if the agent does not possess the reward he desires, he must regulate, delay, or renounce socially disapproved but expedient activities and select only culturally approved means and times for attaining his rewards.

SOME BEHAVIORAL MANIFESTATIONS OF SELF-CONTROL

The withholding or delay of social rewards elicits a variety of responses, some of which have already been discussed in Chapter 3. Nonaggressive responses to frustration are exceedingly diverse and are highly dependent on the previous training of the individual from whom the rewards are withheld. Moreover, largely because of varying social-learning histories, individuals differ considerably in the extent to which they are able to tolerate self-imposed delay of reward and to persist in the pursuit of a goal, the attainment of which requires self-denial and self-restraint. Reactions to frustration also depend on such factors as the length of time for which reward is delayed (Mischel and Metzner, 1962), on the occurrence or nonoccurrence of partial rewards during the course of achievement striving, and on the confidence with which, at any point in the goal-oriented behavior sequence, a favorable outcome may be forecast (Mahrer, 1956).

When barriers to social and material rewards occur, a frustrated person is ideally expected to maintain his orientation toward the goal objects he is seeking, but to strive to acquire these rewards in socially acceptable ways. This solution, as we have seen, may necessitate the expenditure of considerable time and effort and may not always be possible. Under such circumstances, some persons attempt to overcome barriers by illegitimate or culturally disapproved means which involve little delay or effort before the desired goals are attained. An alternative reaction is to devaluate goal objects that appear to be inaccessible or are not readily attained. This is a relatively easy way of maintaining self-control, especially if the frustrated person selects a reference group, the members of which mutually reinforce the devaluating behavior. This kind of response, which in an extreme and pervasive form is encountered among beatnik and Bohemian groups, occurs from time to time in the history of most persons.

The function of devaluating responses as a means of maintaining self-control is apparent in the results of an experiment by Tallman (1962). Junior college students were administered two tests that supposedly provided highly valid measures of academic aptitude. They were informed that if they passed either of these tests, a letter endorsing them for university admission and scholarship aid would be added to their permanent academic record. Both tasks were insoluble, but opportunities were provided to cheat on one of them. Measures of the students' appraisal of the letter of commendation were obtained before the administration of the tests, immediately after the completion of the experiment, and again at a later date. Virtually all students initially attempted to achieve the desired object by legitimate means. After they had exhausted the legitimate alternatives, 52 percent of the students who recognized the possibility of cheating and perceived their performance as poor resorted to deviant means for achieving the goal, while students who did not deviate devaluated the previously desired goal object.

Changes in children's evaluation of a toy with which they were forbidden to play were recorded by Aronson and Carlsmith (1963). Provided the threat of punishment for deviation was relatively mild, the children rated the forbidden toy as relatively low in attractiveness following a play period during which they had complied with the prohibition. When the threat of punishment was more severe, the children's evaluations of the toy were not affected, presumably because their conformity behavior was adequately maintained by their anticipation of the painful consequences of deviation. Devaluation may be initially an outcome of successfully maintained self-control; however, to the extent that the reinforcement value of the object in question has been reduced, the person who devaluates should experience less instigation to deviate on future occasions when the formerly desired goal object presents itself.

Other experimental studies suggest that when subjects perceive themselves as voluntarily undertaking arduous tasks in order to achieve a goal, they tend to evaluate the tasks more highly than if they feel themselves to be coerced (Brehm and Cohen, 1962). In one study fraternity pledges were required to serve in an unexpectedly long and boring piece of psychological research under threat of nonacceptance by their immediate reference group, the fraternity, if they refused to cooperate. These pledges expressed high annoyance with the task and regarded themselves as relatively free to refuse their cooperation; nevertheless, all agreed to participate. Compared to a control group of subjects who felt less annoyed with the task and more compelled to cooperate, these pledges expressed a high evaluation of the task as a potential source of satisfaction.

Both devaluation of not readily attainable or forbidden goals and activities and high evaluation of unpleasant means to a goal that is highly desired appear to be learned ways of maintaining self-control. Although no direct evidence is as yet available, one may suspect that responses of this kind can be readily transmitted by parents and other social models.

Although means of *resisting deviation* have received most attention in the literature relating to self-control, there are other equally important ways in which self-control may be exhibited. For example, a person may possess many rewarding resources, but may regulate the manner in which he administers them to himself. One frequently encounters people who make *self-reward contingent on their performing certain classes of responses* which they come to value as an index of personal merit. Such people may set themselves very explicit standards of achievement, failure to meet which is not considered deserving of self-reward and may even elicit *self-punitive responses;* on the other hand, they may reward themselves generously on those occasions on which they attain their self-imposed standards.

There are marked individual differences in the extent to which persons deny themselves rewards that by others are regarded as socially permissible. Two equally wealthy men may differ considerably in the extent to which they utilize their resources to obtain gratifications for themselves; one may lead an extremely frugal life, while the other may be extremely self-indulgent. Cultural forces sometimes influence the frequency and form of self-rewards and the occasions on which these are administered. Extreme self-denial occurs within some religious sects and subcultural groups; for example, austerity is a cultural norm for the Hutterites (Eaton and Weil, 1955; Kaplan and Plaut, 1956), who strive to preserve their way of life in spite of the increasing availability of consumer goods. In this culture not only are material self-reinforcements sparingly administered, but because of the emphasis on personal responsibility for conduct, self-denial and self-punitive reactions occur with high frequency.

> Control of impulses rather than expression is the rule. Enjoyment of food, drink, music, and sex are rather frowned upon, and are not spoken of publicly. No fighting or verbal abuse is permitted. A spirit of compromise, of giving in to one's opponent, is the accepted guide for interpersonal disagreements and frictions. It is expected that a Hutterite man will not get angry, swear, or lose his temper. It is considered wrong to be interested in the outside world, its activities and values. A Hutterite should not be interested in acquiring possessions, or engaging in politics, but instead should devote himself to living his life according to the rules set down by the Bible (Kaplan and Plaut, 1956, pp. 19–20).

In contrast, in Arapesh society (Mead, 1935) self-rewards are freely dispensed and are not made contingent on the meeting or surpassing of social demands and standards, few of which are rigorously imposed upon the members of this society.

Self-control is also exhibited in the *postponement of culturally approved immediate reinforcements in favor of some potentially more rewarding long-term goal*. Professional status can often be achieved only through long hours of arduous study and training; similarly, the attainment of some valued possession, such as a home, may entail the sacrifice of many day-to-day pleasures. Self-control of this kind occurs in the life-histories of most individuals and is, indeed, such a frequently observed occurrence that it has been largely neglected in the literature on the topic.

The relationship of tolerance for delay of reward and other aspects of self-control has been investigated in several experimental studies. Livson and Mussen (1957) assessed the "ego-control" of nursery-school children from their performances on two persistence tasks, one of which involved the sacrifice of immediately rewarding experiences in order to amass larger resources. Children who showed a high degree of persistence and willingness to delay rewards also expressed less aggression in nursery school, over a two-week observation period, than did children whose "ego-control" was weak. Further evidence of a relationship between preference for delayed, larger rewards (as opposed to more immediate, smaller rewards) and other aspects of self-control is provided in studies by Mischel (1961a, 1961b, 1961c). In the first of these studies, Mischel found that Trinidadian delinquents, in comparison to a control group of nondelinquent boys, were less likely both to delay gratification and to express socially responsible attitudes. Moreover, among nondelinquent children Mischel (1961b) found that preference for delayed reward was positively associated with measures of achievement aspirations, social responsibility scores, and another independent index of "ego-control." In a third study, Mischel and Gilligan (1963) had children perform on a shooting-gallery apparatus. The experimenter controlled the scores in such a way that the children were forced to cheat in order to gain sufficient points to win attractive prizes. Children who preferred delayed, larger rewards exhibited less cheating and completed more shooting trials before falsifying their scores than did children who preferred immediate smaller rewards. These findings are relevant to issues concerning the generality or specificity of self-control responses, a topic that is discussed later in this chapter.

ACQUISITION OF SELF-CONTROL THROUGH MODELING

The social-learning principles set out in the chapters on imitation and direct reinforcement can aid in the understanding of all aspects of self-control, including the development of self-rewarding and self-punitive responses.

The influence of modeling is most clearly apparent in those societies in which the majority of adults consistently display self-denying or self-indulgent behavior. In societies in which denial or indulgence is a cultural norm, the children have little opportunity to observe any other patterns of behavior and consequently are forced to model themselves after the prevalent self-control patterns. As research on the Hutterites (Eaton and Weil, 1955) show, patterns of self-denial may persist for many generations.

The transmission of self-indulgent patterns may be associated with a low level of technology and a precarious economic and social life, which persist in spite of contact with more provident social groups. Among the Siriono of Bolivia, for example, there are relatively few restrictions on the expression of sex and aggression, and there is no obligation for the younger and healthier members to care for the old and infirm, who are abandoned to die when the social group moves on to a new location. Holmberg (1950) attributes the "Siriono personality" to a chronic shortage of food; however, his description of Siriono life indicates that this shortage is largely due to lack of self-denial among the members of the society. On returning from a successful expedition, the Siriono hunter may enter his village empty-handed and signal to his wife to retrieve the game that he has surreptitiously set aside before his entry. He and his family then gorge themselves on the spoils, leaving nothing for a time of shortage. So extreme is this immediate self-indulgence that Siriono females characteristically have distended stomachs, which are, according to Holmberg, attributable to sporadic overeating.

Leighton and his associates (Hughes, Tremblay, Rapoport, and Leighton, 1960) present an account of life in a Nova Scotian county, in which both self-indulgent and self-denial subcultural patterns have co-existed for a number of generations. In "Lavallée," an Acadian community, children are strictly trained in the control of sexual, aggressive, and dependency behavior and are strongly pressured to achieve educational and vocational success. *"Evidently some of these demands are contagious, for the mothers say that their children demand teaching even before entering school"* (p. 133; italics not in original). Both parents spend a considerable amount of time in interacting with their children and thus in transmitting to them the adult patterns which predominate in this cohesive community. While the people of Lavallée emphasize material success, the wealthier members of the community are not expected to be self-indulgent; "the greater economic success a person has, the more he is expected to share it with his family, his church, and his community" (p. 157).

> In terms of time orientation, the main things in life are long-range goals—such as the salvation of the soul, the economic bettering of the area, the preservation and expansion of the Acadian group—*even though some of these are unlikely to be achieved by any individual in his lifetime. . . . Work is a moral activity,* and a man is enjoined not only to do it but also to take pride and pleasure in it under almost any circumstance. . . . Life without work would be life without meaning, and people who try only to get as much money as possible while doing as little as they can are disparaged (pp. 159–160; italics not in original).

Within the same Nova Scotian county there exists a group of settlements in which a very different pattern of life prevails. Community cohesion is lacking, and laziness, drunkenness, fighting, sexual promiscuity, thievery, and other criminal and antisocial activities frequently occur. In contrast to the parents of Lavallée, the parents in these "depressed" settlements are permissive and nondirective and have very low educational and occupational aspirations for their children. Through their own life patterns, they transmit to their children beliefs that work should be avoided, if possible, and that laws are to be defied; and they continually present to them models of drunken, aggressive behavior. Indeed, one of the prevailing sentiments among these people is that "the best thing to do in life is to escape from your problems as quickly as possible."

> The preference for drinking as the modal recreational pattern sets the keynote for this sentiment. The drinking in turn often leads to fighting, another way of attempting to obliterate rather than solve problems. Also popular, though, are some of the "fantastic" types of comic books and violent action movies, through which emotional releases and temporary escapes can be found. Recreation, then, when enjoyed at all,

tends to be at either of two extremes: the drinking which soon results in oblivion, or the fighting and related types of violent action. There is relatively little middle-ground, such as moderately tempered parties or group games. So dominant is the drive for liquor that people are willing to spend exorbitant sums of money to get it from bootleggers after the Government liquor store is closed. They will also drink alcoholic substitutes such as vanilla if the need is not met with regular liquor (p. 307).

A child who grows up in this kind of atmosphere is unlikely to acquire, either through modeling or through reinforcement patterns, habits of self-denial and self-restraint by which he and his children might secure a more stable and prosperous pattern of life.

Parent interview studies (V. J. Crandall, 1963), as well as statistical analyses of demographic and cross-cultural data (McClelland, 1955; McClelland, Atkinson, Clark, and Lowell, 1953), also suggest that high standards of achievement, together with habits of self-restraint in the service of long-term goals, are likely to be transmitted from one generation to another. In one of these studies, Crandall, Katkovsky, and Preston (1962) found that girls whose fathers devoted time to participate in intellectual pursuits with their children were inclined to give up free-play time to engage in intellectual activities. It thus appears that parental modeling may influence not only the standards that govern achievement behavior but also the direction that achievement-striving takes. As Sarason, Davidson, Lighthall, Waite, and Ruebush (1960) have indicated, parental anxiety concerning the evaluative standards of others may be also transmitted to children in the form of an anxious concern about meeting standards set by school authorities.

Further evidence for the influence of parent models in the development of children's habits of self-control comes from Mischel's investigations into self-imposed delay of reinforcement. Anthropological data indicate that adult Trinidadian Negroes are more impulsive and self-indulgent, and less likely to provide for the future, than Grenadian Negroes or Trinidadian Indians. Mischel (1958; 1961c) examined preferences for larger, delayed rewards, as opposed to smaller, immediate rewards, among children of families belonging to each of these three subcultural groups. Children from the highly self-indulgent Trinidadian Negro subculture showed the greatest degree of preference for immediate rewards. Moreover, children who came from homes in which the father was absent were likely to choose smaller, immediate rewards rather than to postpone gratification in order to obtain a larger reward. Assuming that a father's abandonment of his home reflects the family's lack of participation in a delayed-reward culture (Mischel, 1958), this latter finding may be regarded as providing further evidence of the influence of parent models on the self-control of children.

The influence of models in modifying resistance to deviation has been demonstrated in experimental studies having relevance to the problem of deviation. S. Ross (1962) employed a toy-store situation in which nursery-school children alternated in the roles of customer and storekeeper. For children in a deviant-model condition, a peer model, who served as the experimenter's confederate, informed the children that upon completing the game they could select a *single* toy only. The model then proceeded to help himself to three toys. In the conforming-model condition, the model took only one toy and thus exhibited behavior that was consistent with his verbal prohibition. Children in the control group simply received the verbal prohibition. In each condition the peer model left the room while the children made their selections. Relative to the subjects in the conforming-model and the control groups, children who observed the deviant model violated the prohibition more often and exhibited more conflictful behavior as reflected in moralistic comments, self-reassurances about the deviation, self-directed hostility, and concealment while performing the misdeed. Some evidence that a conforming model reinforces the observer's self-controlling tendencies, and thereby reduces conflict in temptation situations, is provided by the finding that control children displayed significantly more conflictful behavior than those who witnessed the conforming model, although both groups were equally conforming.

Lefkowitz, Blake, and Mouton (1955), using an accomplice model who violated a traffic signal, noted an increase in pedestrian violations following exposure to the model, especially if the model was attired as a high-status person. Freed, Chandler, Blake, and Mouton (1955), in an investigation of conditions influencing the violation of a sign prohibiting entry to a building, varied both the strength of a prohibition and the compliance–noncompliance of a model. The combination of a strong prohibition and a compliant model produced the lowest incidence of deviation, whereas deviation was most frequent if the prohibition was weak and the model disobeyed the sign. Using two levels of instigation to deviate, Kimbrell and Blake (1958) prohibited students from drinking from a water fountain. Providing that instigation was not so strong as to force deviation, subjects who observed a model violate a prohibition more readily performed the prohibited act than subjects who observed a conforming model.

The study by Lefkowitz et al. shows that characteristics of the model—in this case, his status position—may increase his effectiveness for reducing inhibitions. The influence of the model is also modified by the observed consequences of his behavior (Walters, Leat, and Mezei, 1963). Children who observe a model rewarded for performing a prohibited act are more likely to deviate than are children who observe the model punished. Indeed, the observation of punishing consequences to the model actually strengthens resistance to deviation.

In the studies referred to above the focus of attention has been on the violation of a prohibited nonaggressive activity. The investigators have, generally speaking, explicitly prohibited responses that in other circumstances would be permitted to the agent. In the case of aggression, particularly intense physical forms, it can be assumed that inhibitions have been developed as a result of past training during the life-histories of the subjects. Lowering of resistance to aggression was demonstrated in previously described studies in which an increase in aggressive responses followed exposure to aggressive models (Chapter 2).

Observation of aggressive models may serve not only to reduce inhibitions but also to teach the observers new ways to deviate. Bandura, Ross, and Ross (1963b) demonstrated that children who observed a model who was rewarded for aggression exhibited imitative aggressive responses that had not previously appeared in their repertory. Moreover, an analysis of aggressive responses which were not precisely imitative revealed that boys and girls were differentially influenced by the behavior of the models and its response consequences. Boys were inclined to inhibit aggression when they either observed an aggressive model punished or had no exposure to displays of aggression, whereas observation of both highly expressive but nonaggressive models and rewarded aggressive models greatly enhanced the boys' aggressive behavior. By contrast, exposure to nonaggressive models had the greatest inhibitory effect on the girls' expression of aggression. These findings suggest that control over aggression can be vicariously transmitted through the influence of models either by the administration of punishment to the model or by the presentation of incompatible prosocial examples of behavior.

The differential effects of prosocial and deviant models on the control of aggression by boys and girls may be partly explained by the relative dominance of aggressive responses in the subjects' repertories. Thus, for boys, in whom physically aggressive responses are relatively strongly established, exposure to a punished model effectively inhibited aggressive behavior, whereas their observation of highly expressive nonaggressive or rewarded aggressive models produced substantial disinhibitory effects. Presumably, a general increase in the boys' activity following exposure to an expressive model resulted in the manifestation of their relatively dominant habits of aggression. On the other hand, girls, who generally exhibit little physical aggression, showed little increase in nonspecifically imitative aggression following exposure to the aggressive models, while exposure to nonaggressive models produced decrements in the girls' aggressive responses.

It is generally assumed that resistance to deviation results from the association of noxious stimuli with the commission of prohibited responses during the life history of an individual. However, as modeling studies demonstrate, children may acquire inhibitions without committing a prohibited act and without themselves receiving any punishment. There is thus considerable evidence that response inhibition and response dis-inhibition can be vicariously transmitted, particularly if the im-mediate consequences to the model are apparent or the model is a person who has evidently been competent or successful in life.

The influence of models in transmitting patterns of self-rewards and self-punishments has received attention in only one experimental study (Bandura and Kupers, 1963). Children participated in a bowling game with an adult or a peer model, the scores, which could range from 5 to 30, being controlled by the experimenter. At the outset of the game, the children and their models were given access to a plentiful supply of candy, from which they could help themselves as they wished. Under one experimental condition the model set a high standard for self-reinforcement; on trials in which the model obtained or ex-ceeded a score of 20, he rewarded himself with candy and made self-approving statements, while on trials in which he failed to meet the adopted standard he took no candy and berated himself. In the other experimental condition, the model exhibited a similar pattern of self-reward and self-disapproval, except that he adopted the standard of 10, a relatively low level of performance. After exposure to their respective models, the children played a series of games on the bowling apparatus in the absence of the models. During these trials the children received a wide range of scores, and the performances for which they rewarded them-selves with candy and self-approval were recorded.

It was found that the children's patterns of self-reinforcement closely matched those of the model to which they had been exposed; moreover, they tended to reproduce the self-approval and self-critical comments of their model. Thus, al-though both groups had access to a plentiful supply of desired material reinforcers, the children who had adopted a high criterion for self-reinforcement through imitation utilized these resources sparingly and only when they achieved relatively high levels of performance, while children who were exposed to the low-standard model rewarded themselves generously even for minimal performance.

A comparison of the results obtained with adult and peer models revealed that children were more influenced by the standard-setting behavior and self-reinforcement patterns exhibited by adults. A control group of children, who had no exposure to models, set no standards for themselves, and tended to reward themselves for minimal performance. Figures 4-1 and 4-2 present graphically, for each of the three groups of children, the distribution of self-reinforcements as a function of level of performance. This experiment demonstrates the influence of vicarious reinforcement, in the form of rewards and punishments *self-administered* by the model, on the process of imitative learn-

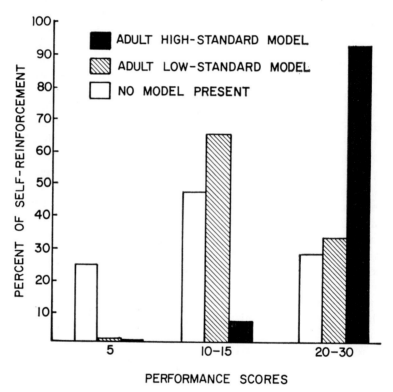

FIG. 4–1. *The regulation of self-reinforcement as a function of level of performance by children in the control group and by those exposed to adult models adopting high and low criteria for self-reinforcement*

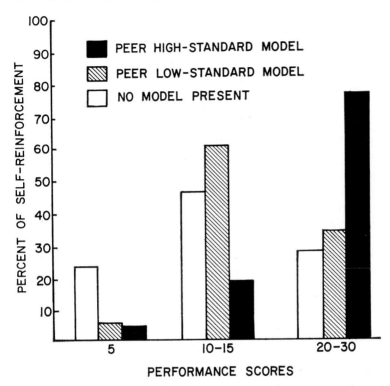

FIG. 4–2. *The regulation of self-reinforcement as a function of level of performance by children in the control group and by those exposed to peer models adopting high and low criteria for self-reinforcement*

ing; it thus indicates clearly one manner in which self-control may be acquired through observational learning.

Demonstrations that inhibitions and self-evaluative responses may be learned without the mediation of direct reinforcement are consistent with common-sense thinking. Socialization agents, for example, parents and teachers, frequently make use of exemplary models and from time to time reward or punish children in front of others in the expectation that the positive or negative reinforcement will influence the future behavior of the observers. Indeed, the administration of well-publicized rewards and penalties is a frequently employed social-influence procedure, whereby those who occupy power positions in society attempt to modify the behavior of many by rewarding and penalizing the behavior of individuals who are already socially visible or who become so as a result of the publicity.

ACQUISITION OF SELF-CONTROL
THROUGH DIRECT REINFORCEMENT

The literature on achievement behavior indicates that parental reinforcement patterns play an important part in determining the extent to which children will make efforts, often involving a good deal of self-denial, in order to attain standards which they have learned to accept for themselves. Rosen and D'Andrade (1959) investigated the manner in which mothers of boys who displayed a great deal of self-reliance and effort responded to their sons' attempts to master a number of tasks. In comparison to mothers of boys who showed less achievement-oriented behavior, the former group of mothers set higher performance standards for their sons, more readily gave approval when their sons' performance was good, and were more critical when the boys' performance failed to reach the desired standards. The effect of positive reinforcement of achievement behavior is also apparent in a study by Crandall, Preston, and Rabson (1960), who found that mothers who spontaneously rewarded and praised their children's efforts to achieve had children who displayed strong and frequent achievement efforts outside the home.

A study by Winterbottom (1953) provides further evidence of the effect of parental training on children's achievement behavior and at the same time suggests a relationship between the development of self-reliance and the attainment of self-control. Winterbottom reported that mothers who trained their children to exhibit little task-oriented dependency, while rewarding person-oriented dependency, had sons who gave a relatively high number of achievement-oriented responses to thematic test stimuli. Winterbottom's findings probably reflect the fact that socially acceptable achievement behavior requires consideration for others, perhaps an outcome of parental fostering of person-oriented dependency and thus of affiliative behavior (Chapter 3), as well as regulative self-direction in the pursuit of long-term goals.

In a number of investigations, the severity of parents' socialization pressures has been related to the extent to which children demonstrate self-control in temptation or achievement situations. The findings, though far from consistent, in general suggest that children who experience relatively early or severe socialization pressures tend to exhibit greater self-control than children who are more leniently trained (W. Allinsmith, 1960; Burton, Maccoby, and Allinsmith, 1961; Cox, 1962; Heinicke, 1953; Whiting and Child, 1953). Assuming that severity-of-socialization measures largely reflect the extent to which parents dispense rewards for conformity with parental standards and punish noncompliance, these results provide indirect evidence that patterns of parental reinforcement are important determinants of the habit strength of the self-control responses of children.

Laboratory studies of reward of aggressive responses provide the only experimental demonstrations of the effects of direct positive reinforcement on the occurrence of socially disapproved responses. Similarly, the role of punishment in the development of response inhibition, although sometimes overemphasized in theoretical expositions, has rarely been explored in experimental studies of human behavior in social situations. The available evidence, some of which was reviewed in Chapter 3, suggests that punishment may have very diverse effects, depending on its timing, intensity, and nature, and on the status of the punitive agent.

According to Mowrer (1960a, 1960b), the execution of a deviant act involves a sequence of response-produced cues, each providing sensory feedback. A painful stimulus (punishment) can be presented at various points in this sequence and so lead to the relatively direct association of a fear response with the response-produced cues occurring at the time of punishment. If the punishment occurs only on the completion of a deviant act, the fear will be most strongly associated with the stimuli accompanying the actual commission of the deviation and less strongly with the stimuli produced by the agent's preparatory responses. On the other hand, punishment occurring early in the sequence should result in a relatively strong association of the stimuli accompanying certain preparatory responses and the emotion of fear; in this latter case, even the initiation of a deviant act may be quickly forestalled. Since, once an act is initiated, numerous not easily identifiable secondary reinforcers may serve to maintain and facilitate the response sequence, and thus counteract the inhibitory effect of fear, punishment administered early in a response sequence should more effectively prevent the actual commission of a deviant act than punishment administered only when the act has occurred.

Walters and Demkow (1963) investigated the effects of timing on children's resistance to temptation. Two groups of children were given a training session, during which they were instructed to look through a book, which was printed in Russian and contained no pictures, while the experimenter "did some work" in another room. An array of toys was set out in front of the children, who were forbidden to touch these during the experimenter's absence. An observer, secreted behind a one-way vision booth, observed each child's responses and administered punishments, in the form of a loud aversive sound, whenever the child deviated. Subjects who were assigned to an early-punishment condition were presented with the aversive stimulus as soon as they began reaching for a toy; subjects assigned to the late-punishment condition received the stimulus only after they had touched the toys. On a subsequent day, the subjects were again brought to the experimental room and once more left with the book, but this time they were not explicitly instructed to refrain from touching the toys. The results for boys, though not for the generally more inhibited girls, supported the hypothesis that early punishment is more effective than late punishment in producing response inhibition.

Additional evidence for the importance of temporal factors in the establishment of response inhibition through punishment is provided in a recent study by Aronfreed and Reber (1963). On each of a series of punishment trials, boys were asked to choose between a highly attractive toy and one which was relatively unattractive. In one training condition punishment was administered as soon as the child's hand approached the attractive toy; in a second condition, the child was punished after he had picked up the toy and held it for a period of time. In the posttraining test for self-control the children were presented with an additional pair of toys and it was noted whether or not they picked up and handled the attractive toy when the punishing agent was absent. The percentages of transgressors in the punishment-at-initiation, punishment-at-completion, and a nonpunished control group were 26, 71, and 80, respectively.

In another study of the timing of punishment, Aronfreed (1963a) investigated its effects on the occurrence of self-punitive responses following transgression. Children were given a series of trials in which a formerly neutral label was paired with the onset of punishment for one group of subjects and with the termination of punishment for another. On two subsequent test trials the punishment was withdrawn and the incidence with which the children emitted the negatively valenced label (self-punitive statement) was recorded. Self-punitive statements were more frequently emitted when labeling had occurred at the termination of punishment than when labeling had occurred at its onset.

Whereas punishments occurring early in a response sequence produce anxiety arousal that inhibits deviant behavior, self-punitive responses associated with the termination of punishment can have an anxiety-reducing function (Aronfreed, 1963a). In the former case, anxiety is reduced by the cessation of the deviant response; in the latter case, it is reduced through the occurrence of the self-punitive response. In neither case is there need to assume that some inner moral agent or faculty has played a role in regulating behavior.

Some suggestive evidence in support of the above interpretation is provided in studies of puppies by Black, Solomon, and Whiting (Mowrer, 1960b). These investigators noted that puppies who were physically punished for approaching attractive but forbidden food showed high resistance to temptation but few emotional responses after transgression, whereas puppies who were punished during the course of consuming the forbidden food were less likely to resist temptation but more likely to exhibit emotional behavior following deviation.

Black *et al.* assume that the emotional behavior of their puppies was indicative of "guilt." However, there is no reason to suppose that emotional behavior following the commission of deviant responses is necessarily equivalent to a self-punitive reaction. In fact, if the completion of a deviant act is frequently paired with the onset of punishment, its commission will elicit anticipatory fear reactions rather than self-punishment. One may suspect that in the majority of cases in which a parent disciplines a child, the child deviates and then is punished; it is rare for the parent to make the termination of punishment contingent on the child's making a self-punitive response. The disciplinary procedures of most parents may consequently be more conducive to the development of fear than to the development of guilt. Indeed, children typically react to their own deviations by attempts to avoid punishment, which may take the form of flight, hiding, concealment, denying responsibility, or attribution of blame to others.

Self-punishment has usually been considered the prototype of guilt reactions. However, self-initiated reactions to deviation are more likely to take the form of apology, restitution, or confession, all of which are usually regarded as indices of guilt. All of these responses, including self-punitive ones, may vary in their function according to the circumstances in which they occur, the person to whom the response is directed, and the social training of the agent. In some cases such responses are aimed primarily at the termination or attenuation of punishment, while in other cases they are designed primarily to secure the reinstatement of positive reinforcers. For example, a child may learn to make self-critical statements as an effective way of forestalling or reducing aversive stimulation in the form of parental punishments and thus acquire a habit of employing self-critical statements as a means of controlling the behavior of others. This parallels an infrahuman organism's learning to press a mildly charged lever in order to avoid or reduce the administration of a painful shock which he cannot directly control. In contrast, a child may learn to criticize himself for transgression because self-criticism has proved a successful means of securing the reinstatement of his parents' affection and approval. In this case, the child's behavior parallels that of an animal who learns to press a mildly charged lever in order to obtain food.

In both of the instances described above, the self-punitive reactions are maintained through the reinforcing responses of external agents. However, transgressions can generate aversive self-stimulation, as, for example, when the agent's behavior fails to meet standards or values that he has already acquired. In this case, the self-generated aversive stimulation can be reduced or terminated by self-punitive responses, in the form of self-criticism, for example, or by increased efforts to reinstate self-administered positive reinforcers. Behavior of this latter kind may demand and reflect a great deal of self-control, yet because of the emphasis in much psychological literature on the internalization of the prohibitions of a punitive agent, is more likely to be regarded as a manifestation of a high achievement drive than of a well-developed self-control system. It may be more profitable to consider such kinds of responses as self-punishment, apology, restitution, and confession, as well as responses usually regarded as indicative of fear (for example, hiding and denial), in terms of their functional utility to the individual, rather than in terms of classes or stages of morality. Indeed, evidence that confession cannot be used unquestionably as an index of guilt has already been provided in an experiment by Rebelsky, Allinsmith, and Grinder (1963), which indicates that this type of response is more characteristic of girls than of boys and bears little relationship to boys' resistance to temptation in a cheating situation.

Direct training in transgression reactions may involve providing a child with opportunities for rewarding and punishing himself in certain ways and in encouraging him to make self-rewarding and self-punishing responses. Aronfreed (1963b) experimentally demonstrated that children who had been taught to deprive themselves of material rewards for "deviant" responses in a training session were more likely to make reparations following an experimentally induced "transgression" than were children from whom rewards had been withdrawn by the experimenter. The effect of the training was enhanced if children were provided with explicit standards of how they should behave. Although the reparation responses made by the children in Aronfreed's experiment were different from the self-depriving actions in which they were trained, both classes of transgression responses were self-initiated. Some evidence that training in self-initiated transgression reactions promotes self-control was provided in the authors' study of adolescents (Bandura and Walters, 1959), in which parents of relatively nonaggressive and high-guilt boys were more inclined to encourage their sons to make restitutive and other conciliatory responses following aggressive and other deviant behavior than were parents of aggressive boys with far more limited self-control.

REINFORCEMENT PATTERNS AND DISCIPLINARY TECHNIQUES

The influence of reinforcement patterns on the development and maintenance of self-controlling responses has been indirectly investigated, within the context of disciplinary methods, in a number of field studies. Considerable attention has, in fact, been paid to the differential effects on children's behavior of disciplinary practices such as physical punishment, verbal attack or criticism, deprivation of privileges, threat of loss of love, isolation, or reasoning. These practices have been sometimes classified under two main headings, psychological and material discipline, on the assumption that self-control is more readily achieved if psychological disciplinary methods predominate. Generally speaking, physical punishment has been considered the prototype of material or nonlove-oriented discipline, and reasoning and threat of loss of love as prototypes of the psychological or love-oriented type. However, there is far from perfect agreement among child psychologists concerning the categorization of other types of disciplinary practices (Bandura and Walters, 1959; Heinicke, 1953; Miller and Swanson, 1960; Sears, Maccoby and Levin, 1957). One reason for disagreement may be that each type of discipline can involve several components and that the accompanying reactions of the disciplinary agent may be crucial in determining the kinds of effect that the discipline has on the child.

Any disciplinary act may involve in varying degrees at least two operations, the *presentation of a negative reinforcer* and the *withdrawal or withholding of positive reinforcement.* For example, threats of loss of love in which the parents depict disastrous consequences to their health resulting from the child's behavior predominantly consist in the presentation of fear-arousing noxious stimuli, whereas threats of loss of love in which the restoration of parental affection and approval is made contingent on the child's conformity to parental wishes involves the withholding of positive reinforcement but little aversiveness. Similarly, a parent who inflicts little pain while impersonally administering mild physical punishment to a child obtains his effects primarily through the withholding of positive reinforcers, whereas a parent who administers very severe physical punishment while assuring the child of his love is dispensing positive reinforcers at the same time as he administers noxious stimuli. Moreover, some parents exhibit pain and self-critical reactions while physically punishing their children, and subsequently apologize to the child or otherwise attempt to make restitution; in such cases, the primary effect may be to model guilt reactions concerning aggression.

Parental modeling of pain and other emotional reactions during the course of disciplinary interventions may in other ways contribute to the development of self-control and so have effects that have been generally attributed to psychological disciplinary practices. The manner in which vicariously acquired emotions may motivate avoidance responses was illustrated in an experiment by Miller, Banks, and Ogawa (1962). Rhesus monkeys were trained to avoid a shock by pressing a bar whenever a stimulus light appeared. The animals were then seated face to face, with the stimulus panel attached to one monkey's chair and the bar to the chair in which the second monkey was seated. The apparatus was wired in such a way that shocks would be simultaneously received by each of the monkeys.

> The task confronting the animals is obvious. The monkey with the light had no means of performing the instrumental response which could avoid the noxious shock

stimulus. The second monkey could perform the response but had no stimulus to inform him when a response was appropriate. However, if the animal with the stimulus was able to communicate to his partner by means of expressive cues the information that the conditioned stimulus (CS) was being presented, the second monkey could then make the appropriate instrumental response which would enable both animals to avoid shock (p. 344).

From our point of view, the most interesting data were obtained from the testing of a pair of monkeys over a twenty-two day period, during which the monkey to whom the stimulus light was presented failed to receive shocks on account of an apparatus defect. Nevertheless, during this period the monkey with the bar learned to avoid shock by attending to the emotional responses of the monkey with the stimulus light. The monkey with the light observed the startle and leg-withdrawal responses of his partner whenever the latter received a shock and reproduced them so precisely that the experimenters failed to detect the fault in their equipment. After eight days of testing, the monkey with the light was behaving emotionally before the shock was delivered, *even though he himself received no shock,* and thus was emitting responses that served as a signal for the other monkey to make an avoidance response. In a similar manner, parents may exhibit anticipatory pain reactions to their children's deviant behavior before their disciplinary actions are carried out. If, at this stage, the child learns to react to his parents' emotional responses by ceasing disapproved activities or complying with parental demands, psychological control of the child's behavior has been largely achieved, no matter what form of discipline the parents originally preferred. Moreover, children often rely on the magnitude of parental emotional arousal to provide the main discriminative cues that compliance is expected and that non-compliant behavior is likely to be punished. In this way, children's behavior comes under the control of emotional-intensity cues that their parents, usually unwittingly, provide.

Experimental studies with children suggest that the immediate effects of presenting a noxious stimulus and of withdrawing or withholding a positive reinforcer may be diametrically opposite. Verbal criticism has been shown to lead to a decrease in both aggressive and dependency behavior in the presence of the disciplinary agent (Hollenberg and Sperry, 1951; Nelsen, 1960) and withholding of rewards to an increase in the strength of instrumental responses (Beller and Haeberle, 1961a, 1961b; Haner and Brown, 1955; Holton, 1961; Olds, 1956). Therefore, the prediction of what effect a particular type of discipline will have is dependent on knowing which operation has predominated. In general, such methods of discipline as threats of withdrawal of love and isolation—usually regarded as examples of psychological discipline—seem to involve predominantly the witholding of positive reinforcers, whereas physical and verbal punishments consist primarily in the presentation of negative reinforcers. Consequently, it is not surprising that some investigators (B. B. Allinsmith, 1960; Burton, Maccoby, and Allinsmith, 1961; Heineke, 1953; MacKinnon, 1938; Unger, 1962) have found that psychological and nonpsychological methods of discipline have differential effects; however, the lack of consistency of results concerning the outcome of these types of discipline and the generally low correlations between parental use of psychological disciplinary methods and the extent to which children show self-control (W. Allinsmith, 1960; Grinder, 1962; Sears, Maccoby, and Levin, 1957) suggest that attention might be more profitably focused on such variables as intensity and timing of presentation of noxious stimuli and completeness and timing of withdrawal of positive reinforcers.

There is ample evidence to suggest that the withholding and withdrawing of positive reinforcers should have a variety of effects, which vary as a function of the prior social-learning experiences of the person who is being disciplined and the context in which the discipline occurs. Under certain circumstances it may have some of the properties of a noxious stimulus and thus produce inhibition of the response with which it is associated (Ferster, 1957, 1958) and active avoidance of the agent. Such effects were evident in an experiment by Brackbill (1958), who first conditioned infants to give smiling responses through the administration of reinforcers in the form of cuddling, reciprocal smiling, cooing, and other forms of affectional demonstrativeness. Following the establishment of the response, the experimenter withdrew the positive reinforcers and remained totally unresponsive when the infant smiled. During this extinction period there was a progressive decline in the frequency of smiling responses made by the infants; in addition, however, these infants made active attempts to avoid looking at the experimenter and manifested other "protest" reactions similar to those produced by the presentation of noxious stimuli.

In other contexts the nonoccurrence of a reward may countercondition fear (Mowrer, 1960a) and thus lead to an increased probability of the occurrence of a formerly punished response. For example, a child may perform a deviant act that, if discovered, would be punished, and then confess his misdeed to his parents. If, under these circumstances, his parents neither reward nor punish him, the nonreward is a welcome outcome and thus may serve, through anxiety reduction, to help maintain the deviant behavior and at the same time to reinforce the subsequent confessional act. Moreover, as we have previously pointed out, nonreward of fairly well established behavior aimed at securing highly desired rewards may lead to at least a temporary intensification of the relevant instrumental responses. Indeed, nonreward can serve as an important discriminative cue, actively influencing the learning process, often in a quite subtle manner (Amsel, 1962).

This latter point of view is strongly supported by two recent studies of the effect of adult nonreward on children's achievement behavior. V. C. Crandall (1963) gave children the task of matching angles with a set of "standards." During a first series of twelve trials, one group of children received verbal approval—for example, "That's good"—on nine occasions; a second group of children were told on nine trials that their responses were wrong; while with the third group of children the experimenter remained silent. All three groups were then given a second set of trials, during which the experimenter remained silent. A measure of each child's expectancy of success was secured at the outset of the session and again after each of the two series of trials. The results of this study demonstrated that nonreward which followed reward had functioned analogously to negative reinforcement, whereas nonreward following punishment had functioned as a positive reinforcer.

Crandall, Good, and Crandall (1964) modified the design of the study just described to include a condition in which the experimenter was removed from the room during the second series of trials. In this way it was possible to differentiate the effects of adult nonreaction from those of extinction (no adult nonreaction). The results obtained in the earlier study were confirmed and, in addition, the changes produced by adult nonreaction were significantly greater than those produced by extinction. "Thus, it was concluded that adult nonreaction acquires active, contrasting reinforcement value of the sign opposite to that of the adult's preceding verbal reinforcements." Moreover, children who had low generalized expectancies of success in achievement situations were more influenced by positive reinforcement, and less influenced by negative reinforcement, from the experimenter than were children who had high generalized expectancies. Since there was evidence that high expectancies of success were the outcome of a history of mostly positive reinforcement in achievement situations and that low expectancies of success were the outcome of a history of negative reinforcement, the study also indicates that children are more sensitive to adult reactions that are contrary to those that they generally experience.

In Chapter 3 it was noted that nonreward following reward may, under some circumstances, have the effect of increasing the intensity of the frustrated response and thus of functioning similarly to a positive reinforcer. As the studies described above indicate, a reward–nonreward sequence may also function analogously to a negative reinforcer. The latter effect may be expected when the reinforcer that is withheld has previously been given for conformity to socialization demands and when the dependent variable is not the conformity response itself, but the self-evaluative responses that are associated with attainment of, or conformity to, standards.

While there is some evidence to suggest that the influence of a particular disciplinary technique on the development of self-control is partly contingent on the operation of other variables, studies of children who show aggressively antisocial response patterns suggest that parental preference for physical punishment as a disciplinary practice is an antecedent of aggressively deviant behavior, while the use of reasoning fosters nonaggressive prosocial behavior (Bandura and Walters, 1959; Glueck and Glueck, 1950; McCord, McCord, and Zola, 1959). The differential effects of aggressive-punitive and nonaggressive disciplinary orientations are also reflected in Bandura's (1960) finding that parents of aggressive boys had made more use of verbal and physical punishment, deprivation of privileges, and isolation in disciplining their children than had parents of very inhibited boys. In contrast, the latter group of parents, consistently with their general behavior patterns, had made more use of reasoning and had more frequently attempted to restore positive relationships with their children when some disciplinary action had been required.

The effects of physical punishment are probably complex and highly dependent upon the intensity of the punishment and the manner in which it is administered. A parent who attempts to modify his child's behavior by inflicting severe physical punishments is providing an aggressive model from whom the child may learn aggressive means of responding in interpersonal situations. Although, because of fear of retaliation, the child may not counteraggress in his parent's presence, he may nevertheless model his behavior after that of his parent when he himself wishes to cope with or control the behavior of others. Indeed, Hoffman (1960) found that mothers who forced compliance with their demands through the use of power-assertive disciplinary techniques, which included verbal and physical aggression, had children who exhibited aggressive power-assertiveness in controlling the behavior of peers and resisted the influence attempts of both teachers and peers. In contrast, one aspect of the use of reasoning as a disciplinary technique may be that the parent provides an example of how to respond nonaggressively in frustrating social interactions.

Chorost (1962) has recently reported significant positive relationships between the overt aggression of adolescent boys, measures of which were obtained from teachers' ratings, and the extent to which their parents employed authoritarian methods of control. The parent behavior was assessed by means of the Parent Attitude Research Instrument (Schaefer and Bell, 1957), which defines authoritarianism in terms of a number of interrelated variables and presents the authoritarian parent as a severe disciplinarian who harshly suppresses aggression. Chorost interprets his findings as reflecting parental modeling of hostile-aggressive behavior and his results may consequently be regarded as consistent with those reported by previous investigators.

Diverse parental disciplinary maneuvers have been regarded as cases of reasoning. These include descriptions of the ways in which the child's undesirable behavior may have un-toward consequences for others—for example, pain, incon-venience, or embarrassment—of which the child may not be aware. To the extent that the child has already been conditioned to avoid producing consequences of these kinds, the parent's account of the effects that may result from the child's behavior may be in itself sufficient to deter the child from acting in the dis-approved way. Reasoning may also involve explanation of pos-sible motives for the placing of restraints on the child's behavior by parents or others, thus forestalling resentment and intense attempts to modify or neutralize the behavior of the controlling agent. Moreover, it sometimes includes symbolic modeling in the form of presenting examples or detailed instructions of alter-native prosocial modes of response that the child can adopt when a similar situation arises at a future time. While focusing on consequences may serve primarily to inhibit behavior that the parent desires to forestall, examples of prosocial behavior and explicit instructions of how to behave in a prosocial manner provide standards by means of which a child can guide and evaluate his actions. The latter effect is demonstrated in ex-periments by Aronfreed (1963b; Aronfreed, Cutlick, and Fagan, 1963), in which children who were provided with explicit instruc-tions concerning how they should behave gave more self-critical responses, when they were led to believe that they had fallen short of the standards that had been presented, than did children for whom the expected pattern of behavior was relatively un-specified.

Evidence that suggesting alternative nonaggressive reactions reduces the incidence of aggressive responses in adults, even when instigation to aggression is present, is provided by Kaufman and Feshbach (1962), who found less hostile attitudes to delinquency in students who had received suggestions for constructive rational approaches than in students for whom such suggestions had not been provided. In contrast, parental use of symbolic negative models, which provide children with opportunities to become aware of, and to acquire, detailed knowledge of the deviant behavior of others, may contribute to the development of aggressive, disruptive behavior in children. Indeed, parents of aggressive children were found by Bandura (1960) to have relatively frequently presented symbolic examples of how their children should not behave.

Whereas physical punishment is frequently an emotionally toned parental reaction to children's completed misdemeanors, reasoning is more likely to be used when the parent anticipates a deviation or interrupts its occurrence in order to forestall undesirable consequences. Thus, reasoning is more likely than physical punishment to occur early in a deviant response sequence, so fostering resistance to deviation. Moreover, the administration of physical punishment is often poorly timed; in fact, unless the transgression is immediately discovered and the parent is present at the time of commission, the punishment is inevitably delayed. Even when the child's misbehavior is immediately noted, physical punishment may be postponed until the parent who usually administers this punishment is present. Since the child anticipates the punishment, he may be "on his good behavior" and thus be performing prosocial acts when the time for administration arrives. Although on most occasions parents symbolically reinstate the offense before punishing the child, the prosocial behavior, as well as the symbolized transgression, gets paired with the aversive stimulation. Although there is little evidence to indicate what precise effect it will have on the child, this procedure is certainly not the best way of promoting alternative prosocial modes of response.

Disciplinary methods may be most effective when termination of punishment is made contingent on the child's compliance with parental demands. In such cases, compliance either terminates the negative reinforcer or reinstates the positive reinforcer; in both cases, the desired behavior may be strongly reinforced. Threats of loss of love in which positive reinforcers are continuously withheld until the child complies with the parents' demands may thus be especially effective in establishing self-control. The finding of Sears, Maccoby, and Levin (1957) that mothers who used withdrawal of love as a preferred disciplinary technique tended to have children whose self-control was well developed, *provided that the mothers were warm and affectionate,* seems to support this point of view. However, if physical punishment or deprivation of privileges were used in a similar way, that is, if their termination were made contingent on the child's complying with his parents' demands, these techniques might be equally effective in establishing self-control (Hill, 1960).

Several investigators have reported relationships between generalized parental response tendencies (such as warmth, affectionate demonstrativeness, and acceptance) and the degree to which children display self-control (Bandura and Walters, 1959; Heinicke, 1953; Hoffman and Saltzstein, 1960; Sears, Maccoby, and Levin, 1957; Shaplin, 1954). Such parental responses may facilitate the development of self-control in ways other than through their contingent withdrawal and reinstatement. In the first place, warm, accepting parents are presumably those who often reward their children's approach responses, thus ensuring frequent parent-child interactions. Consequently, their children are provided with numerous opportunities to observe the behavior exhibited by the parents in many social contexts. Moreover, to the extent that the parents' behavior is associated with positive reinforcements for the child, it acquires reward value, and thus the child has some incentive to reproduce his parents' responses. Finally, when imitative responses occur, warm and affectionate parents are likely to reinforce them, and in turn to find the child's matching responses a source of positive reinforcement for themselves. Provided the parents are not deviant, these conditions should contribute to the acquisition of self-control; on the other hand, the very same conditions could foster the reproduction of the behavior of an antisocial deviant parent.

In two experimental studies, Aronfreed and his co-workers (Aronfreed, 1963a; Aronfreed, Cutlick, and Fagan, 1963) have reported that children who had experienced nurturant interactions with an adult experimenter and children toward whom the experimenter had adopted an aloof, distant attitude did not differ in the extent to which they gave self-critical responses after a transgression. Aronfreed's claim that the association of self-critical responses with the termination of punishment (anxiety reduction) is the crucial factor in establishing habits of self-criticism is probably sound. Nevertheless, for reasons stated above, one might expect that a nurturant disciplinarian would be more effective than a nonnurturant agent of punishment in conditioning self-punitive behavior. Under Aronfreed's nurturance condition, labels and actions presumed to be indicative of conforming behavior were associated also with approval and physical demonstrativeness on the part of an adult model, a procedure whereby these positive evaluative responses should have acquired conditioned reinforcing properties. Aronfreed's finding that children in the nurtured condition failed to reproduce the model's positive evaluative responses raises some doubts concerning the potency of his nurturance manipulation. The experimenter-child interactions were confined to brief periods within a single training session, during which the experimenter's nurturance involved only the expression of positive feelings and a limited amount of physically demonstrated affection. A brief attenuated nurturance interaction of this kind would be unlikely to reproduce any of the conditions described in the preceding paragraph. In contrast, Bandura and Huston (1961), who devoted two fairly lengthy sessions to establishing a rewarding relationship between an adult model and a child before testing commenced, found that children who had been assigned to the nurturance condition reproduced responses resembling those of the model to a substantially greater extent than did children who had been assigned to a nonnurturance condition.

The role of nurturance in the acquisition of self-punitive responses is not independent of the type of discipline employed by the agent of punishment. When the punishment takes the form of withholding or withdrawing positive reinforcers, and their reinstatement is made contingent on the child's performing some form of self-punitive response, the nurturant quality of the disciplinary agent assumes greater significance. Reports of a lack of relationship between parental warmth or nurturance and the self-control of children (Burton, Maccoby, and Allinsmith, 1961; Grinder, 1962) may be expected as long as a possible interaction between parental nurturance and preferred type of disciplinary procedure continues to be overlooked.

The role of the withholding of positive reinforcers and the presentation of noxious stimuli in the learning of self-control has received considerable attention from students of child-training practices. In contrast, the frequently used parental technique of eliciting and reinforcing responses incompatible with an ongoing or incipient deviant activity has been largely overlooked, at least in this context. This technique primarily emphasizes the production of prosocial behavior, involves actively teaching the child what he should do, and focuses relatively little on the deviant or erroneous response. The demonstrated efficacy of programmed learning springs largely from its fostering of correct responses and reduction of the probability of occurrence of undersirable alternatives; in contrast, the relative ineffectiveness of much social training is probably due to its focusing on the modification of deviant responses as they occur, instead of concentrating on the eliciting and rewarding of prosocial behavior.

The incentive used to elicit prosocial behavior may be either some kind of material reward or some positive social response. It has sometimes been assumed that these two types of reward have very different effects, paralleling those obtained from physical and psychological disciplinary measures, respectively. However, it is much more reasonable to suppose that the effect of either kind of reward is highly dependent on the manner in which it is dispensed. If during a child's life history the giving of material rewards has been frequently associated with the bestowing of affection and approval, material rewards acquire the same functional value as praise or other social reinforcers. However, if material rewards have been dispensed in an impersonal manner, and especially if they are used as substitutes for warmth and affection in manipulating and controlling the child's behavior, their social value can be only instrumental. In the former case, the parent is likely to bestow the reward as a spontaneous expression of affection for the child; in the latter case, the reward serves to produce and maintain behavior that the parent finds convenient. The relative effectiveness of different kinds of reinforcers is undoubtedly dependent also on such factors as the age, sex, and socioeconomic status of the recipient. In the case of a young child, material rewards dispensed by a warm, affectionate parent may serve as highly effective reinforcers for producing prosocial behavior.

PERSONALITY CORRELATES
OF AVOIDANCE CONDITIONABILITY

There is ample evidence that the readiness with which conditioned fear responses are acquired is dependent in part on attributes of the subject which are the outcome of prior social-learning experiences or may reflect constitutional differences. Rapidity and adequacy of learning to avoid noxious stimulation appear to be affected by individual differences in emotional responsiveness, which have been conceptualized by Spence (1956, 1958) as reflecting variability in generalized drive or anxiety level. Experimental evidence that subjects who score high on Taylor's Manifest Anxiety Scale (Taylor, 1953) learn more rapidly than low-anxious subjects to avoid a noxious stimulus has been provided by Spence, Taylor, and their coworkers (Spence and Beecroft, 1954; Spence and Farber, 1953; Spence and Taylor, 1953; Taylor, 1951). Spence (1958), in addition, found that avoidance conditioning was faster in subjects who showed high emotional lability, assessed from changes in skin resistance and heart rate in response to a noxious stimulus, than in subjects whose emotional lability was less marked.

Jones (1950) reported that adolescents who showed high emotional reactivity to mild anxiety-arousing stimuli, reflected in their polygraph records during a free-association test, were more inhibited and less expressive and assertive in their social behavior than adolescents who showed little emotionality to the test stimuli. Jones' findings were essentially confirmed by

Block (1957), who demonstrated that medical-school candidates who were high reactors during a lie-detection test were, among other things, more dependent and suggestible than candidates who were low reactors. Taken in conjunction with data from studies of the influence of emotionality on avoidance conditioning, these findings seem to indicate that emotional lability facilitates social conditioning, as well as avoidance learning in a nonsocial situation. Consequently, expressive-aggressive individuals might be expected to learn to inhibit punished responses less readily than more inhibited and socially controlled persons.

A study by Lykken (1957) in part at least confirms this expectation. Lykken selected two groups of prisoners, one sociopathic according to the criteria set forth by Cleckley (1955) and one neurotically psychopathic according to psychoanalytic theorizing, and a group of normal subjects who were comparable to the prisoners in age, intelligence, and socioeconomic status. During galvanic-skin-response conditioning, the prisoners' responses were weaker than those of the normal subjects and they also conditioned more slowly. Moreover, the prisoners were relatively slow in learning to avoid making errors that, in a multiple-choice task, were punished by shock. While this study clearly indicates that readiness to inhibit punished responses is in part a function of emotional reactivity, it provides little support for the assumption that psychopaths are incapable of developing conditioned emotional reactions. Sociopathic and neurotic prisoners differed little in performance on the behavioral tasks; moreover, although somewhat slower to learn to avoid punishment than the normal group, neither type of antisocial personality was incapable of profiting by experience. Indeed, in the avoidance conditioning task, the prisoners' scores showed considerable overlap with those of the normals. Finally, there were no differences among the three groups of subjects in the extent to which the emotional responses acquired through conditioning generalized to a new stimulus.

Walters and Parke (1963) compared the responses of two groups of alcoholics and two groups of control subjects in an avoidance-learning task under conditions similar in some respects to those used by Lykken. One group of alcoholics had criminal and antisocial records extending over a period of years and preceding the onset of their alcoholism; the pattern of behavior reflected in the case histories of these subjects would, by most mental health workers, be regarded as symptomatic of socialization defects. The second group of alcoholics were in voluntary attendance at a clinic and had no criminal records; generally speaking, these patients would be regarded as utilizing alcohol in order to reduce anxiety. The control groups were composed of nonalcoholic, noncriminal unemployed workers and of university undergraduates. All subjects were given a battery of relevant paper-and-pencil tests and were then set a probability-learning task, in which they were required to press one of four levers on each of two hundred trials. Each lever was associated with a predetermined probability of producing shock for the subject. Polygraph records of the subjects' emotional responses were secured throughout the learning trials. Contrary to expectations, the two alcoholic groups displayed similar patterns of response; both groups were high-anxious, showed signs of emotional lability, and exhibited a relatively low incidence of pain-avoidance responses on the probability-learning task. Nevertheless, although their performance throughout the task remained poorer than the controls', the alcoholics clearly profited from experience within the experimental session. Detailed analysis of results in fact indicated that significant differences among the groups were present during the first twenty trials and that these tended to decrease slightly as a result of training. In this study, the subjects inevitably received shock on a proportion of the trials; when punishment cannot be entirely avoided, the *performance* of highly reactive subjects may be initially so disrupted that the occurrence of *learning* may be overlooked if only over-all efficiency is taken into consideration.

Eysenck and his associates (Eysenck, 1957; Franks, 1961) have provided evidence that introverted subjects form conditioned emotional reactions more rapidly than extroverted subjects, and that these responses, once acquired, extinguish less readily in introverted subjects. From this it would follow that introverted children should become socialized more readily and develop stronger self-control than extroverted children (Eysenck,

1959). Eysenck attributes individual differences in condition-ability to variations in cortical excitation and inhibition, which he regards as genetically determined characteristics (Eysenck, 1952b); however, child-training practices that tend to produce introverted children may also be conducive to the acquisition of self-control, and it is consequently difficult to assess the contribution of constitutional factors to the development of the complex and generalized social-behavior patterns to which Eysenck's (1947) dimensions of personality refer. Nevertheless, studies based on Eysenck's theory, as well as those cited in earlier paragraphs, clearly indicate that individual-difference factors may play an important role in facilitating or retarding the acquisition of self-control.

THE GENERALITY OF MORAL BEHAVIOR

According to the point of view presented here, there is no necessary relationship between resistance to temptation and guilt as defined in terms of self-punitive responses. In fact, the learning principles involved in the development of these two modes of response seem to differ radically; whereas resistance to temptation involves the classical conditioning of emotional responses, the habit of responding self-punitively appears to result from instrumental conditioning. It is therefore not surprising that no consistent relationships between resistance to temptation and guilt have emerged from a number of studies in which both variables have been measured (W. Allinsmith, 1960; Burton, 1959; Burton, Maccoby, and W. Allinsmith, 1961; MacKinnon, 1938; Sears, Rau, and Alpert, 1960); moreover, one should not expect to find that these variables are related to precisely the same child-training practices (Hoffman, 1962), since the training procedures necessary for their development appear to be very different.

The issue of the generality or specificity of moral behavior has received considerable attention in both empirical studies and theoretical discussions (Brogden, 1940; Burton, 1962; Durkin, 1961; Hartshorne and May, 1928; Hartshorne, May, and Maller, 1929; Hartshorne, May, and Shuttleworth, 1930; Hoffman, 1962; Maller, 1934). Most of the empirical

studies, of which those by Hartshorne, May, and their collaborators were the forerunners, have involved resistance-to-deviation
measures, primarily ones involving cheating. The results indicate that there is considerable intraindividual inconsistency in
response to specific situations which permit children to misrepresent their level of performance. Since parents are likely to consider cheating as morally reprehensible regardless of the circumstances under which it occurs, one would expect less specificity of
response than that reported by Hartshorne and May. Indeed,
Burton (1963), following a reanalysis of the Hartshorne and May
data, has concluded that there is some generality in moral behavior when this behavior is defined in terms of not cheating on
tests. He proposes that consistency is mediated by two independent generalization gradients. One gradient represents generalization from one situation to another as a function of the
stimulus elements the situations have in common. The other
represents generalization based on verbal labeling; in this case,
the stimulus elements may differ considerably from one situation
to another, but a similar response is elicited because the same
label is attached to each. Burton also points out that most
middle-class parents try to teach both kinds of generalization.
The problem is thus not to explain the degree of generality, but
the marked specificity, of children's responses to opportunities to
deceive.

The evidence cited earlier in this chapter indicates
that resistance to deviation and other forms of self-control can
be transmitted through parental modeling, which is likely to
attenuate the effects of direct training. Thus, while parents may
almost unconditionally label cheating as an undesirable activity,
they may at the same time themselves display violations of social
prohibitions that the child has opportunity to observe. Most
parents frequently violate traffic laws, particularly those relating
to speed limits and parking, sometimes with the child enlisted as
a participant observer. They enter into discussions of how they
can "pad" expense accounts or misrepresent their financial position on income tax returns; they appropriate materials from their
businesses or offices for personal use, and constantly infringe
minor social prohibitions. Moreover, it is not unusual for parents

to boast of their success in outwitting public officials, whom they are apt to depict as easily corruptible, or as getting the better of a bargain through deliberate overrepresentation of the value of their goods or services.

Indeed, Wallerstein and Wyle (1947), in a study of 1,700 predominantly middle-class adults in New York State, found that even seriously deviant behavior was not uncommon among those supposedly law-abiding citizens. Sixty-four percent of the men and 29 percent of the women who were interviewed admitted "off the record" offenses that amounted to felonies under the State law, while 99 percent of the adults acknowledged one or more offenses sufficiently serious to have drawn a sentence of at least one year. Less serious unlawful behavior and breaches of social prohibitions are undoubtedly much more frequent. There can be little doubt that most children are provided with ample opportunities for observing deviation in their parents; such experiences may more than counteract inhibitions that have been established through direct training and may, in fact, promote the learning of means of circumventing social and legal prohibitions.

Even less generality of self-control might be expected in cases in which parents provide precise discriminative training, as they do, for example, in teaching control of aggression. While parents may demand strict self-control of their children's aggression in the home, they may at the same time encourage, instigate, and reward aggression in other situations. In fact, most parents, directly or through modeling, train their children to respond in a highly discriminative manner to situations to which aggression is a possible response; discriminative stimuli, such as the age, sex, and status of the subject, are expected to govern the occurrence, form, and intensity of the response. Under such circumstances, general inhibition of aggression is maladaptive rather than a normal outcome of social training.

In this discussion, emphasis has been placed on factors that make for specificity of self-control. This emphasis, however, is not meant to imply that self-control responses do not generalize to situations similar to those in which they were learned or that parental training is inevitably lacking in consistency. It was noted earlier, for example, that children who prefer larger, delayed rewards to more immediate, smaller gains also show high resistance to deviation, express attitudes reflecting a relatively high degree of social responsibility, and inhibit aggressive behavior (Livson and Mussen, 1957; Mischel, 1961a, 1961b; Mischel and Gilligan, 1963). Grinder (1962) has reported that children who confessed deviations readily at age five to six were, at age eleven to twelve, less likely to deviate when given opportunities to cheat in a game. This finding is especially surprising since mothers' reports were the source of information concerning early childhood confession, while resistance to cheating in later childhood was assessed from the children's performance in a carefully devised experimental situation. By contrast, Burton, Maccoby, and Allinsmith (1961), using four-year-old children, found a negative relationship between children's resistance to deviation and the extent to which they exhibited guilt responses after the commission of a deviant act. Burton *et al.* used the same test of resistance to deviation and the same index of guilt as those used by Grinder; moreover, in their study the measures of resistance and guilt were both secured when the children were four years of age. Grinder attempts to reconcile these discrepant findings by postulating that children have not developed a unitary self-control system by the age of four, but that such a system is present in children who have reached the age of eleven to twelve. It is evident, however, that Grinder's results do not, in fact, support this point of view, since his measures of guilt were secured from data concerning his subjects' behavior when they were still only five or six years old.

The preponderance of contrary findings casts considerable doubt on the utility of theories of morality which assume that self-control is mediated by a unitary, internal moral agent, such as a conscience, superego, or sense of moral obligation. They also call in question theories of moral development, such as that advanced by Piaget (1948 [1932]), in which moral orientations are assumed to emerge in children of specific ages. According to Piaget, one can distinguish two clear-cut stages of moral judgment, demarcated from each other at approximately seven years of age. In the first stage, defined as objective morality, children judge the gravity of a deviant act in terms of the amount of material damages and disregard the intentionality of the action. By contrast, during the second or subjective morality stage, children judge conduct in terms of its intent rather than its material consequences. However, Bandura and McDonald (1963), using a wide variety of verbally described social situations eliciting moral judgments, found that children between five and eleven years of age exhibited highly discriminative moral-judgment repertories, including both objective and subjective judgments, revealing considerable discrimination learning. Moreover, experimental manipulations, based on a social-learning paradigm, revealed that the developmental sequence proposed by Piaget is by no means predetermined or invariant.

In this study, children who exhibited predominantly objective or subjective moral orientations were assigned to one of three experimental conditions. One group of children observed adult models who expressed moral judgments counter to the group's orientation, and the children were reinforced with verbal approval for adopting the model's evaluative responses. A second group observed the models but received no reinforcement for matching the models' behavior. A third group had no exposure to the models, but each child was reinforced whenever he expressed moral judgments that ran counter to his dominant evaluative tendencies. The measures of learning were the percentage of objective judgmental responses produced by the subjective children and the percentage of subjective responses performed by the objectively oriented children in response to sets of stimulus items, each of which depicted a well-intentioned act, resulting in considerable material damage, contrasted with a selfishly or maliciously motivated act that produced only minor consequences. Following the treatment procedure, the stability and generality of the children's judgmental responses were tested in a different social situation in the absence both of the models and of the social reinforcement.

As shown in Figures 4–3 and 4–4, children who were exposed to models and those who were positively reinforced

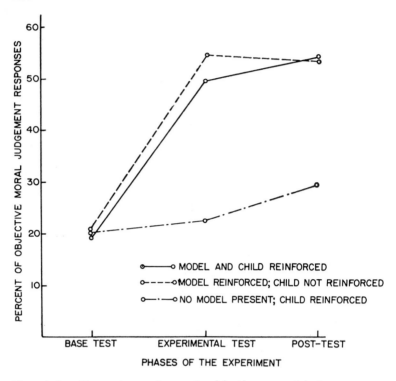

FIG. 4–3. *Mean percentage of objective moral-judgment responses produced by subjective children on each of three test periods for each of three experimental conditions*

for matching their models' moral judgments not only modified their moral orientations but also maintained these changes in their postexperimental judgmental behavior. It is nevertheless apparent from these data that operant-conditioning procedures alone are relatively ineffective in modifying the behavior of subjects who present strong dominant response tendencies and in whom the desired alternative responses are only weakly developed or absent. In such cases, however, the provision of models who exhibit the desired behavior is an exceedingly effective procedure for eliciting from observers appropriate matching re-

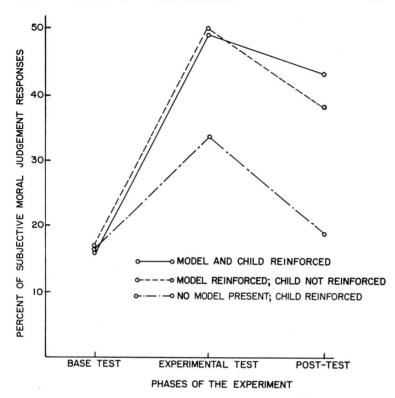

FIG. 4–4. *Mean percentage of subjective moral-judgment responses produced by objective children on each of three test periods for each of three experimental conditions*

sponses early in the learning sequence and thus accelerating the acquisition process. The so-called development stages were readily altered by the provision of adult models who consistently adopted moral orientations that ran counter to those displayed by the child. Increased consistency in the children's moral orientations resulted from consistency on the part of the model and generalized to the new set of social situations. As this study suggests, consistency in moral behavior is probably attained when parent models exhibit widely generalized resistance to deviation or self-punitive responses and at the same time use reinforcement patterns that are consistent with the behavioral examples they provide.

The assumption of a generalized self-control system has led to the practice of conceptualizing deviant response patterns in terms of deficient or overdeveloped superego. For example, a psychopath is depicted as lacking internal controls, whereas a neurotic is presented as suffering on account of an overdeveloped superego. Once he has adopted a unitary theory of morality, the clinician finds himself faced with paradoxes. For example, the psychopath is depicted as being impulse-ridden, yet at the same time as exercising effective control over his behavior in order to gain his own ends. He is said to be free of guilt and shame and yet to exhibit behavior that elicits punishment. These apparent contradictions would undoubtedly disappear if one knew the typical social-learning history of the psychopath and the way in which his discriminations were acquired. Similarly, Redl and Wineman (1955) have depicted "children who hate" as lacking controls from within. In order to account for the occasional resistance to temptation and self-punitive responses displayed by these children, Redl and Wineman invoke the concept of "islands of superego." Not only is their account open to serious misinterpretation, but such concepts as "islands of superego" have no explanatory value. More would have been gained by focusing on the nature of the discriminations that the children had learned than in elaborating the paradox that results from the assumption of a unitary internal moral agent.

PERSISTENCE OF DEVIANT BEHAVIOR

Psychoanalytically oriented writers have frequently attributed repetitive antisocially deviant behavior that persists in spite of punishment to the presence of excessive guilt (Alexander and Staub, 1931; Bromberg, 1948; Freud, 1925b [1915]; Friendlander, 1947; Lindner, 1944). This guilt is thought to spring from unresolved and deeply repressed Oedipal wishes and to lead the offender to commit acts for which he will inevitably be punished.

Delinquency, from a structural point of view, presupposes a weak, absent, or distorted superego. A healthy, strong superego will not permit as flagrantly asocial behavior as stealing. Certain children, however, will steal because of a distorted superego. Bound by a powerful but unconscious sense of guilt, the child feels a need to be punished and thus to make retribution for a "crime," the nature of which he is not conscious. If punishment is obtained the guilt will be relieved. Unable to seek punishment for the primary crime, since its nature is unknown to him, he commits an actual misdeed in order to be punished. He often unconsciously reveals the function his delinquency serves. In committing the delinquent act, be it stealing or any other type of asocial behavior, he does it in a manner that makes detection inevitable. His clumsiness belies his assumed clever misdemeanor or crime. He is caught and punished. If institutionalized he is often the ideal inmate, conforming because he is actually grateful to the administration for the relief from guilt which the punishing situation offers him. Released from the institution, he reverts to his former behavior pattern. He again becomes delinquent. His guilt has not been relieved permanently because the unconscious crime still exists (Josselyn, 1948, pp. 78–79).

This account gives rise to the paradox that guilt, anticipation of which is usually regarded as a major factor in promoting self-control, is depicted as instigating antisocial acts. To resolve this paradox, the exponents of this point of view further assume that the guilt itself is repressed and consequently inoperative as a mechanism whereby antisocial behavior is inhibited. A more usual, but certainly a more parsimonious, view is that persistent offenders, such as psychopaths, have failed to develop an adequate self-control system and react to transgressions with little or no guilt (Cleckley, 1955; Jenkins, 1954; McCord and McCord, 1956). Research into the social backgrounds of persistent delinquents (Andry, 1960; Bandura and Walters, 1959; Bowlby, 1946; Burt, 1925; Glueck and Glueck, 1950; Healy and Bronner, 1925; Lewis, 1954; McCord, McCord, and Zola, 1959; Nye, 1958; Shaw and McKay, 1931) certainly indicates that their environments and the child-training practices to which they are exposed are frequently not conducive to the development of a strong self-control system. However as we noted in the previous section, most antisocial personalities are neither entirely guilt-free nor suffering from pervasive and excessively strong guilt feelings.

The frequently made statement that psychopaths and other habitual offenders do not learn from experience seems to imply that punishment does not alter their behavior. Certainly, punishment does not usually change the antisocial orientation of such offenders or their use of illegitimate means to obtain rewarding resources. However, the efficacy of punishment in modifying antisocial patterns is highly dependent on the extent to which the offender is capable of, or provided with, alternative prosocial modes of response that will permit him to attain desired social goals. Unless prosocial habits are relatively strongly established, the administration of punishment is likely to lead only to minor modifications in the deviant behavior pattern, ones that are aimed at avoiding detection and subsequent punishment but are no more socially acceptable than the behavior the punishment was designed to inhibit.

> The behavior of a person who is primarily fear-controlled will be largely governed by his estimation both of the probability of his being caught and of the severity of the punishment that may follow. There is, of course, an element of error, the magnitude of which depends to a large extent on the offender's ability to learn by experience and to assess the reality circumstances at any given moment. In fact, habitual offenders may the more readily risk punishment because they have consciously changed their techniques on the basis of prior experiences and thus have gained confidence that they will not be caught on future occasions. Moreover, detection of offenses often occurs because of some unusual event which the offender could not have predicted even after careful and prolonged study of the habits of the persons whom he wishes to thwart and deceive. It has been noted that most repeated offenders do not commit offenses that bring extremely severe penalties, nor do they ordinarily carry out their antisocial acts under circumstances in which the probability of being caught is very high, as they might be expected to do if they were motivated by a strong need for punishment (Bandura and Walters, 1959, pp. 367–368).

Thus, antisocial behavior is likely to persist not because punishment does not alter behavior but because the dominant component responses in the repertories of persistent offenders are for the most part antisocial.

The apparent paradox that antisocial behavior persists in the face of punishment might be readily resolved if information were available concerning the outcome of every antisocial act an offender makes. In much of the literature on habitual delinquents, the punished trials are emphasized and the often far more frequent successful and rewarding antisocial acts are consistently overlooked, often of course because they remain unknown. We suspect that most persistent antisocial behavior is maintained through substantial intermittent positive reinforcement which outweighs the inhibitory effects of punishment, except insofar as the latter leads to changes in the form of antisocial acts designed to maximize the offender's chances of securing further reinforcements.

In addition, observation of the successful deviation of others may provide vicarious reinforcement of antisocial behavior, especially if the offender consistently associates, as in fact he usually does, with a delinquent group (Redl, 1945). Moreover, membership of such a group provides opportunities for learning, through observation and direct social reinforcement, of new and safer ways to circumvent the law; at the same time, observing the antisocial activities of others, either while they are committed or symbolically as successful deviations are narrated, may serve to reduce any inhibitions that the offender may have acquired.

Explanations of persistent antisocial behavior that focus on intrapsychic events often totally ignore the fact that a radical change in an offender's behavior may lose him the social and material rewards associated with a delinquent career without providing him with satisfying substitute resources. Indeed, the "ex-con" tends to be rejected by the "law-abiding" members of society and thus to find difficulty in obtaining work, accommodations, and friends outside the delinquent group. Finally, if the offender has been instrumental in aiding his former associates to obtain rewarding resources, he is likely to experience strong coercion to resume gang activities. In the light of the above considerations, change, when it occurs, is usually more difficult to explain than persistence; indeed, the majority of authorities are inclined to attribute its occurrence to a mysterious "maturation" process, usually without reference to the relevant social-learning experiences that probably account for the change.

The critical data cited in support of the view that persistent antisocial activities are motivated by an underlying sense of guilt consist of cases in which an offense is committed in such a way that detection is inevitable. It is true that sometimes persons contrive situations in which others serve as the agents through whom they bring punishment on themselves; however, the reinforcement for behavior of this kind is not inevitably guilt reduction. In the first place, punishment may be invited from others in order to provide an occasion on which hostility or aggression may be expressed in the form of counteraggression, thus reducing the possibility of punishment following the aggressive act. In such cases, if guilt reduction is involved, it is usually in relation to guilt anticipated for the commission of the forthcoming aggressive response and not to antecedent guilt that is generated by repressed Oedipal wishes or transferred from some other area of behavior. In fact, there is evidence from laboratory research that guilt for aggression is less severe when the aggressive response can be made to appear justifiable (Berkowitz, Corwin, and Hieronimus, 1962; Berkowitz and Rawlings, 1962). Secondly, for some individuals institutionalization brings more rewards than life in the community; these individuals may commit crimes in such a way as to ensure detection and consequent institutionalization. In fact, criminals who have become accustomed to life in an institution frequently display emotional behavior as the time for their release approaches and may attempt to delay release through offenses committed in prison during the latter part of their current sentence.

The preceding discussion has focused on a class of persistent deviant behavior that is primarily maintained by intermittent positive reinforcement. Anxiety-motivated deviant behavior is equally resistant to change, although in this case avoidant responses are sustained by the termination or reduction in the strength of conditioned aversive stimulation.

Laboratory studies of avoidance behavior by Miller (1948a) provide an excellent illustration of its acquisition and persistence. Rats were administered electric shocks in a white compartment of a shuttle box and learned to escape the shocks by running through an open door into a black compartment. The formerly neutral cues of the white compartment rapidly acquired fear-producing properties, and the animals continued to make the avoidance responses long after shock stimulation had been discontinued. Escape from the conditioned aversive stimuli thus reinforced the running behavior. The animals were then placed in the white compartment with the door closed, but capable of being released by rotating a wheel. The wheel-turning response was rapidly learned and was probably maintained by intermittent fear reduction. When conditions were changed so that wheel-turning no longer released the door, but the animal could escape from the fear-provoking compartment by pressing a bar, the former response was quickly extinguished while the latter became strongly established. The presence and removal of the conditioned aversive stimuli thus maintained a series of avoidance responses, in spite of the fact that there was no longer any reality basis for emotional reactions since the shock stimulation had been completely discontinued.

Extreme persistence of fear-motivated responses in dogs has been reported by Solomon, Kamin, and Wynne (1953). The animals were trained in a shuttle box to avoid a just-subtetanizing electric shock by jumping over a barrier when a buzzer sounded. The shock was presented on each of the acquisition trials, which were continued until the dog had made ten consecutive avoidance responses; at this point, shock was discontinued and extinction trials began. Under ordinary extinction procedures the dogs continued to jump with just as short a latency for up to two hundred trials without receiving a single further presentation of the unconditioned stimulus.

At this stage in the investigation, various modifications of procedure were introduced. For some dogs, a glass barrier, which prevented the consummation of the jumping responses, was erected between the compartments; for others, a shock was administered for jumping to the compartment into which the dogs had formerly learned to escape. However, these procedures, when used singly, were only moderately successful in producing extinction. Far more effective was a combination of the shock and barrier methods.

The success of the combined methods was apparently due in part to the initial weakening of the dog's classically conditioned emotional responses during those trials on which the animals were forced to remain in the shock compartment for some time after the buzzer had sounded. During these trials, of course, the dogs were prevented from completing their jumps; consequently, no strengthening of the avoidance response through fear reduction could take place. At this stage, the introduction of punishment for jumping could achieve the expected inhibitory effect before the still relatively close conjunction of the buzzer and the presentation of shock had again built up the conditioned emotional reaction.

Solomon *et al.* found that the barrier procedure, when used singly, was relatively ineffective. This procedure, however, was used only on the fourth and seventh of the ten trials which the dogs received during each daily session. As a result, the dogs learned to discriminate between trials on which the barrier was present and those on which it was removed, and continued to jump rapidly on the latter trials. As Carlson and Black (1959) have demonstrated, the response-prevention technique can result in rapid extinction, provided it is employed on every trial in a fairly lengthy series.

It is, nevertheless, reasonable to assume that the persistence of avoidance behavior in social situations is due to some of the maintaining conditions identified by Solomon, Kamin, and Wynne. Relevant data from studies of human subjects are relatively scarce, but there is some evidence that the fear reduction consequent on avoidance behavior has reinforcing properties. For example, Logan (1951) demonstrated that conditioned eye-blink reactions, learned in response to shock, are more resistant to extinction following an avoidance-learning procedure than when the subjects' blinking has served only to terminate shocks which have been consistently administered on every acquisition trial.

Dinsmoor (1954, 1960) has argued that the concept of anxiety- or fear-reduction is unnecessary to account for persistent avoidance behavior, which, according to his exposition, may be explained in terms of the role of the warning signal. "Through its pairing with shock, the warning signal, too, gradually becomes aversive to the subject. Thereafter, any response that removes or reduces *this* stimulus or alters it in some way that it is no longer followed by shock will be learned and maintained through the reinforcing effects of the change in stimulation" (1960, p. 303).

Dinsmoor has been criticized by Mowrer (1960a) for implying that aversiveness is an objective characteristic of the stimulus. However, in describing the manner in which a rat will keep depressing a bar in order to avoid a shock, Dinsmoor writes: "Apparently the stimuli arising *inside the animal* as he begins to let up his pressure serve as adequate warning signals for the punishment that will follow, and the animal learns to remove them by returning to his defensive maneuver with renewed vigor" (1960, p. 304; italics not in original). From this point of view, then, it is the change in internal stimulation which maintains the avoidant behavior, and the difference between Dinsmoor's point of view and that put forward by Mowrer (1960a) becomes largely a matter of semantics.

The resistance to extinction of an avoidance response is particularly strong when the stimulus components present during acquisition are also present during extinction, but resistance weakens as the similarity between the acquisition and extinction situations decreases. By pairing a buzzer with an electric shock, Banks (1963) trained college students to remove their hands from a grid whenever a buzzer sounded. During the acquisition trials, a light was paired with the buzzer on a selected proportion of trials: 100, 75, 50, 25, or 0 percent. During the extinction series, the light was again paired with the buzzer either on the same proportion or on a different proportion of trials. Thus, for different groups of subjects, the frequency of presentation of the paired stimulus during the extinction period differed in varying degrees from its frequency of presentation during the acquisition

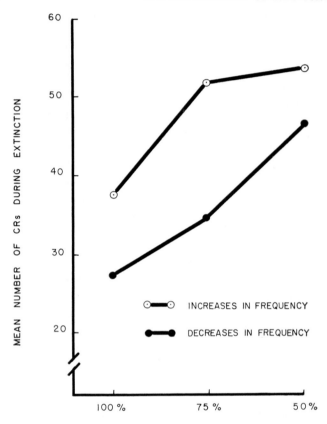

FIG. 4–5.   *Gradients of response strength during extinction trials under increases and decreases in the probability of presentation of PS (paired stimulus) from acquisition to extinction trials (from Banks, 1963)*

period. Figure 4–5, which shows the mean number of conditioned avoidance responses given during extinction by different groups of subjects, indicates that resistance to extinction diminishes as the frequencies with which the paired stimulus is presented during the acquisition and extinction periods become increasingly dissimilar. In view of Banks' finding, one might expect that the elimination of a fear that had generalized would be more easily accomplished in a situation somewhat dissimilar from that in which it had been learned than if extinction were attempted when the originally conditioned stimuli were themselves present. This expectation is supported by studies with animals (Kimble and Kendall, 1953; Wolpe, 1952), which demonstrate effective counterconditioning of fears through the gradual exposure of subjects to a series of stimulus conditions that are increasingly similar to those in which the fear responses were originally learned. Similar methods have, in fact, been applied by Wolpe (1958) as a means of treatment for neurotic patients.

The majority of experimental studies of the effects of aversive stimulation have been concerned with place avoidance, whereas persistent fear-motivated responses in social situations are more likely to take the form of refraining from the performance of previously punished acts. As we have noted earlier (Chapter 1), these latter responses are developed and maintained in the same manner as place-avoidance responses, except that the conditioned aversive stimuli are in this case correlated with certain of the agent's own activities. The principles that account for the maintenance of strong inhibitions are apparently no different from those that explain place-avoidance acts. Since the agent avoids making the fear-arousing responses, the associated emotional responses are difficult to extinguish. Moreover, on those occasions when the agent commences a prohibited activity, the cessation of this response sequence removes the response-produced stimulation and thus helps to maintain incompatible avoidance or prosocial responses. Most inhibitions that are the outcome of ordinary socialization procedures are rarely reinforced through anxiety reduction. Since antagonistic prosocial responses are usually relatively dominant, the conditioned emotional responses associated with the commission of deviant acts are very infrequently aroused in the presence of the conditioned aversive stimuli; consequently, the learned avoidance responses are extinguished only under circumstances that make alternative responses difficult or impossible. Anxiety-motivated deviant and prosocial responses, in fact, seem to differ not in the manner in which they are learned and maintained, but only in respect to the classes of stimulus objects with which fear responses are associated.

Summary

In this chapter attention was primarily focused on the social-learning antecedents of self-controlling and transgression responses. The following three forms of self-controlling behavior were distinguished: resistance to deviation, the regulation of self-administered rewarding resources, and the postponement of immediate reinforcements in favor of some potentially more highly valued delayed reward.

The influence of models on the acquisition and maintenance of self-controlling responses has been demonstrated in a number of experimental studies. It has been shown, for example, that persons who observe models violate prohibitions more readily perform the prohibited acts than persons who are exposed to models who conform. Response inhibition and response disinhibition are most readily effected through modeling if the immediately punishing or rewarding consequences to the model are apparent or if the model is evidently competent, successful, or prestigeful. The self-administered schedules of reinforcement exhibited by models have also been found to be influential in modifying patterns of self-reinforcement. Demonstrations that inhibitions may be strengthened or weakened, and that self-evaluative responses may be learned, without the mediation of direct reinforcement, provide further evidence of the importance of vicarious learning in the socialization process.

The acquisition and maintenance of self-control are influenced also by patterns of direct reinforcement, which generally take the form of disciplinary interventions. Any disciplinary act may involve in varying degrees the presentation of a negative reinforcer and the withdrawal or withholding of positive reinforcement, procedures that may produce very different effects. In order to predict the outcome of any disciplinary intervention on the development of self-control and transgression responses, it is consequently necessary to know to what extent one or the other of these procedures has predominated. The outcome will also, in part, be contingent on the intensity and timing of the aversive stimulation, the completeness and timing of the withdrawal and reinstatement of positive responses, the characteristics of the disciplinary agent, and the prior social-learning experiences of the person who is being disciplined.

Punishment administered at the onset of a response sequence conditions anxiety to the response-generated cues and thus produces response inhibition or resistance to deviation. However, if punishment that is administered following the commission of a deviant act is withdrawn when the recipient makes a self-punitive response, "guilt" reactions may become strongly established. In the former case, aversive stimulation is avoided through the cessation of the deviant response, whereas, in the latter case, it is avoided through the occurrence of self-punitive responses.

In disciplining children, parents on most occasions administer aversive stimuli some time after a deviation has occurred and fail to make its termination contingent on the child's expressing self-punitive responses. Consequently, punitive disciplinary techniques are not generally conducive either to the development of adequate response inhibition or to the acquisition of "guilt." In contrast, when parents withhold or withdraw positive reinforcers, the reinstatement of these rewarding objects or experiences is usually made contingent on the child's complying with parental demands or on his making some kind of restitutive response. Consequently, it is not surprising that some investigators have reported that this method of discipline, especially when used by warm and affectionate parents, is associated with the development in children of self-controlling responses and guilt-reactions to transgression, whereas the use of aversive stimulation as a disciplinary measure is more likely to be associated with avoidance of the disciplinary agents.

While the withholding of positive reinforcers and the presentation of aversive stimuli have received a good deal of attention in the literature on the development of self-control, the technique of eliciting positively reinforcing prosocial responses incompatible with an ongoing or incipient deviant activity has been frequently overlooked. This method of disipline, which is highly effective in inhibiting transgression responses, is often employed by parents who favor reasoning as a means of controlling their children. In investigations into the effects of various parental practices on self-control of children, there has been little attempt to analyze precisely the kinds of parent behavior that may be classified as examples of reasoning. These evidently include descriptions of the painful consequences to others of children's deviant behavior and the provision of examples of alternative prosocial modes of response that the child may adopt when similar situations again arise. The results of controlled experiments with both adults and children have demonstrated that the presentation of prosocial alternatives to aggression reduces the incidence of aggressive responses, even when instigation is present. Consequently, it is not surprising that field studies have supported the hypothesis that parental reasoning is an antecedent of nonaggressive orientations in children.

The social-learning principles presented in this book lead one to expect that most persons will acquire discriminative self-controlling behavior as a consequence of exposure to differential modeling cues and differential patterns of reinforcement. Moreover, from our theoretical standpoint, there is no necessary relationship between response inhibition or "resistance to temptation" and guilt responses to transgression, since different learning principles are involved in the acquisition of these two modes of response. Whereas resistance to deviation involves primarily the classical conditioning of emotional responses, self-punitive behavior is largely maintained through instrumental conditioning.

The readiness with which conditioned anxiety responses are acquired may be partly a function of constitutional or acquired characteristics of the learner. There is some evidence that emotionally reactive and introverted people form conditioned anxiety responses more readily, and also extinguish more rapidly, than less emotionally reactive and more extroverted persons.

The persistence of deviant behavior can be readily accounted for by social-learning principles. Persistent antisocial behavior appears to result from intermittent positive reinforcement; moreover, the persistence of anxiety-motivated avoidance responses can be primarily attributed to the intermittent occurrence of reinforcement through anxiety reduction. There is thus no need to resort to the highly speculative explanatory concepts, for example, "repressed feelings of guilt" and "repetition compulsion," that have been favored by psychodynamic theorists.

In the final chapter of this book we shall be concerned with possible applications of social-learning principles in programs for effecting modifications of behavior. The chapter consequently includes a number of illustrations of how these principles can be used to foster prosocial response patterns, eliminate highly deviant and persistent behavior, and establish self-control.

CHAPTER FIVE

The Modification of Behavior

As Skinner (1956) has pointed out, an experimental analysis that improves man's power to predict human behavior also enables him more effectively to produce behavioral change. In the present chapter, therefore, we have indicated how social-learning principles may be applied to the modification of behavior in desired directions. While the majority of our examples consist of successful attempts to eliminate markedly deviant patterns of response, others are demonstrations of how learning principles may be utilized to modify the behavior of nondeviant children in ways that increase the probability of their gaining rewarding resources during the course of social interactions.

To some extent, most parents and educators from time to time deliberately or unwittingly employ the methods of modifying social responses that are briefly described in this chapter. Rarely, however, do they program or plan the dispensing of reinforcements—positive or negative—to children, or select carefully the models, real-life or symbolic, that children are permitted to observe. Moreover, as we have previously noted, the models adults present are often at variance with the precepts they endorse. In addition, they are apt to have acquired the widely popularized belief that generous amounts of affection are an adequate substitute for planned training and that the best way of producing prosocial behavior is through "unconditional love." If this principle were, in fact, applied in child training, all classes of behavior, prosocial or deviant, would be positively reinforced by demonstrations of affection, and the child could learn no discriminations. "Unconditional love" would thus produce children whose behavior was directionless, asocial, and completely unpredictable. According to this view, a child should receive love, understanding, and affection when he fails to apply himself in school, steals from a neighbor, refuses to eat the food prepared for him, severely injures a sibling, or masturbates openly in public. If all children received this kind of treatment, society would be chaotic. The faith in "unconditional love" exhibited by some child-training authorities is paralleled by the emphasis given in psychodynamic therapies to the therapist-client relationship, the role of which we shall consider in some detail in a later section of this chapter.

It is not our purpose to present a child-training manual or a comprehensive theory of psychotherapy; considerably more detailed accounts of behavioral approaches to therapy have, in fact, been provided elsewhere (Bandura, 1961, 1962c, 1964; Eysenck, 1960; Krasner, 1962; Shaw, 1961; Wolpe, 1958). Our aim is mainly to describe and illustrate the range of problems for which each available social-influence procedure appears to be appropriate and to bring together material from child-training and clinical studies in order to emphasize the wide applicability of the procedures that we advocate. In addition, in the latter part of this chapter we have commented briefly on a number of theoretical issues concerning which the social-learning approach to behavior modification differs from that of conventional psychodynamic theorists.

Methods of Producing Behavioral Change

EXTINCTION

A parent or therapist frequently encounters the problem of eliminating persistent troublesome behavior that may be maintained either by intermittent positive reinforcement or by repeated anxiety-reduction. The process of extinction may in such cases be utilized to eliminate the behavior, though the details of the procedure will vary according to the nature of the reinforcement by which the undesirable responses are maintained.

In the case of behavior that is maintained by positive reinforcement, extinction can sometimes be accomplished simply by withdrawing the reinforcer. A case reported by C. D. Williams (1959) demonstrates the use of this procedure for the elimination of aggressively demanding behavior in a twenty-one-month old boy. This child had been ill for the first eighteen months of his life and had required considerable attention and care. During this period, strong dependency habits were undoubtedly built up. When the child became well, his parents attempted to withdraw some of the attention they had previously given him. The child responded with intense efforts to secure reinforcement, which forced the parents to attend to him and thus to reinforce high-magnitude dependency responses that took the form of crying and demanding the presence and attention of the adults in the family, especially at bedtime. At this stage the child's responses became aversive to the parents, who proceeded to extinguish the behavior in the following manner. The child was put to bed in a leisurely and nonpunitive fashion; then, after the completion of bedtime routines, the parents closed the bedroom door and ignored the child's screaming and raging. There was an immediate sharp drop in the duration of tantrums, and the child's behavior was almost completely extinguished within a few days. However, at this point, the tantrum behavior was reinforced by attention from an aunt. A second series of extinction trials resulted in the complete elimination of the tantrums (Figure 5–1). Behavior of this kind, involving aversive control of parents, is liable, if intermittently reinforced, to generalize and to become increasingly troublesome. In the case described by Williams, the undesirable pattern was readily eliminated, and no side effects were apparent during the follow-up study, which extended over a period of two years.

Ayllon and Michael (1959) provide two illustrations of the use of extinction to eliminate undesirable responses of hospitalized psychotics. A female patient persistently entered the office of the nurses, who reinforced the behavior by attention in the form of leading or pushing her back into the ward. The nurses were instructed by the ward consultant not to respond to the patient's entries in any way whatsoever. There was then a gradual decline in the frequency of the response, which after a

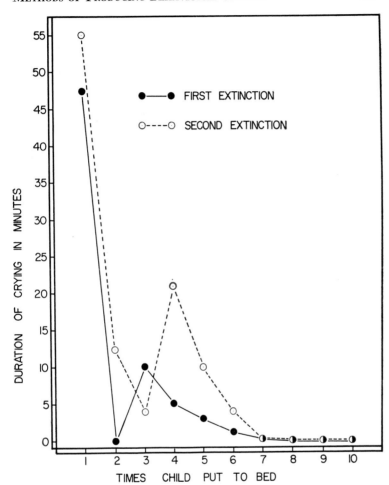

Fig. 5–1. *Length of crying in two extinction series as a function of successive occasions of being put to bed (from Williams, 1959)*

period of eight weeks was almost completely eliminated (Figure 5–2). A second case, which illustrates the role of reinforcement in the maintaining of psychotic behavior, as well as the procedure of extinction, involved the elimination of the psychotic talk of a female patient. While other patients responded negatively

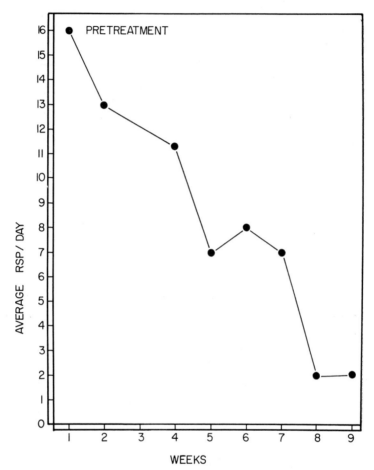

FIG. 5–2. *Extinction of the response "entering the nurses' office"*
(from Ayllon and Michael, 1959)

to this woman's accounts of her "delusions," the nurses from time
to time listened to her sympathetically, thus providing intermittent reinforcement for behavior that was at other times
punished or ignored. The nurses were instructed not to reinforce
psychotic talk and to reinforce only sensible talk. Although the
patient's psychotic responses had persisted over the previous

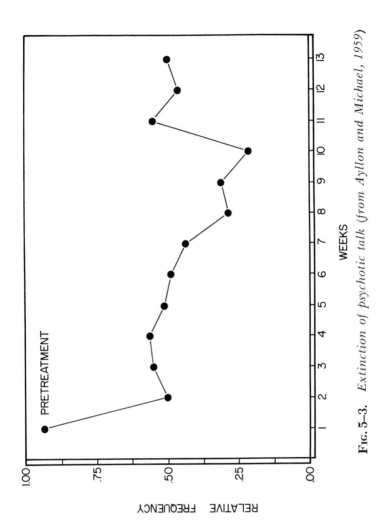

Fig. 5–3. *Extinction of psychotic talk (from Ayllon and Michael, 1959)*

three years, during a relatively brief period of treatment their frequency dropped (Figure 5–3). An increase in psychotic talk during the ninth week of treatment appeared to be due to reinforcement by a social worker, the effects of which generalized to the patient's interactions with other patients and the nurses. Other temporary increases were produced by reinforcements provided by visitors to the ward; even so, the psychotic talk remained less frequent than it had been at the commencement of treatment and therefore no longer elicited hostile and punitive reactions from the other patients.

       Extinction procedures can be effectively applied in cases where the performance of a socially deviant response serves to reduce fear and thus is almost inevitably reinforced. Herzberg (1941) treated a housewife who displayed severe anxiety and psychosomatic reactions whenever she went out alone and consequently refused to leave the house unless she was accompanied by another person or was transported in a taxi. The therapist first assigned her the task of walking by herself in a park, which provided considerably weaker anxiety-producing cues than walking alone in the street. These weaker anxiety reactions were readily extinguished, and she was then instructed to walk alone in a quiet street in her neighborhood. The task had to be undertaken a number of times before her anxiety extinguished and she could proceed to the next step of walking through a more frequented street. Gradual exposure to progressively more anxiety-provoking cues in this case led to extinction of anxiety, so that eventually the housewife could walk alone almost anywhere without any anxiety or psychosomatic reactions.

       Dollard and Miller (1950), on the basis of deductions consistent with psychoanalytic theory (Fenichel, 1939) made from Miller's (1948b) conflict paradigm, recommend that therapists should reduce the anxiety which motivates the avoidance response in an approach-avoidance conflict before attempting to instigate the approach response.

> The person with a severe neurosis who does reach the psychotherapist is a specially selected case with extremely strong avoidance tendencies. Therefore, trying to increase his motivation to approach goals will only increase his fear and conflict. This increase in misery will tend to drive him out of therapy.

> This is indeed what seems to happen. Therapists have found that the first thing to do is to concentrate on reducing the fears motivating avoidance (i.e., to analyze resistances) rather than to try to increase the motivation to approach the feared goal (p. 359).

This point of view implies that the client can be treated only in an interview situation and that no attempt can be made, during the first stages of therapy, to produce the desired behavior. However, Kimble and Kendall (1953) have demonstrated that avoidance responses can be rapidly extinguished if animals are exposed to a graduated series of aversive stimuli that progressively approximate the original intensity of the conditioned fear stimulus. The extinction procedure employed by Herzberg is of this kind. If the therapist had forced the client to expose herself to the most feared stimulus situation at the outset, she might have discontinued psychotherapy, as Dollard and Miller would predict. This does not, however, imply that the therapist must in such cases confine himself to reducing the client's fears by first "analyzing resistances."

Some experimental evidence that favorable outcomes of conventional interview therapy may be due to extinction of anxiety is provided by Dittes (1957a, 1957b), who found that permissive responses on the part of a therapist were followed by a decrease in avoidance responses and galvanic skin reactions accompanying clients' sex expressions.

Extinction may not always be the most effective and economical method of eliminating deviant behavior. In the case of behavior that is maintained by intermittent positive reinforcement, the withdrawal of reinforcers may even produce a temporary increase in the frequency and intensity of undesirable behavior, which may be forestalled or minimized by the procedure of strengthening incompatible prosocial responses. Similarly, fear-motivated behavior can perhaps be more readily modified by active counterconditioning.

COUNTERCONDITIONING

Counterconditioning involves eliciting in the presence of the fear-arousing stimuli responses that are incompatible with anxiety or fear reactions; through the classical conditioning of these incompatible responses to the fear-arousing cues, anxiety is eliminated or reduced. The first systematic application of this method was reported by Jones (1924b) in the treatment of a boy who exhibited severe phobic reactions to furry animals, fur objects, cotton, hair, and mechanical toys. Counterconditioning was achieved by feeding the boy in the presence of a caged rabbit, which was first placed at some distance from him in order not to disturb his eating. Each day the animal was brought nearer to the table at which the boy sat, eventually being released from the cage. During the final stage of treatment, the rabbit was placed on the table and even in the boy's lap. The boy's fear responses were in this way eliminated not only to the rabbit but also, through generalization, to all the furry and other objects he had previously feared.

Jones set up a situation in which the fear-arousing object was itself introduced into the therapy sessions and incompatible consummatory responses were employed in the counterconditioning procedure. In the treatment of most anxiety-motivated deviant behavior, it is difficult or impossible to introduce the fear-provoking objects into the therapy session itself. Wolpe (1958) has devised a method that greatly increases the range of cases that can be treated by counterconditioning procedures. On the basis of historical information, interview data, and psychological test responses, the therapist constructs a ranked list of stimuli to which the client reacts with increasing degrees of anxiety. When counterconditioning is based on relaxation procedures, the client is hypnotized and given relaxation suggestions. He is then asked to imagine a scene representing the weakest item in this hierarchy of anxiety-arousing stimuli and, if the relaxation is unimpaired, he is then asked to imagine the next item in the list and so on throughout the graduated series. In this way the strength of the anxiety-arousing cues is increased from session to session until the most potent phobic stimulus can be presented without disrupting the relaxation state. Consequently, relaxation responses eventually come to be attached to the original anxiety-arousing stimuli.

Lazarus (1960) describes a number of cases in which Wolpe's desensitization procedure has been used with children.

In one of these, a nine-year-old girl who suffered from severe separation anxiety, night terrors, and psychosomatic symptoms in the absence of her mother, necessitating her being excused from school, was given relaxation training. When fully relaxed, the child was asked to imagine that she would be separated from her mother for a period first of five minutes, then of fifteen minutes, and so on, up to one week. After five sessions, extending over a period of ten consecutive days, the child was sufficiently desensitized to return to school, her anxieties having been successfully eliminated. A fifteen-month follow-up revealed that this improvement was maintained.

Counterconditioning techniques have been effectively used for overcoming other specific fears that are often in evidence among nursery-school children, such as fears of the dark, of strange objects or persons, and of large animals (Jersild and Holmes, 1935b). An excellent example of a teacher's use of counterconditioning methods for overcoming a not uncommon fear is provided by Landreth and Read (1942). At sixteen months, a small boy developed a strong fear of having his hair cut, apparently on account of the similarity between the barber's instruments and those used by a doctor who had administered him painful "shots." The teacher, "Miss L.," devised a carefully planned strategy to eliminate this boy's fear.

> Having decided that the points of similarity between the two situations were probably white paint, nickel trim, instruments, and a man in a white coat, Miss L. laid her plans accordingly. She first paid a short visit to the barber. Next morning when she and her assistant, Miss W., called for the children in the school car, she had it stop at the post office. She got out and asked Bud to come in with her. He carried in her letters, dropped them in the box, waved to the postman, and got pleasantly back to the car. At school Miss L. and Miss W. fastened themselves into white uniforms stiff with starch and buttons in place of their customary flowered smocks. Some of the children commented on their change in appearance but Bud paid no attention. Ordinarily the very small children (there were three under two years) did not use the scissors. This morning scissors and colored paper were put on the table in

their room. While they were playing with these, Miss L. sat down beside them with some paper and dressmaking shears and did a little noisy cutting of her own, rousing as far as could be detected nothing more than mild interest on Bud's part. With the scissors there was a small hand hair-clipper, and when Bud and his friend Bill (also eighteen months) were turning it over she showed them how it worked, and made a few illustrative snicks at Bill's hair. Again, the situation aroused only mild interest.

When the children were playing in the sandbox, she brought out one of their white cotton sheets and asked Bill if he would like her to wrap him up. Bill was a docile child who was willing to stand anything in reason from a well-meaning and presumably kindly intentioned adult. Also he was temporarily sated with sand, so out he came. Miss L. wrapped him with a flourish, smiled, and sat him on a box.

"Look, Miss W.," she said, "here's Bill all wrapped up." Miss W.'s smile and interest acknowledged that wrapping up was a very engaging procedure. Miss L. asked Bud if he would like a turn. He came out, was wrapped up and perched on the box for Miss W.'s inspection. Again no signs of fear. Bud was unenthusiastic but pleasantly cooperative.

That noon as the children were taken home, the car stopped outside the barber's shop. Miss L. got out as she had in the morning and asked Bud to come in with her, assuming that they would make a pleasant two-minute call. Bud put his foot out, looked up, saw where the car had stopped, drew his foot in again, and said, "No—no," and started to cry.

This was a distinct set-back after the smoothness of the morning program, but Miss L. said with reassuring hopefulness, "All right, tomorrow," and went in to the barber, who said this was just what he expected. However, he came out of his doorway, and as she got in the car Miss W. said to Bud, "Wouldn't you like to say 'Bye-bye' to the barber?" As the only sort of dealings, social or tonsorial, Bud wanted to have with the barber was to say "Bye-bye" and then "Bye-bye" rapidly, the car drove off with cordial mutual farewells.

Next day was the second day. As the car drove by in the morning, the barber was in his shop window. He waved and the children waved. At noon, going home, the car stopped again. This time Miss L. asked Bill first if he would like to come in with her, and then held out her hand for Bud. At the door his fingers tightened a little, and she lifted him up judging that the situation viewed from an altitude of five-foot-six might look a little more acceptable than it had from his original two-foot-six. Inside the door he gave one look at the barber, clutched Miss L. tightly around the neck, and said, "Bye-bye." The barber and Miss L., however, stood their ground.

He said it was a nice day. She remarked on his large wall clock. Bud had a distinct weakness for clockwork, and she moved a little nearer. "Your clock says 'tick-tock,'" she said to the barber. He said, yes, he'd noticed that too. They exchanged laudatory remarks about the excellence of his mirrors and chairs and again Miss L. suggested that Bud say "Bye-bye." He revived immediately and they left the shop to a chorus of "Bye-bye."

Next day was the third day and a school holiday. Bud's grandmother was to arrive the next morning. Miss L. and Miss W. called first for Bill, who was on the most cordial terms with the barber, and then for Bud.

This time they crossed the doorway without incident. The barber was busy shaving a man in the window and paid no attention to them. In the chair next to the shaving operations was Bud's paternal uncle, almost completely screened by the morning newspaper. As Miss L. surmised then and learned later, he was on hand so that if the worst came to the worst the hair would be removed if not the fear.

His presence was a reminder that though inside there was still quite a way to go. Miss L. sat down in one of the chairs and said, "Miss W., this chair turns around!" and turned around once for her benefit. Miss W. said, "What a nice ride you're having. Wouldn't Bill like one too?" Bill climbed up and he and Miss L. revolved before Miss W.'s appreciative gaze.

Miss L. suggested that Miss W. would also like a ride, and she admitted that she had been craving such an opportunity. As she seated herself, she suggested that of course Bud would want a ride too, and helped him up onto her knee.

As they were successfully completing the second revolution the barber came over. He had been watching their technique and said, "My chairs ride up and down too." While Miss W. and Miss L. registered appropriate appreciation for the versatility of his furnishings, he deftly raised and lowered the chair and adjusted it to working height, and then reached for his cloth. "Let me," said Miss L., and, smiling on Bud, she told him she was going to wrap him up. Miss W. suggested that if he turned around on her knee he would be able to watch himself in her pocket-book mirror.

From then on, the hair-cutting proceeded smoothly and pleasantly and without interruption save from the paternal uncle who came out of ambush to advise that Bill, in undertaking an exploratory survey of the barber's cabinet, was "fixing" to drink some of his hair tonic. Bill was immediately "unfixed," and the now sleek-headed Bud returned to his home with a suggestion that his mother have him call casually at the barber's sometime before his next haircut (pp. 139–141).[1]

It has been sometimes claimed that behavioral therapy is effective only with limited and circumscribed forms of avoidance responses having a very specific noninterpersonal etiology. However, as numerous cases described by Wolpe (1958), Lazarus (1960), and Lazarus and Rachman (1957) indicate, generalized disturbances of interpersonal relationships, which traditional psychotherapists invariably attribute to complex intrapsychic conflicts, have also been successfully treated by "reciprocal inhibition."

MacKay and Laverty (1963) have demonstrated how counterconditioning methods serve to modify clients' emotional responses. Clients' galvanic skin responses were recorded during the course of reciprocal-inhibition treatment. A gradual reduction in the number of spontaneous fluctuations in these responses occurred during the course of treatment. However, small increases in the number of fluctuations were observed whenever new steps in the stimulus hierarchy were introduced or the clients reported that they were feeling anxious.

The counterconditioning method has been used to eliminate strong approach reactions as well as to reduce anxiety-motivated deviant behavior. Raymond (1956) used nausea as the aversion experience in the treatment of a client who presented a fetish for handbags and perambulators, which brought him in frequent contact with the law. This patient repeatedly smeared mucus on ladies' handbags and destroyed perambulators by running into them with his motorcycle, behavior that psychodynamic therapists would undoubtedly attribute to deep-seated sexual conflicts and repressions requiring prolonged depth analysis. However, the client had undergone psychoanalytic treatment and had become fully aware of the origin and sexual significance of his behavior without manifesting any improvement. Raymond's treatment consisted of showing the patient a collection of handbags, perambulators, and colored illustrations just before the onset of nausea produced by injections of apomorphine. Raymond reported that the fetish was in this manner successfully eliminated after the conditioning procedures had been repeated every two hours, day and night, for a week, followed by additional sessions eight days, and six months, later. Moreover, this treatment was accompanied by a vast improvement in the client's social relationships, promotion to a more responsible job, and satisfactory sexual intercourse without the aid of fetish fantasies, which had been necessary cues for sexual arousal before the patient had undergone treatment.

In most instances aversive conditioning has been accomplished through the association of a nauseating or painful stimulus with the deviant pattern of behavior. However, Lazarus (1958) has demonstrated that a psychologically induced aversive experience will bring about results comparable to those produced by the actual presentation of noxious stimuli. An architect whose compulsiveness interfered with his productivity was placed under hypnosis and asked to imagine that he was compulsively and unnecessarily checking his work. It was then suggested to him that he was suddenly becoming anxious. In contrast, relaxation was induced while the client imagined himself carrying out necessary steps in his work and turning to other assignments after these steps had been completed. By thus associating anxiety with the performance of compulsive acts, while at the same time encouraging him to feel relaxed when avoiding compulsive behavior, Lazarus was able to eliminate unnecessary rituals and to considerably increase the client's work productivity.

Aversive conditioning involves the presentation of noxious stimuli and in this respect is analogous to punishment. However, when it is one feature of a psychotherapeutic procedure with clients who voluntarily come for treatment, it is probably viewed by the client as an unpleasant, though necessary, aspect of treatment, comparable to surgery, dentistry, and other painful routines in physical medicine, and not as an interpersonal assault. Consequently, the aversive stimulation presented in this context may have fewer of the side effects that are invariably noted when it is used solely for the purpose of suppressing an undesirable pattern of social behavior.

Positive reinforcement

Operant-conditioning techniques and other methods that rely primarily on the dispensing of rewards are especially appropriate in cases in which there are behavioral deficits. Such procedures have been most frequently used for shaping and maintaining reality-oriented behavior in adult psychotics. King, Armitage, and Tilton (1960) effectively utilized the method of operant conditioning, through successive approximations, to increase the social responsiveness of severely withdrawn schizophrenic patients. Working on the assumption that motor responses could be more easily elicited from these patients than verbal or interpersonal behavior, they first set their subjects the task of depressing a lever, which brought rewards in the form of candy, cigarettes, pictures, and verbal approval. In successive phases, the complexity of the task was increased, and verbal and interpersonal responses were elicited and rewarded. In later phases, rewards were dispensed only when the patients communicated and cooperated with the therapist and other patients in order to solve psychomotor problems of some complexity. Three other groups of patients, matched with the operant-therapy group for severity of illness and length of hospitalization, concurrently participated in verbal therapy, recreational therapy, or received no treatment. "The operant-interpersonal method was more effective than all the control methods in promoting clinical improvement, based both on ward observations and interview assessment" (p. 286). After fifteen weeks' therapy, patients treated by this method displayed more verbal behavior, less resistance to therapy, more interest in occupational therapy, and decreased enuresis, and were more likely to be ready for transfer to another ward, than patients in the other three groups. It is interesting also that patients who received a traditional form of verbal therapy were more verbally withdrawn at the end of treatment than at the beginning.

Ferster (1961), who regards autistic behavior in children as the outcome of parental extinction of social behavior through insufficient reinforcement, has been successful in establishing substantial amounts of reality-oriented responses in autistic children through the dispensing of rewards in an automatically controlled environment. The children have to learn to make increasingly complex discriminative responses in order to obtain coins, which can then be used to operate a wide variety of reinforcement devices within the room (Ferster and DeMyer, 1961, 1962). While this investigation has so far been confined to the developing of relatively simple impersonal responses, it leaves no doubt that autistic children have no serious learning deficits and that they are capable of responding to generalized conditioned reinforcers. Comparable findings have been reported with regressed adult psychotics (Lindsley, 1956; Skinner, Solomon, and Lindsley, 1954).

Most psychotherapeutic procedures have been developed for use with oversocialized, inhibited patients and are unsuitable for undersocialized, aggressive personalities (Bandura and Walters, 1959; Schmideberg, 1959). Delinquents, for example, are usually coerced into treatment by legal and other agencies, with the implication that they will thereby acquire prosocial patterns of behavior which they may have little interest in adopting or may actually devaluate. Moreover, with these patients the therapist's main task is not to reduce anxieties but to eliminate antisocial patterns by inducing incompatible prosocial behavior. In such cases, methods of reward may be the most appropriate and effective means of treatment. Slack and Schwitzgebel (Schwitzgebel, 1960; Slack, 1960; Slack and Schwitzgebel, 1960) set up a "laboratory" in an old store in a delinquency area, made contact with "hard-core" delinquents, and paid them to serve as "subjects." The boys were rewarded with refreshments, candy, and cigarettes, as well as money, for attendance at the laboratory. Through the method of immediate reinforcement, regular attendance and cooperation were readily attained, and in time the therapists were able to substitute social rewards for the material reinforcers that had been necessary in order to bring the boys into treatment. The boys were given opportunities to participate in a variety of activities and to acquire skills that could be utilized to gain rewarding resources in legitimate ways. Their "no-work" ethic began to change and, according to the therapists, their gang and delinquency activities considerably decreased.

The effects of positively reinforcing a wide range of responses that have relevance for therapy have been demonstrated in laboratory studies with children. An increase in assertive-aggressive behavior in social situations, sometimes an objective in the treatment of overinhibited children, has been shown to result from positive reinforcement of aggressive responses in a noninterpersonal context (Walters and Brown, 1963). Other studies indicate that dependency (Nelsen, 1960), cooperative responses (Azrin and Lindsley, 1956), and achievement behavior (Keister, 1938; Updegraff and Keister, 1937) may also be modified through the dispensing of rewards. Generally speaking, the possibility of using planned scheduling of reinforcements for the maintenance of socially desirable behavior in everyday settings has not as yet been fully explored, though Lindsley (1958) has advocated the use of intermittent grading in high schools as a means of improving the achievement motivation of students, while at the same time reducing the routine work of teachers.

In a study by Azrin and Lindsley (1956), children were formed into two-member teams. During a "game," pairs of children were seated at the opposite sides of a table with a stylus and three holes in front of each child. After the experimenter had ascertained that the children knew how to insert their styli into the three holes in front of them, he merely told them that from time to time a jelly bean would fall into a cup placed midway between them and then left them alone in the room. During the experimenter's absence, the children were rewarded with a jelly bean whenever they inserted the styli in opposite holes within a fraction of a second of one another. All teams learned to cooperate, even without specific instructions, within the first ten minutes of play. Leader-follower relations developed, yet the children in eight of the ten teams almost immediately began to share the candy they received. Equitable division of the candy occurred in the remaining two teams after some initial verbal dispute. Following the reinforcement period, no more candies were dispensed, and the cooperative behavior then gradually extinguished. Undoubtedly, this learning process would have been much slower if the task had been more complex or if a larger number of children had been required to coordinate their activities. In such cases, however, cooperation can often be readily achieved and maintained by combining an initial demonstration with the dispensing of rewards. The study nevertheless illustrates how behavior requiring some degree of self-control may be developed and maintained by means of positive reinforcements.

The procedure of positive reinforcement has also been extensively applied in studies of verbal conditioning (Krasner, 1958; Salzinger, 1959). It has been repeatedly demonstrated that this procedure increases the probability of occurrence of classes of verbal responses for which reinforcers are dispensed and that their frequency decreases when reinforcement is withdrawn. Verbal-conditioning experiments generally involve social situations in which the relative effectiveness of different types of reinforcers and the influence of subject and experimenter characteristics on verbal behavior can be investigated. Some of these studies have utilized free-interview or discrimination-learning situations, in which classes of responses that traditional therapists are interested in modifying through psychotherapeutic treatment are positively reinforced. It has been demonstrated that hostile verbalizations (Buss and Durkee, 1958; Weide, 1959), emotional words (Krasner, Ullman, Weiss, and Collins, 1961; Pisoni and Salzinger, 1960), positive self-reference statements (Adams and Hoffman, 1960; Rogers, 1960), negative self-reference statements (Rogers, 1960), hallucinations (Dobie, 1959), confiding responses

(Cairns, 1961), neurotic verbalizations (Everstine and Bendig, 1960), early childhood memories (Quay, 1959), expression of opinion or beliefs (Verplanck, 1955; Walters and Karal, 1960), and affiliative statements (Walters and Henning, 1962) can be readily influenced by the dispensing and withholding of positive reinforcers. Considering the number of interviews that patients receive when undergoing traditional forms of therapy, it is not surprising to find marked changes in their verbal behavior. However, so far there is only very scanty evidence (Lövaas, 1961b) that these changes influence social responses other than verbal ones to any great extent.

SOCIAL IMITATION

In spite of the prevalence of imitative learning in the acquisition of social behavior, it has rarely been deliberately and systematically used in the treatment of behavior disorders. Its incidental use is, however, apparent in many descriptions of traditional and social-learning treatment procedures with children in which the therapist demonstrates the desired responses in play and other interpersonal situations. The potential influence of models is also tacitly recognized in the efforts that are made to set up therapy groups in which the behavior of each participant will favorably influence that of the others.

The influence of modeling is evident in a film (Slavson, 1950a) depicting Slavson's group-therapy procedures (1950b, 1952). The manner in which the therapist elicits and controls behavior through the provision of models is particularly evident in the initial session. For example, when the time for ending the session approaches, the therapist simply takes up a brush and begins to clean up the bench. The more conforming boys in the group follow his example and also begin to tidy up the room. They, in turn, provide models for the more aggressive youngsters, who a little later follow suit. When the therapist goes to the food cupboard, the conforming boys readily respond to his invitation to eat. The aggressive boys first hold back, but when they see the conforming models rewarded by approval and interest, as well as food, they too join the therapist. Finally, merely by putting on his jacket, the therapist provides the final modeling cue for terminating the session.

Jones (1924a) explicitly used the method of social imitation in overcoming children's fears. Fear-reduction was produced by having other children behave in a nonanxious manner in the presence of the avoided object. Jones also demonstrated that a fear could be acquired through social imitation, a finding which suggests that exposure to models who suffer, are punished, or exhibit fear in the course of performing a deviant act may be an effective means of producing conditioned fear reactions, which may be lacking in underinhibited children. Laboratory studies by Bandura (1962b), Bandura, Ross, and Ross (1963b), and Walters, Leat, and Mezei (1963) provide support for the belief that such treatment could, in some cases, be successfully employed for transmitting behavioral control. Provision of a prosocial rewarded model is, nevertheless, a preferable form of treatment. Seeing a model punished for selecting illegitimate means for securing a goal object toward which the observer is strongly oriented may deter the latter from himself selecting these means. However, if the observer has no available alternative prosocial response, he is likely to utilize a different type of illegitimate behavior in order to secure the highly desired goal object. This is essentially the same phenomenon that we discussed in Chapter 1, and refer to later in this chapter, in evaluating the psychodynamic concept of symptom substitution.

In traditional institutional settings, the treatment of patients, such as psychotics, who exhibit gross behavior distortions is usually confined to the dispensing of medications, "occupational therapy" in the form of carrying out hospital routines, participation in recreational activities, group therapy in which the patients are often encouraged to reconstruct their social-learning histories, and occasional individual interviews in which they talk about the interpersonal problems they have encountered both before and during institutionalization. Moreover, the least socially responsive patients are customarily assigned to special wards where they receive only medication and where they mutually extinguish one another's repertory of social behavior. Pilot work with extremely regressed and inhibited chronic schizophrenics, who rarely spoke in the ward setting, has indicated that modeling procedures may be capable of quickly reinstating verbal behavior. Staples, Wilson, and Walters (1963) selected, on the basis of attendants' ratings, a number of patients whose verbal behavior was at a minimum level. Two series of slides, depicting landscapes, animals, and other stimuli, were presented to these patients, who were instructed to talk about what they saw in the pictures. Some patients were exposed to a talkative model, who freely described and reflected on the visually presented material between the exposures of the first and second series of slides. These patients showed a marked increase in verbal responsiveness from the first to the second trials, in comparison to patients who listened only to music between the two series of presentations. Preliminary results suggested that exposure to a model was much more effective in increasing verbal productivity than was the dispensing of cigarettes as rewards for speaking. Generalization of this modeling effect to the ward setting is now under investigation.

Social imitation can be equally effective in the treatment of overinhibited children. The traditional method of overcoming inhibitions has been to provide a permissive atmosphere and wait for desired social behavior to emerge. This procedure is, however, probably minimally effective and highly time-consuming. An illustration of how the eliciting of previously inhibited behavior may be facilitated through modeling is provided in a case treated by Levy (1939). An exceedingly anxious girl was, among other things, afraid of getting her hands dirty. She saw finger paint, wanted to play with it, but was reluctant to get it on her fingers. The therapist played with it himself, and the girl followed suit, at first cautiously but later with complete abandon. Laboratory demonstrations of the disinhibition and shaping of aggressive behavior by social models (Bandura, 1962a) indicate that even children who show high aggression inhibition and are passive and unassertive in their social behavior will exhibit aggressive responses following exposure to aggressive models. This effect is probably not confined to children (Walters and Llewellyn Thomas, 1963).

Therapy based on the principle of social imitation may concentrate on shaping prosocial responses that are incompatible with socially undesirable behavior. This, in effect, was the procedure employed by Chittenden (1942) in modifying children's responses to frustration. After selection on the basis of their responses in five play sessions involving two children and a single toy, highly aggressive children either were assigned to training or served as untrained controls. During training, the experimental group observed a series of "plays," in each of which dolls, representing preschool children, exhibited both an aggressive and a prosocial cooperative frustration reaction under circumstances that the children were likely to encounter in everyday situations. Following the presentation of each pair of alternative responses, the experimenter and the child together discussed the social situation presented in the play and jointly reached a decision concerning the appropriateness of the social responses made by the dolls. In test trials, interspersed among the training situations, the children were required to provide their own solution to an interpersonal conflict involving two dolls. In comparison to the control children, those who had received training showed a decrease in aggressive dominating responses from the initial to the final test session. Moreover, the gain in self-control was manifested also in the social behavior of the children, assessed from nursery-school observations made before training, immediately after training, and a month later. This study is noteworthy for its demonstration that *observational discrimination learning,* coupled with reasoning, fostered cooperative behavior which was incompatible with the initially prepotent aggressive responses, thus leading to their inhibition. In this study, reasoning consisted in part of drawing attention to the adverse consequences of antisocial behavior to both participants in the symbolic social situations. The outcome therefore provides an excellent example of vicarious learning through observation of response consequences to a model.

A study by Anderson (1937) illustrates the manner in which peer models may be used to modify the social behavior of children. Anderson paired relatively assertive orphanage children with one another and also with relatively nonassertive children from the same institution in a series of play situations. Generally speaking, children modified their behavior in the direction of that presented by their companion.

A combination of modeling and social-reinforcement procedures was used by Jack (1934) and Page (1936) to increase the assertiveness of relatively inhibited children. During a series of training sessions, inhibited children were provided with demonstrations of how to cope with tasks of varying degrees of difficulty and were praised for good performance. As a result, they became increasingly less inhibited; moreover, the effects of training appeared to generalize to interactions with peers both in semistructured testing sessions and in free-play situations within the nursery-school setting.

During the course of traditional therapy the client is exposed to many incidental cues involving the therapist's values, attitudes, and patterns of behavior. They are incidental only because they are usually considered secondary or irrelevant to the task of resolving the client's problems. Nevertheless, some of the changes observed in the client's behavior may result, not so much from the intentional interaction between the client and the therapist, as from active learning by the client of the therapist's attitudes and values that the therapist has not directly attempted to teach. Some evidence of this effect is apparent from a study by Rosenthal (1955), who found that in spite of the usual precautions taken by therapists to avoid imposing their values on their clients, the clients who were judged as showing the greatest improvement changed their moral values in the areas of sex, aggression, and authority in the direction of the values of their therapists, whereas clients who were unimproved became less like their therapists. Indeed, if the model adopts a consistent moral orientation, this is likely to be adopted and maintained by the client (Bandura and McDonald, 1963), especially if the client has developed a strong tie to the therapist, a condition that is strongly emphasized in most forms of psychotherapy.

DISCRIMINATION LEARNING

In most theories of psychotherapy, discrimination learning, believed to be accomplished through the gaining of awareness or insight, is strongly emphasized (Dollard and Miller, 1950; Fenichel, 1941; Rogers, 1951; Sullivan, 1953). Almost inevitably, the therapist focuses on producing temporal discriminations involving the client's becoming aware that he has overgeneralized habits learned in childhood in interactions with his parents and is currently responding to authority figures and sex objects in ways that are inappropriate. Once the client gains "insight" into the sources of his inappropriate behavior and realizes that he has in some respects transferred into adult life habits acquired during childhood, it is assumed that his difficulties will begin to disappear and voluntarily guided, discriminative behavior will replace the "unconscious" overgeneralized responses. The widespread acceptance of this view is evident in the almost exclusive reliance placed on interview procedures and interpretative or labeling techniques in all forms of traditional therapy.

Laboratory studies do not clearly support the assumption that awareness plays a crucial role in the establishing of discriminations (Adams, 1957; Eriksen, 1958; Razran, 1949). Eriksen (1956, 1957) presented subjects with a series of stimuli and recorded nonverbal responses (autonomic or motor) as well as verbal responses to the stimulus items. The nonverbal responses were largely independent of the subject's verbalizations and permitted discriminations to occur in the absence of correct verbal labeling. Evidence that discriminations acquired on the basis of nonverbal responses may be sometimes more precise than those based on available verbal labels has led Eriksen (1958) to conclude that language may be an inadequate vehicle for reflecting the discriminations that people are capable of making. Although the tasks employed in his studies were relatively simple, Eriksen's findings cast considerable doubt on the traditional viewpoint that verbalization or labeling is invariably a crucial operation in discrimination learning. This does not, however, imply that the concept of "unconscious" is required in order to explain the occurrence of learning or performance in the absence of verbal labels. There is, for example, no evidence that learning or performance occurs when the relevant nonverbal cues are entirely below threshold level (Eriksen, 1958, 1960) or that delayed recall of previously experienced stimulus situations is due to anything other than an initial absence of cues capable of eliciting the responses in question.

Should one wish to produce discriminative social learning, the best procedure would undoubtedly be to set up actual or symbolic social situations and repeatedly reward desired responses to these stimuli, while punishing undesirable responses or letting these go unrewarded. Freund (1960) used a procedure of a somewhat similar kind for treating clients with well-established homosexual patterns. These clients were administered an emetic mixture by subcutaneous injection, and while the noxious effects of the injection were being experienced, were shown slides of dressed and undressed males. In the second phase of the treatment, the client saw films of nude and semi-nude females approximately seven hours after the administration to testosterone. Freund reported considerable success with those clients who had come voluntarily for treatment. Had the situation been set up in such a way that the clients received a reward instead of merely being sexually stimulated and had reward and punishment sessions been interspersed over a fairly lengthy period of time, Freund's successes might have been far more numerous.

The case of the compulsive architect treated by Lazarus (1958), which was presented as an example of counter-conditioning, also illustrates a discrimination-training procedure. In addition to arousing anxiety concerning the client's compulsive acts, the therapist induced relaxation responses while the patient imagined necessary and productive stages of his work. In the same way, the extinction procedure utilized by Ayllon and Michael (1959) for changing the verbal behavior of the patient who persisted in psychotic talk involved also reward of sensible talk and thus may be regarded as an example of therapy through discrimination learning.

Some Theoretical Issues

THE RELATIONSHIP FACTOR IN PSYCHOTHERAPY

Traditional approaches to the modification of deviant behavior have largely been determined by therapists' affiliations with particular schools, with little consideration of the type of problem presented by the client. For example, orthodox Freudians set out to resolve Oedipal conflicts, Adlerians to alter compensatory power strivings, Rankians to resolve separation anxieties, Rogerians to reduce discrepancies between the real and ideal self, and existentionalists to achieve awareness of self-consciousness. School affiliations not only determine the range of techniques of psychotherapy that a given therapist will employ but even define the client's central conflict or disturbance that the techniques of the school are designed to resolve.

These techniques and goals tend to be preselected with little reference to the diverse forms of behavior deviations that are exhibited by different classes of clients. Since the type of treatment that a given client receives is fortuitously determined by the school affiliation of the therapist, it is highly probable that the therapeutic procedures will in many cases fail to match the problems presented by the client. Consequently, it is not surprising that therapy is often terminated on the initiative of the client after participation in only a few interviews and that the probability of improvement for those who remain is relatively low (Bandura, 1964; Eysenck, 1952a; Levitt, 1957).

According to traditional schools, the main factor promoting therapeutic change is the therapist-patient relationship, in which the therapist should exhibit permissiveness and unconditional positive regard for the client and suspend all adverse judgments. Indeed, therapists who do not identify with a particular school usually rely heavily on such relationship factors, combined with a limited range of intervention techniques governed by trial-and-error experience. It is confidently believed that the relationship, once established, leads to changes that alleviate the patient's initial condition, no matter what this may be. Failure to find differences among schools in the extent to which their methods lead to improvement has been taken as evidence that, given a favorable therapeutic atmosphere, all kinds of techniques are equally capable of remedial effects and that the relationship, not the method, is of primary importance in producing therapeutic success. This point of view implies that any outcome—for example, an *increase* or *decrease* in aggression, dependency, or self-control—can result from the establishment of the relationship in conjunction with almost any technique that the therapist has acquired through his training. It also implies that no significant permanent changes in social behavior can occur if the therapeutic relationship is not firmly established. These assumptions are open to serious question, as the results of research studies indicate. For example, children, and even adults, can acquire quite complex patterns of social behavior by observing a model with whom no prior relationship has been developed (Bandura, 1962a); moreover, it is possible to train children in noninterpersonal situations to make aggressive and other responses of potential social significance, which will then generalize to social interactions (Walters and Brown, 1963).

　　　　Relationship factors may be helpful when the client manifests fairly generalized inhibition, though there are more effective ways of producing disinhibition than through interview methods. On the other hand, clients who lack effective self-control systems are not likely to benefit from unconditional permissiveness, which may instead lead to the inadvertent strengthening of deviant behavior. As a matter of fact, strict adherence to the point of view that therapists should be unconditionally accepting is virtually impossible, as Murray (1956) has demonstrated in a detailed analysis of a case of nondirective therapy. Mild approval and disapproval, silence and nonresponsiveness, avoidance reactions, restatement of clients' expressions, instigation, and topic transition are used by almost every therapist to channel clients' responses (Deutsch and Murphy, 1955; Finesinger, 1948; Gill, Newman and Redlich, 1954; Wolberg, 1954) and have proved useful categories for analyzing therapist-patient interactions in controlled research studies (Bandura, Lipsher, and Miller, 1960; Goldman, 1961; Winder, Ahmad, Bandura, and Rau, 1962). Even if unconditional permissiveness or acceptance were possible, it would be no more meaningful as a possible antecedent of change in psychotherapy than is unconditional love in the social development of children.

　　　　While the establishment of a positive relationship may enhance the value of the therapist as a model and a dispenser of positive and negative reinforcers, such a relationship is not always most readily brought about by a totally acceptant attitude on the part of the therapist. Moreover, granted that a therapist-client relationship in which the client has high esteem and regard for the therapist is maximally effective, modifications of behavior that occur through client-therapist interactions are undoubtedly due to inadvertent applications of learning principles by the therapist, who is usually unaware that he is employing these principles to modify his clients' behavior and may in fact explicitly deny that his behavior determines that of the client. Obviously, the outcomes would be much more predictable and readily attained if the therapist were to apply learning principles in a deliberate and carefully programmed manner, instead of depending on the fortuitous occurrence of client-therapist response sequences that are essential for specified changes to ensue. Indeed, necessary learning contingencies must occur, regardless of the school to which the therapist belongs and of the esoteric rituals that contribute a great deal to the identification of loyalties but which may be irrelevant to the learning process.

TREATMENT OBJECTIVES

Almost without exception, traditional approaches to psychotherapy consider the achievement of "insight" to be an indispensable precondition of the production of reliable and enduring behavioral change. For this reason, the development of "insight" is a primary objective to which most therapists' strategies are devoted. These strategies include the eliciting and maintaining of the client's verbalizations, the channeling of their content into areas that are assumed by the therapist to be loci of emotional conflicts, the timing of interpretations varying in depth, and the handling of the client's resistances. Although the achievement of insight is considered an essential step in the process and supposedly results in a wide variety of beneficial effects, insight has never been clearly defined nor has the manner in which it mediates behavioral change ever been specified or demonstrated. In view of the fact that the client's gain in self-awareness is usually inferred from evidence that he has acquired habits of labeling social-stimulus events, past and present causal sequences, and his own responses and mediating reactions in terms of the theoretical predilections and language of his therapist, it seems probable that the so-called insight is an outcome of learning rather than an indispensable step in treatment. Indeed, in some traditional theoretical expositions of the psychotherapeutic process, insight is regarded as the outcome of change and not as its cause (Alexander and French, 1946).

In contrast to psychodynamic theories, a social-learning approach to psychotherapy necessarily regards the modification of social behavior, rather than of mediating agents and complexes, as the primary objective and maintains that this outcome must be achieved by planned application of social-learning principles for the production of specific forms of behavioral change. In social-learning therapy, the client may be expected to play a major role in determining the direction and nature of the change that is to be produced, though if he is unsure or vague about the outcome he desires, the therapist may need to specify possible alternative changes and their probable consequences to the client before the latter can participate in the selection of a desired treatment outcome. Whereas psychodynamic therapies set up predetermined goals and use preselected and relatively unvarying techniques for producing change, social-learning therapy chooses from a variety of techniques those that seem most appropriate for achieving the objectives that are set in any particular case. The techniques used in the latter type of therapy are, however, all derived from a set of social-learning principles, support for which has been found in carefully controlled research. Willingness to be flexible and to use diverse therapeutic methods does not therefore represent eclecticism. Indeed, learning experiences can combine in a variety of ways to give rise to varying forms of deviant behavior, which may be identified by psychodynamic therapists as Oedipal or compensatory power strivings, separation anxiety, or discrepancies between the real and ideal self.

The social-learning therapist consequently refrains from assuming that the histories of his clients are so uniform in certain vital respects that all disorders are necessarily a manifestation of a single constellation of social-learning experiences, which are thought, in psychodynamic theories, to be present in every case and to be capable of generating a whole host of "symptomatic" behavior patterns. From his point of view, in some families the interactions between parents and child may be such as to produce a so-called Oedipal attachment, though the conditions that could lead to the acquisition of an attachment of this kind probably occur relatively infrequently. Moreover, he regards the diversity of deviant behavior as due to widely varying antecedent conditions producing different consequences, though always in accordance with a set of learning principles that can both serve to explain the acquisition of behavior patterns and be utilized to guide either therapeutic or child-training practices.

As we pointed out in Chapter 1, there is no reason to believe that the direct modification of deviant behavior inevitably results in the appearance of new substitute deviant responses. For example, although, according to psychoanalytic theory, a fetish is regarded as a defense against homosexuality and its removal as creating a danger of substitute homosexual behavior, in the case treated by Raymond with a counterconditioning technique the client not only discarded his fetishistic behavior but also began to participate in satisfactory heterosexual relations. Indeed, in none of the reported cases of behavioristic therapy is there evidence that the removal of one deviant response leads to the emergence of a new one; either the client's behavior changes in the selected direction or, in unsuccessfully treated cases, the original deviant behavior persists (Yates, 1958). Of course, the use of extinction and aversive counterconditioning methods for eliminating deviant responses does not alone ensure that prosocial responses will ensue. Consequently, in any treatment program it is important to include procedures designed to elicit, strengthen, and maintain prosocial responses that are incompatible with the deviant behavior the therapist is attempting to eliminate.

CATHARSIS

As used by Aristotle, catharsis referred to the purging of the passions or sufferings of spectators through vicarious participation in the suffering of a tragic hero as this is portrayed on the stage. In contrast, in psychoanalytic writings (Breuer and Freud, 1955 [1895]; Fenichel, 1945; Freud, 1924a [1914]) catharsis referred to the "liberation of affect" through the re-experiencing of blocked or inhibited emotions, which is supposedly an essential phase in the resolution of unconscious conflicts. In applying this principle to aggressive behavior, Dollard *et al.* (1939) state that "the occurrence of any act of aggression is assumed to reduce the instigation to aggression" (p. 50). So stated, the catharsis hypothesis is not essentially different from the psychoanalytic displacement and projection hypotheses, since all three imply that in some way one aggressive response can serve as a substitute for another in reducing an instinct, urge, or drive of aggression. Whereas the Aristotelian principle of catharsis emphasized the *vicarious* experience of emotional reactions exhibited by social models, the Freudian (and neo-Hullian) hypothesis focused primarily on permitting persons *themselves* to express emotional behavior in fantasy, play, or real life.

Although Freud (1924a [1914]) discarded the belief that cathartic discharge of emotion could by itself serve to produce lasting therapeutic change, nevertheless free expression of affect is widely accepted as an important ingredient in therapy (Menninger, 1948) and in the management of behavior problems (Baruch, 1949). Guided by the catharsis hypothesis, parents and mental-health workers frequently provide hyperaggressive children with opportunities to participate in aggressive recreational activities, encourage them to view aggressive televised programs, and subtly or openly instigate the expression of aggressive behavior in psychotherapeutic playrooms, through the provision of aggressive play materials, in the hope of reducing aggressive impulses that are presumably maintaining the troublesome behavior.

The hydraulic model of personality, the interpretation of deviant behavior as disguised forms of energy discharge, and the therapeutic effects of cathartic drainage are dramatically portrayed in a popular book on discipline widely circulated among parents and teachers.

Another possibility is that the pressure of the unwelcome feelings becomes too great and springs a leak, in the same way that boiling water may spring a leak in a kettle if the steam it generates has no proper channel for release.

Meanwhile, our child is still trying to hide the unwanted feelings from sight. If they were to leak out in their original form, he would recognize them. But this he must not do, so he finds a device for letting them reappear in such a way that he won't recognize them. He *masks* them. He *lets them out in disguises only* and he keeps them disguised in two ways. By changing their form. And by changing their target (Baruch, 1949, p. 35).

When pus accumulates and forms an abscess, the abscess must be opened and drained. If it isn't done the infection spreads. In the end, it may destroy the individual. Just so with feelings. The "badness" must come out. The hurts and fears and anger must be released and drained. Otherwise, these too may destroy the individual (pp. 38–39).

Many times this is the way it happens. When enough of the hurt and fear and anger have been released, they diminish. They stop pushing from within. They stop springing out in compulsive ways, disguising what lies underneath so that it can not be dealt with. After enough of the "badness" has come out, the "goodness" appears (p. 44).

For, curious as it may seem, this has been observed many times over:

When unwanted NEGATIVE FEELINGS
have been emptied out sufficiently
then—
warm and good POSITIVE FEELINGS
flow in

When muddy water, which has dammed up, drains out from a pool, then fresh, clear water can flow in. So it is with these feelings. But the change does not happen quickly. It often takes a long time (p. 45).[2]

---

[2] Reprinted by permission from Dorothy W. Baruch, *New ways in discipline*. New York, McGraw-Hill, 1949.

While the encouragement of expressive behavior may be of value in the treatment of overinhibited children, this procedure is quite evidently inappropriate for overexpressive clients. Indeed, consistent with the social-learning theory presented in this book, evidence from controlled research studies of children indicates that far from producing a cathartic reduction of aggression, direct or vicarious participation in aggressive activities within a permissive setting maintains the behavior at its original level and may actually increase it.

Kenny (1952) tested the hypothesis that participation in doll-play sessions of the "release-therapy" type would lead to a reduction of aggression. The aggressive responses of young children to the first half of a story-completion test formed the pretest measure. Two "therapy" sessions in which physical and verbal aggression were fostered provided the fifteen children in the experimental group with opportunities for catharsis. Control children were instead given two sessions of nonaggressive play. Following the play sessions, the second half of the story-completion test, which supplied the posttest measure of aggression, was administered to both experimental and control subjects. The control group showed a significantly greater decrease in aggression than the experimental therapy group, a finding that provides no support at all for the catharsis hypothesis.

Feshbach (1956) used both high-aggressive and low-aggressive children in a study of the extent to which play with aggressive toys modified aggression in school situations. Children under the aggressive-toy condition listened to stories and records with aggressive themes and played with objects, such as guns, selected to stimulate the expression of aggression. Another group of children participated in play sessions in which nonaggressive themes and objects were introduced, while a third group followed their regular classroom schedule. Pretest-to-posttest changes in aggression, based on ratings made by observers, failed to reveal any significant decrease in aggression in the group that had been encouraged to exhibit aggressive behavior in play. This study, like Kenny's, therefore fails to supply evidence for cathartic drive-reduction.

Studies in which children have vicariously participated in the aggressive activities of models have invariably shown
that this kind of participation results in an increase in aggression,
provided the model's behavior brings rewarding consequences or
goes unpunished (Bandura, Ross, and Ross, 1961, 1963a, 1963b;
Lövaas, 1961a; Mussen and Rutherford, 1961; Siegel, 1956; Walters, Leat, and Mezei, 1963; Walters and Llewellyn Thomas,
1963; Walters, Llewellyn Thomas, and Acker, 1962). If, in treating
hyperaggressive children, a therapist were to use procedures based
on the catharsis energy-reduction principle, it is highly probable
that the behavior the treatment was designed to eliminate would
be inadvertently reinforced.

Findings from adult studies are less clear-cut than
those obtained with children. Generally speaking, participation,
direct or vicarious, by nonangered adults seems to increase the
incidence of subsequent aggression, both in the same and different stimulus situations (Buss, 1961; Walters and Llewellyn
Thomas, 1963). Feshbach (1955, 1961) has reported that adults
who have initially been angered and then are permitted to express aggression through fantasy or are exposed to aggressive
models show a subsequent decrease in aggression. In contrast,
Kahn (1960) reported an increase in aggression in angered subjects, following a display of anger in a social situation in which
hostile remarks were permitted and accepted. This study is
especially relevant since the subjects' expressions of anger were
addressed to a sympathetic "physician" in an interview, thus
making the interaction similar to many that occur in therapy
sessions. Moreover, the effects reported by Feshbach may reflect
guilt-motivated inhibition following open aggressive displays
(Berkowitz, 1958, 1962), while similar outcomes in other studies
are certainly not interpretable as due to the reduction of anger
(Rosenbaum and deCharms, 1960; Thibaut and Coules, 1952).

The persistence of the "drainage" hypothesis, in
spite of criticism (Allport, 1954; McClelland, 1956) and largely
negative experimental findings, reflects the resilience of the hydraulic model of personality popularized through psychoanalytic
writings. Its application is nevertheless by no means consistent.

While therapists, educators, and parents are frequently heard to defend the exposure of children to violent television and movie material, as well as children's participation in highly aggressive body-contact sports, on the grounds that aggressive impulses will thereby be reduced, few adults in North American society are likely to argue that vicarious participation in sexual activities will bring about a decrease in the observers' sexual responses. Indeed, considerable care is taken to exclude adolescents from "restricted admission" movies, presumably on the grounds that such exposure may generate sexual excitation and premature imitative sexual behavior.

IMPLEMENTATION OF PSYCHOTHERAPY PROCEDURES

A considerable amount of heated discussion and argument has centered around the qualifications necessary for a therapist, and there has been much concern about the discrepancy between the available number of qualified practitioners and the increasing demand for psychotherapeutic services. Difficulties in resolving these problems are in part a function of professional jealousies, economic rivalries, and status considerations. In part, too, they are a function of the esoteric psychodynamic models of psychotherapy, which have generated prolonged methods of training in rituals, yet at the same time give no clear instructions concerning the manner in which behavioral change may be achieved.

Perhaps greater progress would be made in resolving these problems if more attention were devoted to establishing the principles whereby behavioral changes may be brought about and to utilizing the large pool of competent persons who are already available to apply those of the principles that have been convincingly established. In fact, some of the illustrative cases cited in this chapter indicate that nurses, teachers, and parents can serve as effective therapeutic agents under the guidance of well-informed behavioral scientists. Indeed, the primary tasks of the professionally qualified clinician should be to develop effective therapeutic procedures based on social-learning principles, to train available persons in the application of these principles, and set up programs which these persons may implement under his guidance and direction. In this way, more people would receive more help than they do under current professional practices.

References

Adams, J. K.   Laboratory studies of behavior without awareness. *Psychol. Bull.*, 1957, *54*, 383–405.

Adams, J. S. & Hoffman, B.   The frequency of self-reference statements as a function of generalized reinforcement. *J. abnorm. soc. Psychol.*, 1960, *60*, 384–389.

Aldrich, C. A., Sung, C., & Knop, C.   The crying of newly born babies: II. The individual phase. *J. Pediat.*, 1945, *27*, 89–96.

Alexander, F., & French, T. M. (Eds.).   *Psychoanalytic therapy.* New York: Ronald, 1946.

Alexander, F., & Staub, H.   *The criminal, the judge, and the public.* New York: Free Press, 1956.

Allinsmith, Beverly B.   Expressive styles: II. Directness with which anger is expressed. In D. R. Miller & G. E. Swanson (Eds.).   *Inner conflict and defense.* New York: Holt, 1960, pp. 315–336.

Allinsmith, W.   The learning of moral standards. In D. R. Miller & G. E. Swanson (Eds.).   *Inner conflict and defense.* New York: Holt, 1960, pp. 141–176.

Allport, F. H.   *Social psychology.* Cambridge, Mass.: Riverside Press, 1924.

Allport, G. W.   *The nature of prejudice.* Reading, Mass.: Addison-Wesley, 1954.

Amsel, A.   A three-factor theory of inhibition: An addition to Hull's two-factor theory. Paper read at the Annual Meeting of the Southern Soc. for Philosophy and Psychology, Roanoke, Va., 1951.

Amsel, A.   The role of frustrative nonreward in noncontinuous reward situations. *Psychol. Bull.*, 1958, *55*, 102–119.

Amsel, A.   Frustrative nonreward in partial reinforcement and discrimination learning: Some recent history and a theoretical extension. *Psychol. Rev.*, 1962, *69*, 306–328.

Anastasi, Anne, & Foley, J. P., Jr. *Differential psychology* (rev. ed.). New York: Macmillan, 1949.

Anderson, H. H. Domination and integration in the social behavior of young children in an experimental play situation. *Genet. Psychol. Monogr.*, 1937, *19*, 341–408.

Andry, R. G. *Delinquency and parental pathology.* London: Methuen, 1960.

Appel, M. H. Aggressive behavior of nursery school children and adult procedures in dealing with such behavior. *J. exp. Educ.*, 1942, *11*, 185–199.

Aronfreed, J. The origins of self-criticism. *Psychol. Rev.*, 1963, in press (a).

Aronfreed, J. The effects of experimental socialization paradigms upon two moral responses to transgression. *J. abnorm. soc. Psychol.*, 1963, in press (b).

Aronfreed, J., Cutlick, R. A., & Fagan, S. A. Cognitive structure, punishment, and nurturance in the experimental induction of self-criticism. *Child Develpm.*, 1963, in press.

Aronfreed, J., & Reber, A. The internalization of social control through punishment. Unpublished manuscript, Univer. of Pennsylvania, 1963.

Aronson, E., & Carlsmith, J. M. The effect of severity of threat on the devaluation of forbidden behavior. *J. abnorm. soc. Psychol.*, 1963, in press.

Asch, S. E. The doctrine of suggestion, prestige, and imitation in social psychology. *Psychol. Rev.*, 1948, *55*, 250–276.

Ausubel, D. P. Relationships between shame and guilt in the socializing process. *Psychol. Rev.*, 1955, *62*, 378–390.

Ayllon, T., & Michael, J. The psychiatric nurse as a behavioral engineer. *J. exp. anal. Behav.*, 1959, *2*, 323–334.

Azrin, N. H. Punishment and recovery during fixed-ratio performance. *J. exp. anal. Behav.*, 1959, *2*, 301–305.

Azrin, N. H. Effects of punishment intensity during variable-interval reinforcement. *J. exp. anal. Behav.*, 1960, *3*, 123–142.

Azrin, N. H., & Lindsley, O. R. The reinforcement of cooperation between children. *J. abnorm. soc. Psychol.*, 1956, *52*, 100–102.

Bach, G. R. Young children's play fantasies. *Psychol. Monogr.*, 1945, *59*, No. 2 (Whole No. 272).

Bach, G. R.   Father-fantasies and father-typing in father-separated children. *Child Develpm.*, 1946, *17*, 63–80.

Baer, D. M.   A technique of social reinforcement for the study of child behavior: Behavior avoiding reinforcement withdrawal. *Child Develpm.*, 1962, *33*, 847–858.

Baldwin, A. L., Kalhorn, Joan, & Breeze, Fay H.   Patterns of parent behavior. *Psychol. Monogr.*, 1945, *58*, No. 3 (Whole No. 268).

Bandura, A.   Relationship of family patterns to child behavior disorders. Progress Report, U.S.P.H. Research Grant M-1734. Stanford Univer., 1960.

Bandura, A.   Psychotherapy as a learning process. *Psychol. Bull.*, 1961, *58*, 143–159.

Bandura, A.   Social learning through imitation. In M. R. Jones (Ed.). *Nebraska symposium on motivation.* Lincoln: Univer. of Nebraska Press, 1962, pp. 211–269 (a).

Bandura, A.   The influence of rewarding and punishing consequences to the model on the acquisition and performance of imitative responses. Unpublished manuscript, Stanford Univer., 1962 (b).

Bandura, A.   Punishment revisited. *J. consult. Psychol.*, 1962, *26*, 298–301(c).

Bandura, A.   *Behavioristic psychotherapy.* New York: Holt, 1964, in press.

Bandura, A., & Huston, Aletha. C.   Identification as a process of incidental learning. *J. abnorm. soc. Psychol.*, 1961, *63*, 311–318.

Bandura, A., & Kupers, Carol J.   The transmission of patterns of self-reinforcement through modeling. *J. abnorm. soc. Psychol.*, in press.

Bandura, A., Lipsher, D., & Miller, Paula E.   Psychotherapists' approach-avoidance reactions to patients' expressions of hostility. *J. consult. Psychol.*, 1960, *24*, 1–8.

Bandura, A., & McDonald, F. J.   The influence of social reinforcement and the behavior of models in shaping children's moral judgments. *J. abnorm. soc. Psychol.*, 1963, in press.

Bandura, A., Ross, Dorothea, & Ross, Shiela A.   Transmission of aggression through imitation of aggressive models. *J. abnorm. soc. Psychol.*, 1961, *63*, 575–582.

Bandura, A., Ross, Dorothea, & Ross, Shiela A. Imitation of film-mediated aggressive models. *J. abnorm. soc. Psychol.*, 1963, *66*, 3–11 (a).

Bandura, A., Ross, Dorothea, & Ross, Shiela A. Vicarious reinforcement and imitation. *J. abnorm. soc. Psychol.*, 1963, in press (b).

Bandura, A., Ross, Dorothea, & Ross, Shiela A. A comparative test of the status envy, social power, and the secondary-reinforcement theories of identificatory learning. *J. abnorm. soc. Psychol.*, 1963, in press (c).

Bandura, A., & Walters, R. H. *Adolescent aggression*. New York: Ronald, 1959.

Bandura, A., & Walters, R. H. Aggression. In *Child psychology: The sixty-second yearbook of the National Society for the Study of Education*, Part 1. Chicago: The National Society for the Study of Education, 1963, pp. 364–415.

Banks, R. K. Extinction of avoidance behavior as a function of variations in the frequency of a stimulus paired with shock. Unpublished doctoral dissertation, Univer. of Toronto, 1963.

Banks, R. K., & Walters, R. H. Prior reinforcement as a determinant of visual recognition thresholds. *Percept. mot. Skills*, 1959, *9*, 51–54.

Barker, R. G., Dembo, Tamara, & Lewin, K. Frustration and regression: An experiment with young children. *Univer. Ia. Stud. Child Welf.*, 1941, *18* (Whole No. 386).

Barker, R. G., Wright, Beatrice A., & Gonick, M. R. Adjustment to physical handicap and illness: A survey of the social psychology of physique and disability. *Soc. Sci. Res. Counc. Bull.*, 1946, No. 55.

Baruch, Dorothy W. *New ways in discipline*. New York: McGraw-Hill, 1949.

Bateson, G. *The Naven*. Stanford: Stanford Univer. Press, 1936.

Bateson, G. The frustration-aggression hypothesis and culture. *Psychol. Rev.*, 1941, *48*, 350–355.

Bayroff, A. G., & Lard, K. E. Experimental social behavior of animals: III. Imitational learning of white rats. *J. comp. Psychol.*, 1944, *37*, 165–171.

Beller, E. K. Dependency and independence in young children. *J. genet. Psychol.*, 1955, *87*, 25–35.

Beller, E. K., & Haeberle, Ann W.   Dependency and the frustration-aggression hypothesis. Unpublished manuscript, Child
  Develpm. Center, New York City, 1961 (a).

Beller, E. K., & Haeberle, Ann W.   Dependency and the frustration-aggression hypothesis: II. Paper read at the Annual
  Meeting of the Eastern Psychol. Assoc., Philadelphia, 1961
  (b).

Benedict, Ruth.   *The chrysanthemum and the sword: Patterns
  of Japanese culture.* Boston: Houghton Mifflin, 1946.

Berg, I. A., & Bass, B. M. (Eds.).   *Conformity and deviation.*
  New York: Harper, 1961.

Berger, S. M.   Conditioning through vicarious instigation.
  Psychol. Rev., 1962, *69,* 450–466.

Berkowitz, L.   The expression and reduction of hostility. *Psychol. Bull.,* 1958, *55,* 257–283.

Berkowitz, L.   *Aggression: A social psychological analysis.* New
  York: McGraw-Hill, 1962.

Berkowitz, L., Corwin, R., & Hieronimus, M.   Film violence
  and subsequent aggressive tendencies. Unpublished manuscript, Univer. of Wisconsin, 1962.

Berkowitz, L., & Rawlings, Edna.   An examination of the effects
  of movie scenes of justified and unjustified aggression
  upon the expression of hostility by angered audience members. Unpublished manuscript, Univer. of Wisconsin,
  1962.

Bettelheim, B.   Individual and mass behavior in extreme situations. *J. abnorm. soc. Psychol.,* 1943, *38,* 417–452.

Biderman, A. D., & Zimmer, H. (Eds.).   *The manipulation of
  human behavior.* New York: Wiley, 1961.

Bijou, S. W., & Baer, D. M.   The laboratory-experimental study
  of child behavior. In P. H. Mussen (Ed.).   *Handbook of
  research methods in child development.* New York: Wiley,
  1960, pp. 140–197.

Bijou, S. W., & Baer, D. M.   *Child development:* Vol. 1. *A systematic and empirical theory.* New York: Appleton, 1961.

Binder, A., McConnell, D., & Sjoholm, Nancy A.   Verbal conditioning as a function of experimenter characteristics. *J.
  abnorm. soc. Psychol.,* 1957, *55,* 309–314.

Bindra, D.   *Motivation: A systematic reinterpretation.* New
  York: Ronald, 1959.

Bitterman, M. E., & Kniffin, C. W.   Manifest anxiety and "perceptual defense." *J. abnorm. soc. Psychol.*, 1953, *48*, 248–252.

Blake, R. R., Mouton, Jane S., & Hain, J. D.   Social forces in petition signing. *Southwestern soc. sci. Quart.*, 1956, *36*, 385–390.

Blake, R. R., Rosenbaum, M. E., & Duryea, R.   Gift-giving as a function of group standards. *Hum. Rel.*, 1955, *8*, 61–73.

Block, J.   A study of affective responsiveness in a lie-detection series. *J. abnorm. soc. Psychol.*, 1957, *55*, 11–15.

Block, Jeanne, & Martin, B.   Predicting the behavior of children under frustration. *J. abnorm. soc. Psychol.*, 1955, *51*, 281–285.

Bowlby, J.   *Forty-four juvenile thieves: Their characters and home life.* London: Ballière, 1946.

Bowlby, J.   *Maternal care and mental health.* Geneva: World Health Organization, 1952 (WHO Monogr. Series, No. 2).

Brackbill, Yvonne.   Extinction of the smiling response in infants as a function of reinforcement schedules. *Child Develpm.*, 1958, *29*, 115–124.

Brehm, J. W., & Cohen, A. R.   *Explorations in cognitive dissonance.* New York: Wiley, 1962.

Breuer, J., & Freud, S.   Studies on hysteria. In J. Strachey (Ed.). *Standard edition.* Vol. II. London: Hogarth, 1955 (First German ed., 1895).

Brogden, H. E.   A factor analysis of 40 character traits. In H. Woodrow (Ed.).   Studies in quantitative psychology. *Psychol. Monogr.*, 1940, *52*, No. 3 (Whole No. 234), pp. 39–55.

Bromberg, W.   *Crime and the mind: An outline of psychiatric criminology.* Philadelphia: Lippincott, 1948.

Brown, D. G.   Sex role preference in young children. *Psychol. Monogr.*, 1956, *70*, No. 14 (Whole No. 421).

Brown, J. S.   Gradients of approach and avoidance responses and their relation to level of motivation. *J. comp. physiol. Psychol.*, 1948, *41*, 450–465.

Brown, J. S.   *The motivation of behavior.* New York: McGraw-Hill, 1961.

Brown, J. S., & Farber, I. E.   Emotions conceptualized as intervening variables—with suggestions toward a theory of frustration. *Psychol. Bull.*, 1951, *48*, 465–495.

Brown, J. S., & Jacobs, A.   The role of fear in the motivation and acquisition of responses. *J. exp. Psychol.*, 1949, *39*, 747–759.

Brown, R. W.   Mass phenomena. In G. Lindzey (Ed.).   *Handbook of social psychology.* Vol. 2. Reading, Mass.: Addison-Wesley, 1954, pp. 833–876.

Bugelski, B. R.   *The psychology of learning.* New York: Holt, 1956.

Burnstein, E., Stotland, E., & Zander, A.   Similarity to a model and self-evaluation. *J. abnorm. soc. Psychol.*, 1961, *62*, 257–264.

Burt, C.   *The young delinquent.*   London: London Univer. Press, 1925.

Burton, R. V.   Some factors related to resistance to temptation in four-year-old children. Unpublished doctoral dissertation, Harvard Univer., 1959.

Burton, R.V.   The generality of honesty reconsidered. *Psychol. Bull.*, 1963, in press.

Burton, R. V., Maccoby, Eleanor E., and Allinsmith, W. Antecedents of resistance to temptation in four-year-old children. *Child Develpm.*, 1961, *32*, 689–710.

Buss, A. H.   *The psychology of aggression.* New York: Wiley, 1961.

Buss, A. H., & Durkee, Ann.   Conditioning of hostile verbalizations in a situation resembling a clinical interview. *J. consult. Psychol.*, 1958, *22*, 415–418.

Buss, A. H., & Foliart, R.   Role-playing aggression and the catharsis hypothesis. Unpublished research, 1958. (Cited in A. H. Buss.   *The psychology of aggression.* New York, Wiley, 1961.)

Cairns, R. B.   The influence of dependency inhibition on the effectiveness of social reinforcers. *J. Pers.*, 1961, *29*, 466–488.

Cairns, R. B.   Antecedents of social reinforcer effectiveness. Unpublished manuscript, Indiana Univer., 1962.

Cairns, R. B., & Lewis, M.   Dependency and the reinforcement value of a verbal stimulus. *J. consult. Psychol.*, 1962, *26*, 1–8.

Cameron, N.   *The psychology of behavior disorders: A biosocial interpretation.* Boston: Houghton Mifflin, 1947.

Cameron, N., & Magaret, Ann. *Behavior pathology*. Boston: Houghton Mifflin, 1951.

Carlson, N. J., & Black, A. H.   Traumatic avoidance learning: Note on the effect of response prevention during extinction. *Psychol. Rep.*, 1959, *5*, 409–412.

Cattell, R. B.   *The description and measurement of personality*. New York: Harcourt, 1946.

Child, I. L., Potter, E. H., & Levine, Estelle M.   Children's textbooks and personality development: An exploration in the social psychology of education. *Psychol. Monogr.*, 1946, *60*, No. 3 (Whole No. 279).

Chittenden, Gertrude E.   An experimental study in measuring and modifying assertive behavior in young children. *Monogr. Soc. Res. Child Develpm.*, 1942, *7*, No. 1 (Serial No. 31).

Chorost, S. B.   Parental child-rearing attitudes and their correlates in adolescent hostility. *Genet. Psychol. Monogr.*, 1962, *66*, 49–90.

Church, R. M.   Transmission of learned behavior between rats. *J. abnorm. soc. Psychol.*, 1957, *54*, 163–165.

Clark, R. A., & Sensibar, Minda R.   The relationship between symbolic and manifest projections of sexuality with some incidental correlates. *J. abnorm. soc. Psychol.*, 1955, *50*, 327–334.

Cleckley, H.   *The mask of sanity* (3rd ed.). St. Louis: Mosby, 1955.

Cloward, R. A., & Ohlin, L. E.   *Delinquency and opportunity: A theory of delinquent gangs*. New York: Free Press, 1960.

Cohen, A. K.   *Delinquent boys: The culture of the gang*. New York: Free Press, 1955.

Cowan, P. A., & Walters, R. H.   Studies of reinforcement of aggression. I. Effects of scheduling. *Child Develpm.*, 1963, *34*, 543–552.

Cowen, E. L., & Beier, E. G.   Threat-expectancy, word frequencies, and perceptual prerecognition hypotheses. *J. abnorm. soc. Psychol.*, 1954, *49*, 178–182.

Cowen, E. L., Landes, J., & Schaet, D. E.   The effect of mild frustration on the expression of prejudiced attitudes. *J. abnorm. soc. Psychol.*, 1959, *58*, 33–38.

Cox, F. N.   Some effects of frustration: I. A methodological programme. *Austral. J. Psychol.*, 1952, *4*, 94–106.

Cox, F. N. An assessment of children's attitudes toward parent figures. *Child Develpm.*, 1962, *33*, 821–830.

Crandall, V. J. Achievement. In *Child psychology: The sixty-second yearbook of the National Society for the Study of Education,* Part. 1. Chicago: The National Society for the Study of Education, 1963, pp. 416–459.

Crandall, V. J., Katkovsky, W., & Preston, Anne. Motivational and ability determinants of young children's intellectual achievement behaviors. *Child Develpm.*, 1962, *33*, 643–662.

Crandall, V. J., Preston, Anne, & Rabson, Alice. Maternal reactions and the development of independence and achievement behavior in young children. *Child Develpm.*, 1960, *31*, 243–251.

Crandall, Virginia C. The reinforcement effects of adult reactions and non-reactions on children's achievement expectations. *Child Develpm.*, 1963, in press.

Crandall, Virginia C., Good, Suzanne, & Crandall, V. J. The reinforcement effects of adult reactions and non-reactions on children's achievement expectations: A replication study. *Child Develpm.*, 1964, in press.

Crawford, M. P., & Spence, K. W. Observational learning of discrimination problems by chimpanzees. *J. comp. Psychol.*, 1939, *27*, 133–147.

Davis, A. Child training and social class. In R. G. Barker, J. S. Kounin, & H. F. Wright (Eds.). *Child behavior and development.* New York: McGraw-Hill, 1943, pp. 605–619.

Davis, A., & Havighurst, R. J. *The father of the man: How your child gets his personality.* Boston: Houghton Mifflin, 1947.

Davitz, J. R. The effects of previous training on postfrustrative behavior. *J. abnorm. soc. Psychol.*, 1952, *47*, 309–315.

deCharms, R., & Rosenbaum, M. E. Status variables and matching behavior. *J. Pers.*, 1960, *28*, 492–502.

Deese, J. *The psychology of learning.* New York: McGraw-Hill, 1952.

Deutsch, F., & Murphy, W. F. *The clinical interview.* New York: International Universities, 1955.

Dinsmoor, J. A. Punishment: I. The avoidance hypothesis. *Psychol. Rev.*, 1954, *61*, 34–46.

Dinsmoor, J. A. Studies of abnormal behavior in animals. In R. H. Waters, D. A. Rethlingshafer, & W. E. Caldwell.

Principles of comparative psychology. New York: McGraw-Hill, 1960, pp. 289–324.

Dittes, J. E. Extinction during psychotherapy of GSR accompanying "embarrassing" statements. *J. abnorm. soc. Psychol.,* 1957, *54,* 187–191 (a).

Dittes, J. E. Galvanic skin response as a measure of patient's reaction to therapist's permissiveness. *J. abnorm. soc. Psychol.,* 1957, *55,* 295–303 (b).

Dobie, Shirley I. Operant conditioning of verbal and hallucinatory responses with nonverbal reinforcement. Paper read at the Annual Meeting of the Midwestern Psychol. Assoc., Chicago, 1959.

Dollard, J., Doob, L. W., Miller, N. E., Mowrer, O. H., & Sears, R. R. *Frustration and aggression.* New Haven: Yale Univer. Press, 1939.

Dollard, J., & Miller, N. E. *Personality and psychotherapy.* New York: McGraw-Hill, 1950.

Duncker, K. Experimental modification of children's food preferences through social suggestion. *J. abnorm. soc. Psychol.,* 1938, *33,* 489–507.

Durkin, Dolores. The specificity of children's moral judgments. *J. genet. Psychol.,* 1961, *98,* 3–13.

Easterbrook, J. A. The effect of emotion on cue utilization and the organization of behavior. *Psychol. Rev.,* 1959, *66,* 183–201.

Eaton, J. W., & Weil, R. J. *Culture and mental disorders.* New York: Free Press, 1955.

Ehrmann, W. *Premarital dating behavior.* New York: Holt, 1959.

Eisenberg, L. The fathers of autistic children. *Amer. J. Orthopsychiat.,* 1957, *27,* 715–724.

Elkin, F., & Westley, W. A. The myth of adolescent culture. *Amer. sociol. Rev.,* 1955, *20,* 680–684.

Epstein, R., & Liverant, S. Verbal conditioning and sex-role identification in children. *Child Develpm.,* 1963, *34,* 99–106.

Eriksen, C. W. An experimental analysis of subception. *Amer. J. Psychol.,* 1956, *69,* 625–634.

Eriksen, C. W. Prediction from and interaction among multiple concurrent discriminative responses. *J. exp. Psychol.,* 1957, *53,* 353–358.

Eriksen, C. W. Unconscious processes. In M. R. Jones (Ed.). *Nebraska symposium on motivation.* Lincoln, Ne.: Univer. of Nebraska Press, 1958, pp. 169–227.

Eriksen, C. W. Discrimination and learning without awareness: A methodological survey and evaluation. *Psychol. Rev.,* 1960, *67,* 279–300.

Erikson, E. H. *Childhood and society.* New York: Norton, 1950.

Eron, L., Walder, L. O., Toigo, R., & Lefkowitz, M. M. The relationship between social class and parental punishment for aggression and of both to an independent measure of child aggression. *Child Develpm.,* 1963, in press.

Estes, W. K. An experimental study of punishment. *Psychol. Monogr.,* 1944, *57,* No. 3 (Whole No. 263).

Estes, W. K., & Skinner, B. F. Some quantitative properties of anxiety. *J. exp. Psychol.,* 1941, *29,* 390–400.

Everstine, L., & Bendig, A. W. Conditioning neurotic verbalizations. *Amer. Psychologist,* 1960, *15,* 430 (Abstract).

Eysenck, H. J. *Dimensions of personality.* London: Routledge, 1947.

Eysenck, H. J. The effects of psychotherapy: An evaluation. *J. consult. Psychol.,* 1952, *16,* 319–324 (a).

Eysenck, H. J. *The scientific study of personality.* London: Routledge, 1952 (b).

Eysenck, H. J. *The dynamics of anxiety and hysteria.* New York: Praeger, 1957.

Eysenck, H. J. The development of moral values in children: VII. The contribution of learning theory. *Brit. J. Educ. Psychol.,* 1959, *29,* 11–21.

Eysenck, H. J. (Ed.). *Behavior therapy and the neuroses.* New York: Pergamon, 1960.

Fenichel, O. *Problems of psychoanalytic technique.* Albany, N.Y.: Psychoanalytic Quarterly, 1941.

Fenichel, O. *The psychoanalytic theory of neurosis.* New York: Norton, 1945.

Ferguson, P. E. The influence of isolation, anxiety, and dependency on reinforcer effectiveness. Unpublished M.A. thesis, Univer. of Toronto, 1961.

Ferster, C. B. Withdrawal of positive reinforcement as punishment. *Sci.,* 1957, *126,* 509.

Ferster, C. B. Control of behavior in chimpanzees and pigeons by time out from positive reinforcement. *Psychol. Monogr.*, 1958, *72*, No. 8 (Whole No. 461).

Ferster, C. B. Positive reinforcement and behavioral deficits in autistic children. *Child Develpm.*, 1961, *32*, 437–456.

Ferster, C. B., & deMyer, Marian K. The development of performances in autistic children in an antomatically controlled environment. *J. chronic Dis.*, 1961, *13*, 312–345.

Ferster, C. B., & deMyer, Marian K. A method for the experimental analysis of the behavior of autistic children. *Amer. J. Orthopsychiat.*, 1962, *32*, 89–98.

Ferster, C. B., & Skinner, B. F. *Schedules of reinforcement.* New York: Appleton, 1957.

Feshbach, S. The drive-reducing function of fantasy behavior. *J. abnorm. soc. Psychol.*, 1955, *50*, 3–11.

Feshbach, S. The catharsis hypothesis and some consequences of interaction with aggressive and neutral play objects. *J. Pers.*, 1956, *24*, 449–462.

Feshbach, S. The stimulating versus cathartic effects of a vicarious aggressive activity. *J. abnorm. soc. Psychol.*, 1961, *63*, 381–385.

Festinger, L., Riecken, H. W., & Schachter, S. *When prophecy fails.* Minneapolis: Univer. of Minnesota Press, 1956.

Finesinger, J. E. Psychiatric interviewing. *Amer. J. Psychiat.*, 1948, *105*, 187–195.

Fisher, A. E. The effects of differential early treatment on the social and exploratory behavior of puppies. Unpublished doctoral dissertation, Penn. State Univer., 1955.

Fleck, S. Family dynamics and origin of schizophrenia. *Psychosomat. Med.*, 1960, *22*, 333–344.

Ford, C. S., & Beach, F. A. *Patterns of sexual behavior.* New York: Harper, 1951.

Franks, C. M. Conditioning and abnormal behavior. In H. J. Eysenck (Ed.). *Handbook of abnormal psychology.* New York: Basic, 1961, pp. 457–487.

Freed, A., Chandler, P. J., Blake, R. R., & Mouton, Jane S. Stimulus and background factors in sign violation. *J. Pers.*, 1955, *23*, 499.

Freeman, J. T. Set or perceptual defense? *J. exp. Psychol.*, 1954, *48*, 283–288.

French, J. R. P., Jr., Morrison, H. W., & Levinger, G. Coercive power and forces affecting conformity. *J. abnorm. soc. Psychol.*, 1960, *61*, 93–101.

French, J. R. P., Jr., & Raven, B.   The bases of power. In D. Cartwright (Ed.).   *Studies in social power.* Ann Arbor, Mich.: Inst. Soc. Res., 1959, pp. 150–167.

Freud, Anna.   *The ego and the mechanisms of defense.* New York: International Universities, 1946 (First German ed., 1936).

Freud, Anna, & Burlingam, Dorothy T.   *Infants without families.* New York: International Universities, 1944.

Freud, S.   *A general introduction to psychoanalysis.* New York: Liveright, 1920 (First German ed., 1917).

Freud, S.   On the history of the psychoanalytic movement. In E. Jones (Ed.).   *Collected papers.* Vol. I. London: Hogarth, 1924, pp. 284–359. (First published in the *Jahrbuch der Psychoanalyse,* Bd. VI, 1914.)

Freud, S.   The dynamics of transference. In E. Jones (Ed.). *Collected papers.* Vol. II. London: Hogarth, 1924, pp. 312–322. (First published in *Zentralblatt,* Bd. II, 1912.)

Freud, S.   Mourning and melancholia. In E. Jones (Ed.).   *Collected papers.* Vol. IV. London: Hogarth, 1925, pp. 152–170. (First published in *Zeitschrift,* Bd., IV, 1917).

Freud, S.   Some character types met in psychoanalytic work. In E. Jones (Ed.).   *Collected papers.* Vol. IV. London: Hogarth, 1925, pp. 318–344. (First published in *Imago,* Bd. IV, 1915.)

Freud, S.   *An outline of psychoanalysis.* New York: Norton, 1949. (First published in *Internationale Zeitschrift für psychoanalyse und Imago,* Bd. XXV, 1940.)

Freund, K.   Some problems in the treatment of homosexuality. In H. J. Eysenck (Ed.).   *Behavior therapy and the neuroses.* New York: Pergamon, 1960, pp. 312–326.

Friedlander, Kate.   *The psychoanalytic approach to juvenile delinquency.* London: Routledge, 1947.

Gallagher, J. R., & Harris, H. I.   *Emotional problems of adolescents.* New York: Oxford Univer. Press, 1958.

Gelfand, Donna M.   The influence of self-esteem on rate of verbal conditioning and social matching behavior. *J. abnorm. soc. Psychol.*, 1962, *65*, 259–265.

Gerard, H. B., & Rabbie, J. M.   Fear and social comparison. *J. abnorm. soc. Psychol.*, 1961, *62*, 586–592.

Gesell, A., & Ilg, Frances L. *Infant and child in the culture of today.* New York: Harper, 1943.

Gewirtz, J. L. Three determinants of attention seeking in young children. *Monogr. Soc. Res. Child Develpm.,* 1954, *19,* No. 2 (Serial No. 59).

Gewirtz, J. L. A learning analysis of the effects of normal stimulation, privation, and deprivation on the acquisition of social motivation and attachment. In B. M. Foss (Ed.). *Determinants of infant behavior.* New York: Wiley, 1961, pp. 213–283.

Gewirtz, J. L., & Baer, D. M. The effects of brief social deprivation on behaviors for a social reinforcer. *J. abnorm. soc. Psychol.,* 1958, *56,* 49–56 (a).

Gewirtz, J. L., & Baer, D. M. Deprivation and satiation of social reinforcers as drive conditions. *J. abnorm. soc. Psychol.,* 1958, *57,* 165–172 (b).

Giedt, F. H. Changes in sexual behavior and attitudes following class study of the Kinsey Report. *J. soc. Psychol.,* 1951, *33,* 131–141.

Giffin, Mary E., Johnson, Adelaide M., & Litin, E. M. Antisocial acting out: 2. Specific factors determining antisocial acting out. *Amer. J. Orthopsychiat.,* 1954, *24,* 668–684.

Gill, M., Newman, R., & Redlich, F. C. *The initial interview in psychiatric practice.* New York: International Universities, 1954.

Glueck, S., & Glueck, Eleanor. *500 Criminal careers.* New York, Knopf, 1930.

Glueck, S., & Glueck, Eleanor. *Unraveling juvenile delinquency.* Cambridge: Harvard Univer. Press, 1950.

Goffman, E. *The presentation of self in everyday life.* New York: Doubleday, 1959.

Goldfarb, W. Infant rearing and problem behavior. *Amer. J. Orthopsychiat.,* 1943, *13,* 249–265.

Goldman, Jeri R. The relation of certain therapist variables to the handling of psychotherapeutic events. Unpublished doctoral dissertation, Stanford Univer., 1961.

Goodenough, Florence L. Anger in young children. *Inst. Child Welf. Monogr. Ser.,* No. 9. Minneapolis: Univer. of Minnesota Press, 1931.

Graham, Frances K., Charwat, Wanda A., Honig, Alice S., & Weltz, Paula C. Aggression as a function of the attack and the attacker. *J. abnorm. soc. Psychol.*, 1951, *46*, 512–520.

Grinder, R. E. Parental childrearing practices, conscience, and resistance to temptation of sixth-grade children. *Child Develpm.*, 1962, *33*, 8   820.

Grossman, H. J., & Green   g. N. H. Psychosomatic differentiation in infancy: I. Autonomic activity in the newborn. *Psychosomat. Med.*, 1957, *19*, 293–306.

Hagman, R. R. A study of fears of children of preschool age. *J. exp. Educ.*, 1932, *1*, 110–130.

Hall, J. F. *Psychology of motivation.* Philadelphia: Lippincott, 1961.

Hammar, S. L. A study of adolescent obesity. Paper read at the Annual Meeting of the Western Society for Pediatric Research, San Francisco, 1961.

Haner, C. F., & Brown, Patricia A. Clarification of the instigation to action concept in the frustration-aggression hypothesis. *J. abnorm. soc. Psychol.*, 1955, *51*, 204–206.

Hartshorne, H., & May, M. A. *Studies in the nature of character:* Vol. I. *Studies in deceit.* New York: Macmillan, 1928.

Hartshorne, H., May, M. A., & Maller, J. B. *Studies in the nature of character:* Vol. 2. *Studies in service and self-control.* New York: Macmillan, 1929.

Hartshorne, H., May, M. A., & Shuttleworth, F. K. *Studies in the nature of character:* Vol. 3. *Studies in the organization of character.* New York: Macmillan, 1930.

Hartup, W. W. Nurturance and nurturance-withdrawal in relation to the dependency behavior of preschool children. *Child Develpm.*, 1958, *29*, 191–201.

Hartup, W. W. Sex and social reinforcement effects with children. Paper read at the Annual Meeting of the Amer. Psychol. Assoc., New York, 1961.

Hartup, W. W., & Himeno, Yayoi. Social isolation vs. interaction with adults in relation to aggression in preschool children. *J. abnorm. soc. Psychol.*, 1959, *59*, 17–22.

Hartup, W. W., & Keller, E. D. Nurturance in preschool children and its relation to dependency. *Child Develpm.*, 1960, *31*, 681–689.

Hathaway, S. R., & McKinley, J. C. *The Minnesota Mul-*

tiphasic Personality Inventory (rev. ed.). Minneapolis: Univer. of Minnesota Press, 1943.

Hayes, Catherine. *The ape in our house.* New York: Harper, 1951.

Hayes, K. J., & Hayes, Catherine. Imitation in a home-raised chimpanzee. *J. comp. phys. Psychol.,* 1952, *45,* 450–459 (a).

Hayes, K. J., & Hayes, Catherine. *Imitation in a home-raised chimpanzee (*16 mm. silent film). State College, Pa.: Psychol. Cinema Register, 1952 (b).

Healy, W., & Bronner, Augusta. *Delinquents and criminals: Their making and unmaking.* New York: Macmillan, 1925.

Heathers, G. Emotional dependence and independence in a physical threat situation. *Child Develpm.,* 1953, *24,* 169–179.

Heineke, C. M. Some antecedents and correlates of guilt and fear in young boys. Unpublished doctoral dissertation, Harvard Univer., 1953.

Helson, H., Blake, R. R., Mouton, Jane S., & Olmstead, J. A. Attitudes as adjustments to stimulus, background, and residual factors. *J. abnorm. soc. Psychol.,* 1956, *52,* 314–322.

Herbert, J. J., & Harsh, C. M. Observational learning by cats. *J. comp. Psychol.,* 1944, *37,* 81–95.

Herzberg, A. Short treatment of neuroses by graduated tasks. *Brit. J. Med. Psychol.,* 1941, *19,* 36–51.

Hilgard, E. R. *Theories of learning.* New York: Appleton, 1956.

Hill, W. F. Learning theory and the acquisition of values. *Psychol. Rev.,* 1960, *67,* 317–331.

Himmelweit, Hilde T., Oppenheim, A. N., & Vince, Pamela. *Television and the child: An empirical study of the effect of television on the young.* New York: Oxford University Press, 1958.

Hockman, C. H., & Lipsitt, L. P. Delay-of-reward gradients in discrimination learning with children for two levels of difficulty. *J. comp. physiol. Psychol.,* 1961, *54,* 24–27.

Hoffman, M. L. Power assertion by the parent and its impact on the child. *Child Develpm.,* 1960, *31,* 129–143.

Hoffman, M. L. Child-rearing practices and moral development: Generalizations from empirical research. Unpublished manuscript, the Merrill-Palmer Institute, 1962.

Hoffman, M. L., & Salzstein, H. D. Parent practices and the child's moral orientation. Interim research report presented at the Amer. Psychol. Assoc. Annual Meeting, Chicago, 1960.

Hogbin, H. I. Marriage in Wogeo, New Guinea. *Oceania,* 1945, *15,* 324–352.

Hollenberg, Eleanor, & Sperry, Margaret. Some antecedents of aggression and effects of frustration in doll play. *Personality,* 1951, *1,* 32–43.

Hollingshead, A. B. *Elmstown's youth: The impact of social classes on youth.* New York: Wiley, 1949.

Hollingshead, A. B., & Redlich, F. C. *Social class and mental illness.* New York: Wiley, 1958.

Holmberg A. R. *Nomads of the long bow.* Washington, D.C.: U.S. Govt. Print. Off., 1950.

Holt, E. B. *Animal drive and the learning process.* Vol. I. New York: Holt, 1931.

Holton, Ruth B. Amplitude of an instrumental response following the withholding of reward. *Child Develpm.,* 1961, *32,* 107–116.

Hops, H., & Walters, R. H. Studies of reinforcement of aggression. II. Influence of some antecedent variables. *Child Develpm.,* 1963, *34,* 553–562.

Hovland, C. I., Janis, I. L., & Kelley, H. H. *Communication and persuasion.* New Haven: Yale Univer. Press, 1953.

Hughes, C. C., Tremblay, M., Rapoport, R. N., & Leighton, A. H. *People of cove and woodlot: Communities from the viewpoint of social psychiatry.* New York: Basic, 1960.

Hull, C. L. *Principles of behavior.* New York: Appleton, 1943.

Humphrey, G. Imitation and the conditioned reflex. *Ped. Sem.,* 1921, *28,* 1–21.

Hunt, J. McV. *Intelligence and experience.* New York: Ronald, 1961.

Hurlock, Elizabeth B. *Adolescent development.* New York: McGraw-Hill, 1955.

Jack, Lois M. An experimental study of ascendant behavior in preschool children. *Univer. Ia. Stud. Child Welf.,* 1934, *9,* 3–65.

Jacobs, R. C., & Campbell, D. T. The perpetuation of an

arbitrary tradition through several generations of a laboratory microculture. *J. abnorm. soc. Psychol.,* 1961, *62,* 649–658.

Jakubczak, L. F., & Walters, R. H. Suggestibility as dependency behavior. *J. abnorm. soc. Psychol.,* 1959, *59,* 102–107.

Jegard, Suzanne F., & Walters, R. H. A study of some determinants of aggression in young children. *Child Develpm.,* 1960, *31,* 739–747.

Jenkins, R. L. *Breaking patterns of defeat.* Philadelphia: Lippincott, 1954.

Jenkins, R. L., & Hewitt, L. E. Types of personality structure encountered in child guidance clinics. *Amer. J. Orthopsychiat.,* 1944, *14,* 84–95.

Jellinek, E. M. *The disease concept of alcoholism.* New Haven: Hillhouse, 1960.

Jersild, A. T., & Holmes, Frances B. Children's fears. *Monogr. Soc. Res. Child Develpm.,* 1935, *6* (Serial No. 20) (a).

Jersild, A. T., & Holmes, Frances B. Methods of overcoming children's fears. *J. Psychol.,* 1935–1936, *1,* 75–104 (b).

Johnson, Adelaide M., & Szurek, S. A. The genesis of antisocial acting out in children and adults. *Psychoanal. Quart.,* 1952, *21,* 323–343.

Johnson, Elizabeth Z. Attitudes of children toward authority as projected in their doll play at two age levels. Unpublished doctoral dissertation, Harvard Univer., 1951.

Jones, H. E. The study of patterns of emotional expression. In M. L. Reymert (Ed.). *Feelings and emotions.* New York: McGraw-Hill, 1950, pp. 161–168.

Jones, Mary C. The elimination of children's fears. *J. exp. Psychol.,* 1924, *7,* 383–390 (a).

Jones, Mary C. A laboratory study of fear: The case of Peter. *Pedagog. Sem. & J. genet. Psychol.,* 1924, *31,* 308–315 (b).

Jones, Mary C. The later careers of boys who were early—or late—maturing. *Child Develpm.,* 1957, *28,* 113–128.

Josselyn, Irene M. *Psychosocial development of children.* New York: Family Service Assoc. of America, 1948.

Kagan, J., & Moss, H. A. The stability of passive and dependent behavior from childhood to adulthood. *Child Develpm.,* 1960, *31,* 577–591.

Kagan, J., & Mussen, P. H. Dependency themes on the TAT and group conformity. *J. consult. Psychol.,* 1956, *20,* 29–32.

Kahn, M. A polygraph study of the catharsis of aggression. Unpublished doctoral dissertation, Harvard Univer., 1960.

Kanareff, Vera T., & Lanzetta, J. T. Effects of success-failure experiences and probability of reinforcement upon the acquisition and extinction of an imitative response. *Psychol. Rep.*, 1960, *7,* 151–166.

Kaplan, B., & Plaut, T. F. A. *Personality in a communal society: An analysis of the mental health of the Hutterites.* Lawrence, Kansas: Univer. of Kansas Publications, Social Science Studies, 1956.

Kaufman, Edna L., & Miller, N. E. Effect of number of reinforcements on strength of approach in an approach-avoidance conflict. *J. comp. physiol. Psychol.*, 1949, *42,* 65–74.

Kaufman, H., & Feshbach, S. The modification of aggressive behavior through cognitive restructuring. Unpublished manuscript, Univer. of Pennsylvania, 1962.

Kausler, D. H., & Trapp, E. P. Motivation and cue utilization in intentional and incidental learning. *Psychol. Rev.*, 1960, *67,* 373–379.

Keister, Mary E. The behavior of young children in failure: An experimental attempt to discover and to modify undesirable responses of preschool children to failure. *Univer. Ia. Stud. Child Welf.*, 1938, *14,* 27–82.

Keller, Helen. *The story of my life.* New York: Doubleday, 1927.

Kellogg, W. N., & Kellogg, L. A. *The ape and the child: A study of environmental influence upon early behavior.* New York: McGraw-Hill, 1933.

Kenny, D. T. An experimental test of the catharsis theory of aggression. Unpublished doctoral dissertation, Univer. of Washington, 1952.

Kessen, W., & Mandler, G. Anxiety, pain, and the inhibition of distress. *Psychol. Rev.*, 1961, *68,* 396–404.

Kessen, W., Williams, E. Jane, & Williams, Joanna P. Selection of test of response measures in the study of the human newborn. *Child. Develpm.*, 1961, *32,* 7–24.

Kimble, G. A. *Hilgard and Marquis' "Conditioning and Learning."* New York: Appleton, 1961.

Kimble, G. A., & Kendall, J. W., Jr. A comparison of two methods of producing experimental extinction. *J. exp. Psychol.*, 1953, *45,* 87–90.

Kimbrell, D., & Blake, R. R.   Motivational factors in the violation of a prohibition. *J. abnorm. soc. Psychol.*, 1958, *56*, 132–133.

King, G. F., Armitage, S. G., & Tilton, J. R.   A therapeutic approach to schizophrenics of extreme pathology. *J. abnorm. soc. Psychol.*, 1960, *61*, 276–286.

Kinsey, A. C., Pomeroy, W. B., & Martin, C. E.   *Sexual behavior in the human male.* Philadelphia: Saunders, 1948.

Kinsey, A. C., Pomeroy, W. B., Martin, C. E., & Gebhard, P. H.   *Sexual behavior in the human female.* Philadelphia: Saunders, 1953.

Krasner, L.   Studies of the conditioning of verbal behavior. *Psychol. Bull.*, 1958, *55*, 148–170.

Krasner, L.   The psychotherapist as a social reinforcement machine. In H. H. Strupp and L. Luborsky (Eds.).   *Research in psychotherapy*, Vol. II. Washington, D.C.: American Psychological Association, 1962, pp. 61–94.

Krasner, L., Ullman, L. P., Weiss, R. L., & Collins, Beverly J.   Responsivity to verbal conditioning as a function of three different examiners. *J. clin. Psychol.*, 1961, *17*, 411–415.

Lacy, O. W., Lewinger, Nancy, & Adamson, J. F.   Foreknowledge as a factor affecting perceptual defense and alertness. *J. exp. Psychol.*, 1953, *45*, 169–174.

Landreth, Catherine, & Read, Katherine H.   *Education of the young child: A nursing school manual.* New York: Wiley, 1942.

Lanzetta, J. T., & Kanareff, Vera T.   The effects of a monetary reward on the acquisition of an imitative response. *J. abnorm. soc. Psychol.*, 1959, *59*, 120–127.

Larder, Diane L.   Effect of aggressive story content on nonverbal play behavior. *Psychol. Rep.*, 1962, *11*, 14.

Lawrence, D. H.   Acquired distinctiveness of cues: I. Transfer between discriminations on the basis of familiarity with the stimulus. *J. exp. Psychol.*, 1949, *39*, 770–784.

Lawrence, D. H.   Acquired distinctiveness of cues: II. Selective association in a constant stimulus situation. *J. exp. Psychol.* 1950, *40*, 175–188.

Lawrence, D. H., & Festinger, L.   *Determinants and reinforcements: The psychology of insufficient rewards.* Stanford: Stanford Univer. Press, 1962.

Lawson, R., & Marx, M. H. Frustration: Theory and experiment. *Genet. Psychol. Monogr.*, 1958, *57*, 393–464.

Lazarsfeld, M., & Zeisl, H. Die arbeitslosen von Marienthal. *Psychol. Monographen,* 1933, *5.*

Lazarus, A. A. New methods in psychotherapy: A case study. *South African Med. J.,* 1958, *33*, 660–663.

Lazarus, A. A. The elimination of children's phobias by deconditioning. In H. J. Eysenck (Ed.). *Behavior therapy and the neuroses.* New York: Pergamon, 1960, pp. 114–122.

Lazarus, A. A., & Rachman, S. The use of systematic desensitization in psychotherapy. *South African Med. J.,* 1957, *31*, 934–937.

Lazowick, L. M. On the nature of identification. *J. abnorm. soc. Psychol.,* 1955, *51*, 175–183.

Lefkowitz, M. M., Blake, R. R., & Mouton, Jane S. Status factors in pedestrian violation of traffic signals. *J. abnorm. soc. Psychol.,* 1955, *51*, 704–706.

Leighton, Dorothy, & Kluckhohn, C. *Children of the people.* Cambridge, Mass.: Harvard Univer. Press, 1947.

Leiman, A. H., & Epstein, S. Thematic sexual responses as related to sexual drive and guilt. *J. abnorm. soc. Psychol.,* 1961, *63*, 169–175.

Lesser, G. S., & Abelson, R. P. Personality correlates of persuasibility in children. In I. L. Janis & C. I. Hovland (Eds.). *Personality and persuasibility.* New Haven: Yale Univer. Press, 1959, pp. 187–206.

Levin, H., & Baldwin, A. L. Pride and shame in children. In M. R. Jones (Ed.). *Nebraska symposium on motivation.* Lincoln: Univer. of Nebraska Press, 1959, pp. 138–173.

Levin, H., & Sears, R. R. Identification with parents as a determinant of doll-play aggression. *Child Develpm.,* 1956, *27*, 135–153.

Levin, H., & Turgeon, Valerie. The influence of the mother's presence on children's doll-play aggression. *J. abnorm. soc. Psychol.* 1957, *55*, 304–308.

Levitt, E. E. The results of psychotherapy with children: An evaluation. *J. consult. Psychol.,* 1957, *21*, 189–196.

Levy, D. M. Trends in therapy: III. Release therapy. *Amer. J. Orthopsychiat.,* 1939, *9*, 713–737.

Levy, D. M. *Maternal overprotection.* New York: Columbia Univer. Press, 1943.

Lewin, K. *A dynamic theory of personality.* New York: McGraw-Hill, 1935.

Lewin, K., Lippitt, R., & White, R. K. Patterns of aggressive behavior in experimentally created "social climates." *J. soc. Pyschol.,* 1939, *10,* 271–299.

Lewis, Hilda. *Deprived children.* London: Oxford Univer. Press, 1954.

Lewis, O. *Children of Sanchez.* New York: Random House, 1961.

Lidz, T., Cornelison, Alice R., Fleck, S., & Terry, Dorothy. The intrafamilial environment of the schizophrenic patient: I. The father. *Psychiat.,* 1957, *20,* 329–342 (a).

Lidz, T., Cornelison, Alice R., Fleck, S., & Terry, Dorothy. The intrafamilial environment of the schizophrenic patient: II. Marital schism and marital skew. *Amer. J. Psychiat.,* 1957, *114,* 241–248 (b).

Lidz, T., Cornelison, Alice R., Fleck, S., & Terry, Dorothy. Intrafamilial environment of schizophrenic patients: VI. The transmission of irrationality. *AMA Arch. Neurol. Psychiat.,* 1958, *79,* 305–316.

Lindner, R. M. *Rebel without a cause: The hypnoanalysis of a criminal psychopath.* New York: Grune & Stratton, 1944.

Lindsley, O. R. Operant conditioning methods applied to research in chronic schizophrenia. In N. S. Kline (Ed.). *Psychiatric Research Reports* 5. Washington: Amer. Psychiat. Assoc., 1956, pp. 118–139.

Lindsley, O. R. Intermittent grading. *The Clearing House,* 1958, *32,* 451–454.

Lindzey, G. An experimental investigation of the scapegoat theory of prejudice. *J. abnorm. soc. Psychol.,* 1950, *45,* 296–309.

Lippitt, R. An experimental study of the effect of democratic and authoritarian group atmospheres. *Univer. Ia. Stud. Child Welf.,* 1940, *16,* 43–195.

Lippitt, R., Polansky, N., Redl, F., & Rosen, S. The dynamics of power: A field study of social influence in groups of children. *Hum. Rel.,* 1952, *5,* 37–64.

Lipsitt, L. P., & Castaneda, A. Effects of delayed reward on choice behavior and response speeds in children. *J. comp. physiol. Psychol.*, 1958, *51*, 65–67.

Lipsitt, L. P., Castaneda, A., & Kemble, J. D.   Effects of delayed reward pretraining on discrimination learning of children. *Child Develpm.*, 1959, *30*, 273–278.

Litin, E. M., Giffin, Mary E., & Johnson, Adelaide M.   Parental influences in unusual sexual behavior in children. *Psychoanal. Quart.*, 1956, *25*, 37–55.

Livson, N., & Mussen, P. H.   The relation of ego control to overt aggression and dependency. *J. abnorm. soc. Psychol.*, 1957, *55*, 66–71.

Lloyd Morgan, C.   *Habit and instinct.* London: Arnold, 1896.

Logan, F. A.   A comparison of avoidance and nonavoidance eyelid conditioning. *J. exp. Psychol.*, 1951, *42*, 390–393.

Longstreth, L. E.   The relationship between expectations and frustration in children. *Child Develpm.*, 1960, *31*, 667–671.

Lorenz, K.   Der Kumpan in der Umvelt des Vogels, *J. Ornithol.*, 1935, *83*, 137–214, 289–413.

Lövaas, O. I.   Effect of exposure to symbolic aggression on aggressive behavior. *Child Develpm.*, 1961, *32*, 37–44 (a).

Lövaas, O. I.   Interaction between verbal and nonverbal behavior. *Child Develpm.*, 1961, *32*, 329–336 (b).

Lowrey, L. G.   Personality distortion and early institutional care. *Amer. J. Orthopsychiat.*, 1940, *10*, 576–586.

Lundin, R. W.   *Personality: An experimental approach.* New York: Macmillan, 1961.

Lykken, D. T.   A study of anxiety in the sociopathic personality. *J. abnorm. soc. Psychol.*, 1957, *55*, 6–10.

McBrearty, J. F., Marston, A. R., & Kanfer, F. H.   Conditioning a verbal operant in a group setting: Direct vs. vicarious reinforcement. *Amer. Psychologist,* 1961, *16*, 425 (abstract).

McClelland, D. C.   *Personality.* New York: Sloane, 1951.

McClelland, D. C.   Some social consequences of achievement motivation. In M. R. Jones (Ed.). *Nebraska symposium on motivation.* Lincoln: Univer. of Nebraska Press, 1955, pp. 41–65.

McClelland, D. C.   Personality. In P. R. Farnsworth & Q. McNemar (Eds.). *Annual review of psychology.* Stanford: Annual Reviews, Inc., 1956, pp. 39–62.

McClelland, D. C., & Apicella, F. S. A functional classification of verbal reactions to experimentally induced failure. *J. abnorm. soc. Psychol.*, 1945, *40*, 376–390.

McClelland, D. C., Atkinson, J. W., Clark, R. A., & Lowell, E. L. *The achievement motive.* New York: Appleton, 1953.

McCord, W., & McCord, Joan. *Psychopathy and delinquency.* New York: Grune & Stratton, 1956.

McCord, Joan, & McCord, W. The effects of parental role models on criminality. *J. soc. Issues*, 1958, *14*, 66–74.

McCord, W., McCord, Joan, & Zola, I. K. *Origins of crime: A new evaluation of the Cambridge-Somerville Youth Study.* New York: Columbia Univer. Press, 1959.

McDougall, W. *An introduction to social psychology.* London: Methuen, 1908.

McGinnies, E. Emotionality and perceptual defense. *Psychol. Rev.*, 1949, *56*, 244–251.

McGinnies, E., & Sherman, H. Generalization of perceptual defense. *J. abnorm. soc. Psychol.*, 1952, *47*, 81–85.

McNulty, J. A., & Walters, R. H. Emotional arousal, conflict, and susceptibility to social influence. *Canad. J. Psychol.*, 1962, *16*, 211–220.

MacKay, H. A., & Laverty, S. G. A new techinque for examining traumatic conditioning. Unpublished manuscript, Queen's University, Ontario, 1963.

MacKinnon, D .W. Violations of prohibition. In H. A. Murray *et al. Explorations in personality.* New York: Oxford Univer. Press, 1938, pp. 491–501.

Maccoby, Eleanor, E. Role-taking in childhood and its consequences for social learning. *Child Develpm.*, 1959, *30*, 239–252.

Mackworth, N. H., & Llewellyn Thomas, E. Head-mounted eye-marker camera. *J. opt. Soc. America*, 1962, *52*, 713–716.

Mahrer, A. R. The role of expectancy in delayed reinforcement. *J. exp. Psychol.*, 1956, *52*, 101–106.

Malinowski, B. *The sexual life of savages in north-western Melanesia.* New York: Harcourt, 1929.

Maller, J. B. General and specific factors in character. *J. soc. Psychol.*, 1934, *5*, 97–102.

Marquis, Dorothy P. Learning in the neonate: The modification of behavior under three feeding schedules. *J. exp. Psychol.*, 1941, *29*, 263–282.

Marx, M. H. Some relations between frustration and drive. In M. R. Jones (Ed.). *Nebraska symposium on motivation*. Lincoln: Univer. of Nebraska Press, 1956, pp. 92–130.

Maslow, A. H. Deprivation, threat, and frustration. *Psychol. Rev.*, 1941, *48*, 364–366.

Mausner, B. Studies in social interaction: III. Effect of variation in one partner's prestige on the interaction of observer pairs. *J. appl. Psychol.*, 1953, *37*, 391–393.

Mausner, B. The effect of prior reinforcement on the interaction of observer pairs. *J. abnorm. soc. Psychol.*, 1954, *49*, 65–68 (a).

Mausner, B. The effect of one partner's success in a relevant task on the interaction of observer pairs. *J. abnorm. soc. Psychol.*, 1954, *49*, 557–560 (b).

Mausner, B., & Bloch, B. L. A study of the additivity of variables affecting social interaction. *J. abnorm. soc. Psychol.*, 1957, *54*, 250–256.

Mead, G. H. *Mind, self, and society*. Chicago: Univer. of Chicago Press, 1934.

Mead, Margaret. *Sex and temperament in three savage tribes*. New York: Morrow, 1935.

Mead, Margaret. Some anthropological considerations concerning guilt. In M. L. Reymert (Ed.). *Feelings and emotions*. New York: McGraw-Hill, 1950, pp. 362–373.

Menninger, W. C. Recreation and mental health. *Recreation*, 1948, *42*, 340–346.

Merton, R. K. *Social theory and social structure* (rev. ed.). New York: Free Press, 1957.

Miller, D. R., & Swanson, G. E. (Eds.). *Inner conflict and defense*. New York: Holt, 1960.

Miller, N. E. The frustration-aggression hypothesis. *Psychol. Rev.*, 1941, *48*, 337–342.

Miller, N. E. Studies of fear as an acquirable drive: I. Fear as motivation and fear-reduction as reinforcement in the learning of new responses. *J. exp. Psychol.*, 1948, *38*, 89–101 (a).

Miller, N. E. Theory and experiment relating psychoanalytic displacement to stimulus-response generalization. *J. abnorm. soc. Psychol.*, 1948, *43*, 155–178 (b).

Miller, N. E. Liberalization of basic S-R concepts: Extension to conflict behavior, motivation, and social learning. In S.

Koch (Ed.). *Psychology: A study of a science.* Vol. 2. New York: McGraw-Hill, 1959, pp. 196–292.

Miller, N. E., & Bugelski, B. R.   Minor studies of aggression: II. The influence of frustrations by the in-group on attitudes expressed toward out-groups. *J. Psychol.,* 1948, *25,* 437–442.

Miller, N. E., & Dollard, J.   *Social learning and imitation.* New Haven: Yale Univer. Press, 1941.

Miller, N. E., & Kraeling, Doris.   Displacement: Greater generalization of approach than avoidance in a generalized approach-avoidance conflict. *J. exp. Psychol.,* 1952, *43,* 217–221.

Miller, N. E., & Murray, E. J.   Displacement and conflict: Learnable drive as a basis for the steeper gradient of avoidance than of approach. *J. exp. Psychol.,* 1952, *53,* 227–231.

Miller, N. E., & Stevenson, S. S.   Agitated behavior of rats during experimental extinction and a curve of spontaneous recovery. *J. comp. Psychol.,* 1936, *21,* 205–231.

Miller, R. E., Banks, J. H., & Ogawa, N.   Communication of affect in "cooperative conditioning" of Rhesus monkeys. *J. abnorm. soc. Psychol.,* 1962, *64,* 343–348.

Mischel, W.   Preference for delayed reinforcement: An experimental study of a cultural observation. *J. abnorm. soc. Psychol.,* 1958, *56,* 57–61.

Mischel, W.   Preference for delayed reinforcement and social responsibility. *J. abnorm. soc. Psychol.,* 1961, *62,* 1–7 (a).

Mischel, W.   Delay of gratification, need for achievement, and acquiescence in another culture. *J. abnorm. soc. Psychol.,* 1961, *62,* 543–552 (b).

Mischel, W.   Father-absence and delay of gratification: Cross-cultural comparisons. *J. abnorm. soc. Psychol.,* 1961, *63,* 116–124 (c).

Mischel, W., & Gilligan, Carol F.   Delay of gratification and resistance to temptation. Unpublished manuscript, Stanford Univer., 1962.

Mischel, W., & Metzner, R.   Preference for delayed reward as a function of age, intelligence, and length of delay interval. *J. abnorm. soc. Psychol.,* 1962, *64,* 425–431.

Mohr, G. S., & Despres, M. A.   *The stormy decade: Adolescence.* New York: Random House, 1958.

Moreno, J. L.   Who shall survive? *Nerv. & ment. Dis. Monogr. Ser.*, 1934, No. 58.

Mowrer, O. H.   An experimental analogue of "regression," with incidental observations on "reaction formation." *J. abnorm. soc. Psychol.*, 1940, *35*, 56–87.

Mowrer, O. H.   *Learning theory and personality dynamics.* New York: Ronald, 1950.

Mowrer, O. H.   Speech development in the young child: The autism theory of speech development and some clinical applications. *J. Speech & Hearing Dis.*, 1952, *17*, 263–268.

Mowrer, O. H.   Hearing and speaking: An analysis of language learning. *J. Speech Dis.*, 1958, *23*, 143–152.

Mowrer, O. H.   *Learning theory and behavior.* New York: Wiley, 1960 (a).

Mowrer, O. H.   *Learning theory and the symbolic processes.* New York: Wiley, 1960 (b).

Mowrer, O. H., & Kluckhohn, C.   Dynamic theory of personality. In J. McV. Hunt (Ed.).   *Personality and the behavior disorders.* Vol. I. New York: Ronald, 1944, pp. 69–135.

Murray, E. J.   A content-analysis method for studying psychotherapy. *Psychol. Monogr.*, 1956, *70*, No. 13 (Whole No. 420).

Murray, E. J., & Berkun, M. M.   Displacement as a function of conflict. *J. abnorm. soc. Psychol.*, 1955, *51*, 47–56.

Mussen, P. H.   Some antecedents and consequents of masculine sex-typing in adolescent boys. *Psychol. Monogr.*, 1961, *75*, No. 2 (Whole No. 506).

Mussen, P. H., & Distler, L.   Masculinity, identification, and father-son relationships. *J. abnorm. soc. Psychol.*, 1959, *59*, 350–356.

Mussen, P. H., & Jones, Mary C.   Self-conceptions, motivations, and interpersonal attitudes of late– and early–maturing boys. *Child Develpm.*, 1957, *28*, 243–256.

Mussen, P. H., & Rutherford, E.   Effects of aggressive cartoons on children's aggressive play. *J. abnorm. soc. Psychol.*, 1961, *62*, 461–464.

Mussen, P. H., & Scodel, A.   The effects of sexual stimulation under varying conditions on TAT sexual responsiveness. *J. consult. Psychol.*, 1955, *19*, 90.

Muste, M. J., & Sharpe, D. F.   Some influential factors in the determination of aggressive behavior in preschool children. *Child Develpm.*, 1947, *18*, 11–28.

Nash, M. *Machine age Maya: The industrialization of a Guatemalan community. Amer. Anthropologist,* 1958, *60*, No. 2, Part 2 (Memoir No. 87).

Nelsen, E. A. The effects of reward and punishment of dependency on subsequent dependency. Unpublished manuscript, Stanford Univer., 1960.

Newcomb, T. M. *Personality and social change.* New York: Holt, 1943.

Newcomb, T. M. *Social psychology.* New York: Holt, 1950.

Nye, F. I. *Family relationships and delinquent behavior.* New York: Wiley, 1958.

Olds, J. The influence of practice on the strength of secondary approach drives. *J. exp. Psychol.,* 1953, *46*, 232–236.

Olds, J. *The growth and structure of motives.* New York: Free Press, 1956.

Osgood, C. E., Suci, G. J., & Tannenbaum, P. H. *The measurement of meaning.* Urbana, Ill.: Univer. of Illinois Press, 1957.

Otis, Nancy B., & McCandless, B. Responses to repeated frustrations of young children differentiated according to need area. *J. abnorm. soc. Psychol.,* 1955, *50*, 349–353.

Page, Marjorie L. The modification of ascendant behavior in preschool children. *Univer. Ia. Stud. Child Welf.,* 1936, *12*, 7–69.

Parsons, T. Psycho-analysis and the social structure. *Psychoanal. Quart.,* 1950, *19*, 371–384.

Parsons, T. *The social system.* New York: Free Press, 1951.

Parsons, T. Family structure and the socialization of the child. In T. Parsons and R. F. Bales. *Family, socialization, and interaction process.* New York: Free Press, 1955, pp. 35–131.

Pastore, N. The role of arbitrariness in the frustration-aggression hypothesis. *J. abnorm. soc. Psychol.,* 1952, *47*, 728–731.

Patterson, G. R., Ludwig, M., & Sonoda, Beverly. Reinforcement of aggression in children. Unpublished manuscript, Univer. of Oregon, 1961.

Payne, D. E., & Mussen, P. H. Parent-child relations and father identification among adolescent boys. *J. abnorm. soc. Psychol.,* 1956, *52,* 358–362.

Pearson, G. H. J. *Adolescence and the conflict of generations.* New York: Norton, 1958.

Penney, R. K. The effects of non-reinforcement of response strength as a function of number of previous reinforcements. *Canad. J. Psychol.,* 1960, *14,* 206–215.

Piaget, J. *The moral judgment of the child.* New York: Free Press, 1948. (First published in French, 1932.)

Piaget, J. *The construction of reality in the child.* New York: Basic, 1954. (First published in French, 1937.)

Piers, G., & Singer, M. B. *Shame and guilt.* Springfield, Ill.: Thomas, 1953.

Pisoni, Stephanie, & Salzinger, K. The unidimensionality of verbal affect and its distinctiveness from verbal nonaffect. *Amer. Psychologist,* 1960, *15,* 431 (abstract).

Postman, L., Bronson, Wanda C., & Gropper, G. L. Is there a mechanism of perceptual defense? *J. abnorm. soc. Psychol.,* 1953, *48,* 215–224.

Powdermaker, Hortense. *Life in Lesu.* New York: Norton, 1933.

Powers, E., & Witmer, Helen. *An experiment in the prevention of deliquency: The Cambridge-Somerville Youth Study.* New York: Columbia Univer. Press, 1951.

Prince, A. I. Relative prestige and the verbal conditioning of children. *Amer. Psychologist,* 1962, *17,* 378 (abstract).

Quay, H. C. The effect of verbal reinforcement on the recall of early memories. *J. abnorm. soc. Psychol.,* 1959, *59,* 254–257.

Radke-Yarrow, Marian, Trager, Helen G., & Miller, Jean. The role of parents in the development of children's ethnic attitudes. *Child Develpm.,* 1952, *23,* 13–53.

Raymond, M. S. Case of fetishism treated by aversion therapy. *Brit. med. J.,* 1956, *2,* 854–856.

Razran, G. Stimulus generalization of conditioned responses. *Psychol. Bull.,* 1949, *46,* 337–365.

Rebelsky, Freda G., Allinsmith, W., & Grinder, R. E. Resistance to temptation and sex differences in children's use of fantasy confession. *Child Develpm.,* 1963, in press.

Redl, F. The psychology of gang formation and the treatment

of juvenile delinquents. *Psychoanal. Study Child,* 1945, *1,* 367–377.

Redl, F., & Wineman, D.   *Children who hate.* New York: Free Press, 1951.

Redl, F., & Wineman, D.   *The aggressive child.* New York: Free Press, 1955.

Reichard, Gladys, A.   Social life. In F. Boas (Ed.).   *General anthropology.* Boston: Heath, 1938, pp. 409–486.

Reider, N.   The demonology of modern psychiatry. *Amer. J. Psychiat.,* 1955, *111,* 851–856.

Rheingold, Harriet L.   The modification of social responsiveness in institutional babies. *Monogr. Soc. Res. Child Develpm.,* 1956, *21,* No. 2 (Serial No. 63).

Riesman, D.   *The lonely crowd.* New Haven: Yale Univer. Press, 1950.

Rogers, C. R.   *Client-centered therapy.* Boston: Houghton Mifflin, 1951.

Rogers, J. M.   Operant conditioning in a quasi-therapy setting. *J. abnorm. soc. Psychol.,* 1960, *60,* 247–252.

Rokeach, M.   *The open and the closed mind.* New York: Basic, 1960.

Rosanoff, A. J.   *Manual of psychiatry and mental hygiene.* Boston: Houghton Mifflin, 1938.

Rosen, B., & D'Andrade, R.   The psychosocial origins of achievement motivation. *Sociometry,* 1959, *22,* 185–218.

Rosenbaum, M. E.   The effect of stimulus and background factors on the volunteering response. *J. abnorm. soc. Psychol.,* 1956, *53,* 118–121.

Rosenbaum, M. E., & Blake, R. R.   Volunteering as a function of field structure. *J. abnorm. soc. Psychol.,* 1955, *50,* 193–196.

Rosenbaum, M. E., & deCharms, R.   Direct and vicarious reduction of hostility. *J. abnorm. soc. Psychol.,* 1960, *60,* 105–111.

Rosenbaum, M. E., & Tucker, I. F.   The competence of the model and the learning of imitation and nonimitation. *J. exp. Psychol.,* 1962, *63,* 183–190.

Rosenberg, M. J., & Abelson, R. P.   An analysis of cognitive balancing. In M. J. Rosenberg, C. I. Hovland, W. J. McGuire, R. P. Abelson, & J. W. Brehm.   *Attitude organi-*

zation and change. New Haven: Yale Univer. Press, 1960, pp. 112–163.

Rosenberg, M. J., & Gardner, C. W. Some dynamic aspects of posthypnotic compliance. *J. abnorm. soc. Psychol.,* 1958, *57,* 351–366.

Rosenblith, Judy F. Learning by imitation in kindergarten children. *Child Develpm.,* 1959, *30,* 69–80.

Rosenblith, Judy F. Imitative color choices in kindergarten children. *Child Develpm.,* 1961, *32,* 211–223.

Rosenthal, D. Changes in some moral values following psychotherapy. *J. consult. Psychol.,* 1955, *19,* 431–436.

Rosenzweig, S. An outline of frustration theory. In J. McV. Hunt (Ed.). *Personality and the behavior disorders.* New York: Ronald, 1944, pp. 379–388.

Ross, Dorothea. The relationship between dependency, intentional learning, and incidental learning in preschool children. Unpublished doctoral dissertation, Stanford Univer., 1962.

Ross, Shiela A. The effect of deviant and nondeviant models on the behavior of preschool children in a temptation situation. Unpublished doctoral dissertation, Stanford Univer., 1962.

Rotter, J. B. *Social learning and clinical psychology.* Englewood Cliffs, N.J.: Prentice-Hall, 1954.

Salzinger, K. Experimental manipulation of verbal behavior: A review. *J. gen. Psychol.,* 1959, *61,* 65–94.

Sarason, S. B., Davidson, K. S., Lighthall, F. F., Waite, R. R., & Ruebush, B. K. *Anxiety in elementary school children.* New York: Wiley, 1960.

Sarbin, T. R. Role theory. In G. Lindzey (Ed.). *Handbook of social psychology.* Vol. I. Reading, Mass.: Addison-Wesley, 1954, pp. 223–258.

Schachter, S. Deviation, rejection, and communication. *J. abnorm. soc. Psychol.,* 1951, *46,* 190–207.

Schachter, S. *The psychology of affiliation.* Stanford: Stanford Univer. Press, 1959.

Schachter, S., & Hall, R. Group-derived restraints and audience persuasion. *Hum. Rel.,* 1952, *5,* 397–406.

Schachter, S., & Singer, J. E. Cognitive, social, and physiological determinants of emotional state. *Psychol. Rev.,* 1962, *69,* 379–399.

Schachter, S., & Wheeler, L.   Epinephrine, chlorpromazine, and amusement. *J. abnorm. soc. Psychol.*, 1962, *65*, 121–128.

Schaefer, E. S., & Bell, R. O.   Patterns of attitudes toward child-rearing and the family. *J. abnorm. soc. Psychol.*, 1957, *54*, 391–395.

Schein, E. H.   The effect of reward on adult imitative behavior. *J. abnorm. soc. Psychol.*, 1954, *49*, 389–395.

Schmideberg, Melitta.   Psychotherapy of juvenile delinquents. *Int. ment. Hlth. Res. Newsltr.*, 1959, *1*, 1–2.

Schramm, W., Lyle, J., & Parker, E. B.   *Television in the lives of our children.* Stanford: Stanford Univer. Press, 1961.

Schwitzgebel, R.   A new approach to understanding delinquency. *Fed. Probation*, 1960, *24*, 31–35.

Screven, C. G.   The effects of interference on response strength. *J. comp. physiol. Psychol.*, 1954, *47*, 140–144.

Sears, Pauline S.   Doll play aggression in normal young children: Influence of sex, age, sibling status, father's absence. *Psychol. Monogr.*, 1951, *65*, No. 6 (Whole No. 323).

Sears, Pauline S.   Child-rearing factors relating to playing sex-typed roles. *Amer. Psychologist*, 1953, *8*, 431 (abstract).

Sears, R. R.   Nonaggressive reactions to frustration. *Psychol. Rev.*, 1941, *48*, 343–346.

Sears, R. R.   A survey of objective studies of psychoanalytic concepts. *Soc. Sci. Res. Counc. Bull.*, 1943, No. 51.

Sears, R. R.   A theoretical framework for personality and social behavior. *Amer. Psychologist*, 1951, *6*, 476–483.

Sears, R. R.   Identification as a form of behavioral development. In D. B. Harris (Ed.). *The concept of development.* Minneapolis: Univer. of Minnesota Press, 1957, pp. 149–161.

Sears, R. R.   Relation of early socialization experiences to aggression in middle childhood. *J. abnorm. soc. Psychol.*, 1961, *63*, 466–492.

Sears, R. R., Maccoby, Eleanor E., and Levin, H.   *Patterns of child rearing.* New York: Harper, 1957.

Sears, R. R., Rau, Lucy, & Alpert, R.   Identification and child training: The development of conscience. Interim research report presented at Amer. Psychol. Assoc. Annual Meeting, Chicago, 1960.

Sears, R. R., Whiting, J. W. M., Nowlis, V., & Sears, Pauline S.   Some child-rearing antecedents of aggression and dependency in young children. *Genet. Psychol. Monogr.,* 1953, *47,* 135–234.

Setterington, R. G., & Walters, R. H. Effects of concurrent delay of material rewards and punishments on problemsolving in children. *Child Develpm.,* 1963, in press.

Shaplin, J. S. Child training and the identification of preadolescent boys. Unpublished doctoral thesis, Harvard Univer., 1954.

Shaw, C. R., & McKay, H. Social factors in juvenile delinquency. In *Report on the causes of crime,* Vol. II. Washington, D.C.: U.S. Government Printing Office, 1931.

Shaw, C. R., & McKay, H. *Juvenile delinquency and urban areas.* Chicago: Univer. of Chicago Press, 1942.

Shaw, F. J. *Behavioristic approaches to counseling and psychotherapy.* Tuscaloosa: Univer. of Alabama Press, 1961.

Sheffield, F. D. Theoretical considerations in the learning of complex sequential tasks from demonstration and practice. In A. A. Lumsdaine (Ed.). *Student response in programmed instruction: A symposium.* Washington, D.C.: National Academy of Sciences—National Research Council, 1961, pp. 13–32.

Sheldon, W. H., Hartl, E. M., & McDermott, E. *Varieties of delinquent youth.* New York: Harper, 1949.

Sidman, M. Operant techniques. In A. J. Bachrach (Ed.). *Experimental foundations of clinical psychology.* New York: Basic, 1962, pp. 170–210.

Siegel, Alberta E. Film-mediated fantasy aggression and strength of aggressive drive. *Child Develpm.,* 1956, *27,* 365–378.

Siegel, Alberta E., & Kohn, Lynette G. Permissiveness, permission, and aggression: The effect of adult presence or absence on aggression in children's play. *Child Develpm.,* 1959, *30,* 131–141.

Simkins, L. Effects of examiner attitudes and type of reinforcement on the conditioning of hostile verbs. *J. Pers.,* 1961, *29,* 380–395.

Skinner, B. F. *The behavior of organisms.* New York: Appleton, 1938.

Skinner, B. F. *Science and human behavior.* New York: Macmillan, 1953.

Skinner, B. F. Some issues concerning the control of human behavior. *Sci.*, 1956, *124*, 1057–1060, 1064–1066.

Skinner, B. F., Solomon, H. C., & Lindsley, O. R. A new method for the experimental analysis of the behavior of psychotic patients. *J. nerv. ment. Dis.*, 1954, *120*, 403–406.

Slack, C. W. Experimenter-subject psychotherapy: A new method of introducing intensive office treatment for unreachable cases. *Ment. Hygiene*, 1960, *44*, 238–256.

Slack, C. W., & Schwitzgebel, R. A handbook: Reducing adolescent crime in your community. Privately printed, 1960.

Slavson, S. R. *Activity group therapy.* (16 mm. sound film.) New York: Columbia Univer. Press, 1950 (a).

Slavson, S. R. *Analytic group psychotherapy with children, adolescents, and adults.* New York: Columbia Univer. Press, 1950 (b).

Slavson, S. R. *Child psychotherapy.* New York: Columbia Univer. Press, 1952.

Solley, C. M., & Murphy, G. *Development of the perceptual world.* New York: Basic, 1960.

Solomon, R. L., Kamin, L. J., & Wynne, L. C. Traumatic avoidance learning: The outcomes of several extinction procedures with dogs. *J. abnorm. soc. Psychol.*, 1953, *48*, 291–302.

Spence, K. W. *Behavior theory and conditioning.* New Haven: Yale Univer. Press, 1956.

Spence, K. W. A theory of emotionally based drive (D) and its relation to performance in simple learning situations. *Amer. Psychologist*, 1958, *13*, 131–141.

Spence, K. W., & Beecroft, R. S. Differential conditioning and level of anxiety. *J. exp. Psychol.*, 1954, *48*, 399–403.

Spence, K. W., & Farber, I. E. Conditioning and extinction as a function of anxiety. *J. exp. Psychol.*, 1953, *45*, 116–119.

Spence, K. W., & Taylor, Janet A. The relation of conditioned response strength to anxiety in normal, neurotic, and psychotic subjects. *J. exp. Psychol.*, 1953, *45*, 265–272.

Spitz, R. A. Hospitalism: An inquiry into the genesis of psychiatric conditions in early childhood. *Psychoanal. Study Child*, 1945, *1*, 53–74.

Stagner, R., & Congdon, C. S. Another failure to demonstrate displacement of aggression. *J. abnorm. soc. Psychol.*, 1955, *51*, 695–696.

Staples, F. R., & Walters, R. H. Anxiety, birth order, and susceptibility to social influence. *J. abnorm. soc. Psychol.*, 1961, *62*, 716–719.

Staples, F. R., & Walters, R. H. Studies of reinforcement of aggression: IV. Influence of strength of initial inhibition. Unpublished manuscript, Ontario Hospital, New Toronto, and University of Waterloo, 1963.

Staples, F. R., Wilson, F. S., & Walters, R. H. Increasing the verbal responsiveness of chronic schizophrenics. Unpublished research. Ontario Hospital, New Toronto, and University of Waterloo, 1963.

Stevenson, H. W., & Cruse, D. B. The effectiveness of social reinforcement with normal and feebleminded children. *J. Pers.*, 1961, *29*, 124–135.

Stevenson, H. W., & Fahel, Leila S. The effect of social reinforcement on the performance of institutionalized and noninstitutionalized normal and feebleminded children. *J. Pers.*, 1961, *29*, 136–147.

Stolz, Lois Meek & collaborators. *Father relations of war-born children.* Stanford: Stanford Univer. Press, 1954.

Stotland, E., & Dunn, R. Empathy, self-esteem, and birth order. *J. abnorm. soc. Psychol.*, 1963, in press.

Stotland, E., & Patchen, M. Identification and changes in prejudice and in authoritarianism. *J. abnorm. soc. Psychol.*, 1961, *62*, 265–274.

Sullivan, H. S. *The interpersonal theory of psychiatry.* New York: Norton, 1953.

Tallman, I. An experimental study of normlessness. Unpublished doctoral dissertation, Stanford Univer., 1962.

Tarde, G. *The laws of imitation.* New York: Holt, 1903.

Taylor, Janet A. The relationship of anxiety to the conditioned eyelid response. *J. exp. Psychol.*, 1951, *41*, 81–92.

Taylor, Janet A. A personality scale of manifest anxiety. *J. abnorm. soc. Psychol.*, 1953, *48*, 285–290.

Thibaut, J. W., & Coules, J. The role of communication in the reduction of interpersonal hostility. *J. abnorm. soc. Psychol.*, 1952, *47*, 770–777.

Thorndike, E. L. Animal intelligence: An experimental study of the associative processes in animals. *Psychol. Rev. Monogr. Suppl.*, 1898, *2*, No. 4 (Whole No. 8).

Thorpe, W. H. *Learning and instinct in animals.* London: Methuen, 1956.

Toch, H. H., & Schulte, R. Readiness to perceive violence as a result of police training. *Brit. J. Psychol.,* 1961, *52,* 389–394.

Unger, J. M. On the functioning of guilt potential in a conflict dilemma. *Amer. Psychologist,* 1962, *17,* 303 (abstract).

Updegraff, Ruth, & Keister, Mary E. A study of children's reactions to failure and an experimental attempt to modify them. *Child Develpm.,* 1937, *8,* 241–248.

Verplanck, W. S. The control of the content of conversation: Reinforcement of statements of opinion. *J. abnorm. soc. Psychol.,* 1955, *51,* 668–676.

Wallerstein, J. A., & Wyle, C. I. Our law-abiding law-breakers. *Probation,* 1947, *25,* 107–112, 118.

Walters, J. C., Pearce, Doris, & Dahms, Lucille. Affectional and aggressive behavior of preschool children. *Child Develpm.,* 1957, *28,* 15–26.

Walters, R. H. Conditioning of attention as a source of autistic effects in perception. *J. abnorm. soc. Psychol.,* 1958, *57,* 197–201.

Walters, R. H. Emotionality and discrimination learning of children. Unpublished manuscript, Univer. of Toronto, 1962.

Walters, R. H., Banks, R. K., & Ryder, R. R. A test of the perceptual defense hypothesis. *J. Pers.,* 1959, *27,* 47–55.

Walters, R. H., Bowen, Norma V., & Parke, R. D. Experimentally induced disinhibition of sexual responses. Unpublished manuscript, University of Waterloo, 1963.

Walters, R. H., & Brown, M. Studies of reinforcement of aggression: III. Transfer of responses to an interpersonal situation. *Child Develpm.,* 1963, *34,* 563–572.

Walters, R. H., & Demkow, Lillian. Timing of punishment as a determinant of resistance to temptation. *Child Develpm.,* 1963, *34,* 207–214.

Walters, R. H., & Henning, G. B. Isolation, effect of instructions, and verbal behavior. *Canad. J. Psychol.,* 1962, *16,* 202–210.

Walters, R. H., & Karal, Pearl. Social deprivation and verbal behavior. *J. Pers.,* 1960, *28,* 89–107.

Walters, R. H., Leat, Marion, & Mezei, L. Response inhibition and disinhibition through empathetic learning. *Canad. J. Psychol.*, 1963, *17*, 235–243.

Walters, R. H., & Llewellyn Thomas, E. Enhancement of punitiveness by visual and audiovisual displays. *Canad. J. Psychol.*, 1963, *17*, 244–255.

Walters, R. H., Llewellyn Thomas, E., & Acker, C. W. Enhancement of punitive behavior by audiovisual displays. *Sci.*, 1962, *136*, 872–873.

Walters, R. H., Marshall, W. E., & Shooter, J. R. Anxiety, isolation, and susceptibility to social influence. *J. Pers.*, 1960, *28*, 518–529.

Walters, R. H., & Parke, R. D. Emotionality and avoidance conditioning in alcoholic and nonalcoholic males. Unpublished manuscript, Univer. of Waterloo, 1963.

Walters, R. H., & Ray, E. Anxiety, social isolation, and reinforcer effectiveness. *J. Pers.*, 1960, *28*, 358–367.

Walters, R. H., & Zaks, M. S. Validation studies of an aggression scale. *J. Psychol.*, 1959, *47*, 209–218.

Warden, C. J., Fjeld, H. A., & Koch, A. M. Imitative behavior in Cebus and Rhesus monkeys. *Pedagog. Sem. & J. genet. Psychol.*, 1940, *56*, 311–322.

Warden, C. J., & Jackson, T. A. Imitative behavior in the Rhesus monkey. *Pedagog. Sem. & J. genet. Psychol.*, 1935, *46*, 103–125.

Watson, J. B. Recent literature on mammalian behavior. *Psychol. Bull.*, 1908, *5*, 195–205.

Watson, J. B., & Rayner, Rosalie. Conditioned emotional reactions. *J. exp. Psychol.*, 1920, *3*, 1–14.

Weatherley, D. Anti-semitism and the expression of fantasy aggression. *J. abnorm. soc. Psychol.*, 1961, *62*, 454–457.

Weide, T. N. Conditioning and generalization of the use of affect-related words. Unpublished doctoral dissertation, Stanford Univer., 1959.

Westley, W. A., & Elkin, F. The protective environment and adolescent socialization. *Social Forces*, 1956, *35*, 243–249.

Whiting, J. W. M. *Becoming a Kwoma.* New Haven: Yale Univer. Press, 1941.

Whiting, J. W. M. The frustration complex in Kwoma society. *Man.* 1944, *44*, 140–144.

Whiting, J. W. M. Sorcery, sin, and the superego. In M. R.

Jones (Ed.). *Nebraska symposium on motivation.* Lincoln: Univer. of Nebraska Press, 1959, pp. 174–195.

Whiting, J. W. M.   Resource mediation and learning by identification. In I. Iscoe & H. W. Stevenson (Eds.). *Personality development in children.* Austin: Univer. of Texas Press, 1960, pp. 112–126.

Whiting, J. W. M., & Child, I. L.   *Child training and personality.* New Haven: Yale Univer. Press, 1953.

Whiting, J. W. M., & Mowrer, O. H.   Habit progression and regression—a laboratory study of some factors relevant to human socialization. *J. comp. Psychol.,* 1943, *36,* 229–253.

Whyte, W. F.   *Street-corner society.* Chicago: Univer. of Chicago Press, 1937.

Williams, C. D.   The elimination of tantrum behavior by extinction procedures. *J. abnorm. soc. Psychol.,* 1959, *59,* 269.

Williams, R. I.   Verbal conditioning in psychotherapy. *Amer. Psychologist,* 1959, *14,* 388 (abstract).

Winder, C. L., Ahmad, Farrukh Z., Bandura, A., & Rau, Lucy C.   Dependency of patients, psychotherapists' responses, and aspects of psychotherapy. *J. consult. Psychol.,* 1962, *26,* 129–134.

Winterbottom, Marian R.   The relation of childhood training in independence to achievement motivation. Unpublished doctoral dissertation, Univer. of Michigan, 1953.

Wolberg, L. R.   *The technique of psychotherapy.* New York: Grune & Stratton, 1954.

Wolff, P. H.   Observations on new-born infants. *Psychosomat. Med.,* 1959, *21,* 110–118.

Wolpe, J.   Experimental neuroses as learned behavior. *Brit. J. Psychol.,* 1952, *43,* 243–268.

Wolpe, J.   *Psychotherapy by reciprocal inhibition.* Stanford: Stanford Univer. Press, 1958.

Wright, G. O.   Projection and displacement: A cross-cultural study of folktale aggression. *J. abnorm. soc. Psychol.,* 1954, *49,* 523–528.

Wright, M. E.   Constructiveness of play as affected by group organization and frustration. *Char. & Pers.,* 1942, *11,* 40–49.

Wright, M. E.   The influence of frustration upon the social relations of young children. *Char. & Pers.,* 1943, *12,* 111–122.

Yarrow, L. J.   The effect of antecedent frustration on projective play. *Psychol. Monogr.,* 1948, *62,* No. 6 (Whole No. 293).

Yarrow, L. J.   Maternal deprivation: Toward an empirical and conceptual reevaluation. *Psychol. Bull.,* 1961, *58,* 459–490.

Yates, A. J.   Symptoms and symptom substitution. *Psychol. Rev.,* 1958, *65,* 371–374.

Zedek, Meira E.   The conditioning of verbal behavior with negative cultural connotations. *J. Pers.,* 1959, *27,* 477–486.

Zigler, E. F., Hodgden, Laurel, & Stevenson, H. W.   The effect of support on the performance of normal and feebleminded children. *J. Pers.,* 1958, *26,* 106–122.

Zigler, E. F., & Kanzer, P.   The effectiveness of two classes of verbal reinforcers on the performance of middle- and lower-class children. *J. Pers.,* 1962, *30,* 157–163.

Zipf, Sheila G.   Resistance and conformity under reward and punishment. *J. abnorm. soc. Psychol.,* 1960, *61,* 102–109.

Zubek, J. P., & Solberg, Patricia A.   *Doukhobors at war.* Toronto: Ryerson Press, 1952.

AUTHOR INDEX

SUBJECT INDEX

Abnormal behavior
  abnormal-normal dichotomy, 32–33, 35–38, *44–45*
  disease model of, *29–31, 44–45*
  labeling of, 32–35
  modification of, 212–213, 225–248
  persistence of, 210–220
  social-learning model of, 30–32, 37–38, *44*
  see also Deviant behavior
Acadia, *173–175*
Achievement anxiety, parental modeling of, *175*
Achievement behavior
  cross-cultural data on, *171–176*
  and delay of reward, *170–172*
  demands for in North America, *166–167*
  and independence training, *182–183*
  modeling of, *173–176*
  positive reinforcement of, *182, 192–193, 240*
  restrictions on, *166–168*
  and self-control responses, *168–172, 175–176, 187*
  and self-denial, *171–174*
  and social-class variables, *165–167, 173–175*
Achievement demands, and social mobility, *166–167*
Adolescence
  aggression in, *26, 129*

conflict of values in, *25–26*
continuity in social development in, *25–26*
and delinquency, *26*
dependency conflicts in, *25–26, 147*
modeling of aggression in, *68–69, 118, 193–195*
and rebellion, *25–26*
reinforcement of aggression in, *119–120*
sex behavior in, *76, 150–154*
stability of behavior in, *25–26*
and stage theories of development, *25–26*
timing of development in, *27*
Affiliative behavior
  as response to frustration, *135–136*
  and reward for dependency, *142–143, 182–183*
Aggression
  age-changes in, *127–128*
  definition of, *112–115*
  and dependency frustration, *137, 144, 146–147*
  and disciplinary techniques, *127–130, 193–196*
  discrimination training in, *9, 18, 20–21, 117–122, 129–130, 167, 205*
  disinhibition of, *72–76, 81–82, 107, 158*

307

Models (*cont.*)

aggressive, *57–58, 61–64, 68–70, 73–76, 81–82, 87, 95–96, 100–106, 117–118, 158, 174, 194–195*

consequences to

inhibitory and disinhibitory effects of, *57–59, 70–79, 81–84, 103, 177–178, 220–243*

inferred, *55, 81, 84, 177*

of cooperative behavior, *171, 173–174, 245*

dependent, *64–65*

distortion of, *71–72*

effects of exposure to

eliciting effect, *60, 79–81, 106, 242–243*

inhibitory and disinhibitory effects, *60, 70–79, 81–84, 106–107, 171–182, 220, 243–244, 257*

modeling effect, *60–72, 81, 106*

exemplary, *50, 90–91, 181–182, 195–196*

film-mediated, *49, 55–58, 61–63, 73–79, 81–83, 88, 117*

influence of characteristics of, *10–11, 84, 107, 117*

inhibited, *61, 64, 69*

in language learning, *3, 52–54, 79, 93–94*

modes of presentation of, *49–51*

multiple, *91–100*

negative, *50, 60, 196*

normative, *50–51, 90*

pictorially presented, *49, 56–57, 65*

positive, *50, 195–196*

prestigeful, *10–11, 50, 84, 86, 94–100, 177, 220*

in psychotherapy, *242–246*

symbolic, *49–51, 61–63, 65, 73–79, 81–83, 86, 90, 195–196*

at variance with precepts, *68–69, 176, 194, 204–205*

verbally presented, *49–50, 73–74, 90–91, 185–186*

Moral behavior

generality-specificity issue concerning, *187, 203–210, 222*

Piaget's stage theory of, *206–210*

and social models, *172–182*

see also Guilt reactions, Self-control, Self-denial, *and* Self-punitive responses

Navaho, *49*

Negative attention getting, *see* Aggression *and* Dependency

Negative models

as means of learning deviant behavior, *50, 60, 96*

parental use of, *50, 60*

Negative reinforcement

of aggression, *18, 119, 127–130, 158–159, 191*

of dependency, *21, 143–148, 159–160, 191*

of sex behavior, *149–150, 152–153, 157*

see also Avoidance conditioning, Disciplinary techniques, Punishment, *and* Reinforcement patterns

Neurotic behavior

and alcoholism, *201–202*

persistence of, *214–220*

and psychopathy, *201, 210–212*

treatment of, *230–236, 243–244, 246–248*

Nonreward

active properties of, *133–135, 192–193*

as an aversive stimulus, *191–193*

as extinction procedure, *12, 135, 193, 224–230*

as frustration, *115–117, 134*

as positive reinforcer, *132, 191–193*